I would like to dedicate this book to my family, my safe harbor through all of life's transitions (and there were many; those who know me are well aware).

To my mother, who dedicated her life to caring for me and my siblings, and who taught me the meaning of genuine love for another person.

To my father (in memoriam), who showed me the value of hard work and dedication. Though he is no longer here to witness this achievement, he remains my greatest inspiration to be as good a father as he was.

To you, the reader, for believing that my experience can contribute to your own journey of growth.

– Marlon Vidal Ferreira

Contributors

About the author

Marlon Vidal Ferreira is a technology executive with a 15-year career and more than 7 years of experience in digital marketing, a unique combination of technical expertise and business vision. He is currently an Engineering Manager at TELUS Digital, an official Cursor Ambassador in Brazil for the cities of Belo Horizonte, MG, and Porto Alegre, RS, and the owner of a digital marketing agency focused on online advertising.

His career includes stints at companies such as Banco BS2, Avenue Code, Gap, Fanatics, BMG Money, Grupo Fácil, Minds Digital, and Grupo Boticário, progressing from developer to Head of Technology. Along the way, he also founded two companies, further strengthening his entrepreneurial vision.

Connect with the author:

`https://linkedin.com/in/marlonvidal`

`https://github.com/marlonvidal`

`https://marlonvidal.com.br/#en`

About the reviewers

Andrii Derevianko is a Chief Quality Officer and QA Architect with over 15 years of experience spanning software engineering, IoT hardware integration, and industrial automation. Holding an M.Sc. in Automation Engineering, he specializes in scaling QA infrastructure through AI-driven workflows and rigorous shift-left methodologies. Andrii's expertise encompasses modern test automation frameworks, digital twin virtualization, and CI/CD quality gates. A strong advocate of clean code and strict architectural contracts, he champions Spec-Driven Development to eliminate chaotic implementation patterns, ensuring enterprise systems are built on resilient, testable, and deeply validated foundations.

Tim Dickey is a product development and business agility coach who helps teams connect strategy, delivery, and real-world product work. A 2024–2025 LinkedIn Top Voice, he shares practical, human-centered insights on product development, coaching, and new ways of working. Before consulting, Tim served for nearly 25 years in the U.S. Navy, on active duty and in the reserve, including service in the submarine force and in support of deployed special operations units, where he learned servant leadership under pressure. He has worked with organizations such as Carnival Cruise Lines, Verizon, IBM, and Improving. Today, Tim helps product teams become more AI-fluent through experimentation, collaboration, systems thinking, and rapid MVP learning.

Table of Contents

Preface xiii

Free benefits with your book ... xviii

Chapter 1: Introducing Spec-Driven Development and BMAD Method 1

Technical requirements ... 2
Why SDD is the future of development ... 3
Looking at the BMAD method ... 4
Understanding the BMAD workflows ... 4
Understanding BMAD modules ... 5
BMAD Builder • 5
Creative Intelligence Suite (CIS) • 6
Game Dev Studio (GDS) • 6
Test enterprise architect (TEA) • 6
Moving forward: our focus on quality • 6
Context engineering: the foundation of good specs ... 7
The context gap challenge • 7
Context drift • 7
What is context engineering? • 7
The three pillars of upstream context ... 8
The first pillar: the who • 8
The second pillar: the why • 8
The third pillar: the what • 9
A real-world context example • 9
Building a full feature using the complete BMAD cycle ... 10
Configuring BMAD in the project ... 12
The _bmad-output folder • 15
Differences between v4 and v6 ... 15
Progressive disclosure ... 16
What is new in v6 ... 17

Modular architecture • 17
Workflows without agents • 17
QuickSpec workflow • 17
BMAD Help • 17
Party Mode • 18
Project context • 18
BMAD Agile and TEA workflows 18
Analysis phase • 18
Planning phase • 19
Solutioning phase • 19
Implementation phase • 20
TEA workflows • 21
The importance of project-context.md 22
Installing v6 and updating from v4 23
Prerequisites • 23
Fresh installation • 23
Upgrading from v4 to v6 • 23
Recommended workflow for getting started 24
New projects • 24
Existing projects • 24
Summary 24

Chapter 2: Upstream Phase: Analysis, Planning and Solutioning 25

The analysis phase 26
Brainstorming the product idea • 28
Performing market research • 31
Creating the product brief • 33
Working backwards with PRFAQ • 34
The planning phase 35
Working with John, the product manager • 35
Creating the PRD • 37
Updating and validating the PRD • 39
Working with Sally, the UX designer • 39
Creating the UX design • 40
The solution phase 43

Working with Winston, the architect • 43
Creating the architecture • 45
Generating project context • 46
Working with Murat, the test architect • 48
Designing the test strategy • 49
Creating epics and stories • 51
Checking implementation readiness • 53
Summary **54**

Chapter 3: Downstream Phase: Implementing and Sprinting 55

The implementation phase **56**
Working with Amelia, the developer • 56
Initializing the sprint plan • 58
The development cycle • 59
Creating a story • 59
Implementing the story • 61
Reviewing the Code • 62
The quick dev workflow • 64
Handling Mid-Sprint changes • 65
The testing cycle • 66
Setting up the test framework • 67
Configuring the CI pipeline • 68
Generating test scaffolds before implementation • 69
Expanding coverage after implementation • 71
The coverage gate • 73
The epic retrospective • 74
Summary **76**

Chapter 4: Applying BMAD to an Existing Project 77

Technical requirements **79**
Knowing the project and installing dependencies **79**
Knowing the problems and installing BMAD v6 .... **80**
Setting up BMAD • 80
Understanding the installed folder structure • 81
Running the TEA framework **82**

Documenting the project 85
Creating the project context 88
Adding new customers via QuickSpec 91
Understanding the Clarify-and-Route step • 92
Using TEA automate to create E2E tests 94
Adding new tags via quick spec 96
Using TEA ATDD to generate tests before implementation 97
Wrapping up implementation and using TEA automate 98
Validating tests and real-world scenarios 100
Recommended workflow for quick spec 101
Creating a dashboard through a PRD 101
Advanced elicitation • 102
Party mode • 104
Creating epics and stories 105
Validating implementation readiness 106
Sprint planning 107
Creating test scenarios 108
Risk-based testing strategy • 108
Creating the story 109
Vertical slicing and team extensibility • 110
Creating tests using ATDD 110
Developing the story 112
Reviewing the code 113
Automating tests 114
Wrapping up the entire workflow 115
Correcting the course during the sprint 116
Performing the retrospective 116
Summary 118

Chapter 5: Applying BMAD to a New Project 119

Recommended workflow 120
Brainstorming session 121
Research customers, competitors and technology 127
Creating the product brief 129
Creating the PRD 132

Creating the UX ... 134
Creating the architecture ... 143
Creating the test design and setting up test framework ... 146
Creating project context, epics and stories and wrapping up ... 148
Summary ... 151

Chapter 6: BMAD in Practice: Answers to Real-World Questions 153

On skipping steps ... 154

Can I skip stages if context already exists? • 154

When is it acceptable to skip the UX step entirely? • 154

Does a validated Figma prototype mean I can skip UX? • 154

When does running the UX step cost more than it delivers? • 154

What about quick dev – does it replace the UX step for small changes? • 155

On structuring work ... 155

How should I break up PRDs? By user journey, by feature, or by epic? • 155

Should I generate all stories for all epics at once, or epic by epic? • 155

Can I run multiple stories in parallel? • 156

How complex should a single PRD be? We have a product with dozens of sub-features • 156

The BMAD agent asked me about endpoints and request parameters during PRD creation. is that appropriate? • 156

What's the difference between a product brief and a PRD? • 157

On context management ... 157

Our PRD is picking up technical context we didn't include – it seems biased toward certain technology choices even after we cleaned it • 157

We work across three separate repositories. How do we share context without duplicating everything? • 157

Should the _bmad artifacts be versioned in git? • 158

On teams and processes ... 158

What team composition works best with BMAD? • 158

How do we handle work cycles? Do we still do sprints? • 158

How do multiple product managers work with BMAD? Do they share PRD creation? • 159

On architecture ... 159

We're trying to evolve our data architecture from an existing pattern to a reference architecture. Can BMAD help? • 159

Should I provide architecture context before generating the architecture document, or let BMAD suggest one? • 159

We want to reuse corporate components across all applications. How do we prevent teams from building things that already exist? • 160

Who should own each workflow? • 160

On UX and design systems 160

Our design team works directly in HTML rather than Figma. Does the UX workflow still apply? • 160

How do we ensure BMAD doesn't generate components that contradict our design system? • 161

The UX workflow didn't help us explore unhappy paths. It mostly validated what we already had. • 161

We receive prototypes from stakeholders built in informal tools. Can we use those as a BMAD starting point? • 161

How do we validate early concepts without going through the full BMAD process? • 161

On quality and testing 162

What is the recommended sequence for the testing workflow? • 162

Why not generate all ATDD tests at the beginning of an epic? • 162

What is the relationship between test design and ATDD? • 162

We tried running ATDD on a legacy system and most of our tests failed immediately • 163

Can test design documents be modified after the fact? • 163

Should test coverage percentages be configured in BMAD or in the pipeline? • 163

We want to use our organization's custom test framework, but BMAD keeps generating tests for the default frameworks • 163

Our test repository is separate from our application repository. Can BMAD generate tests there? • 164

Does BMAD support the concept of tests that must pass before code is accepted? • 164

On governance and maintenance 164

How do we prevent teams from using different versions of BMAD and getting inconsistent results? • 164

How do we handle breaking changes when BMAD releases new versions? 165

The BMAD help command – is it actually useful for day-to-day questions? • 165

Crosscutting themes 165

Chapter 7: Unlock the Code Bundle and the PDF Version 167

Unlock this book's free benefits in three easy steps 168

Other Books You May Enjoy 173

Index 177

Preface

There is a moment most developers recognize. You have a capable AI model in front of you, a clear feature to build, and an afternoon of back-and-forth that produces something that mostly works. Then, two weeks later, in a fresh conversation, the same model has forgotten everything. The context is gone. The decisions are gone. You are explaining the same project from scratch, and the output is different from what you built before.

That moment was where this book started for me.

I came to AI-assisted development with the same instinct most developers bring: start writing, iterate fast, and let the model fill the gaps. What I found was that the faster I moved, the more fragile the result became. Each session was a fresh negotiation. Each change introduced new inconsistencies. The AI was capable, but the process had no structure. There was no shared memory, no contract between what I wanted and what the model understood. I was getting code, but I was not building software.

I started looking for a better approach.

Discovering BMAD

The BMAD Method is a framework for AI-assisted software development built around a simple premise: the model is not the problem. The process is. Most failures in AI-driven development happen before a single line of code is written because the work of defining what to build, why to build it, and how to structure it has been skipped. BMAD does not skip that work. It makes it explicit, structured, and artifact-driven.

I found BMAD through Brian Madison's YouTube masterclass. At the time of writing, it remains the most complete video resource on the method. Beyond that, the documentation is the primary source of knowledge. There is no ecosystem of tutorials and no abundance of secondary explanations. Learning BMAD means reading, experimenting, and building.

That constraint turned out to be useful. It forced me to go beyond surface familiarity and develop a working understanding of why each phase exists and what it produces.

Applying it in Practice

I began applying BMAD to personal projects first. The early results were different enough from what I had experienced with unstructured AI development that I continued. The artifacts produced during the analysis and planning phases gave the implementation agents real

context to work from. The work did not restart with each session. The decisions accumulated rather than dissolved.

At my current company, TELUS Digital, I extended that practice to professional projects. The conditions were more demanding: a larger scope, real stakeholders, and production constraints. BMAD held. The method scales because it separates concerns cleanly: analysis is not the same work as planning, planning is not the same work as solutioning, and solutioning is not the same work as implementation. Each phase produces artifacts that the next phase depends on. That chain of dependencies is what makes AI-assisted development reproducible rather than accidental.

Working through those projects gave me enough confidence in the method to teach it. This book is the result of that teaching.

Who this book is for

This book is for developers who are already using AI tools and want to do so more deliberately. It assumes you have worked with a model-native coding tool and encountered its limits. You do not need prior experience with BMAD. You do need a willingness to slow down during the planning phases to move faster and more reliably during implementation.

The book is not for readers looking for a comparison of AI coding tools or an introduction to AI-assisted development in general. The focus is narrow and intentional: the BMAD Method, how it works, and how to use it.

What this book covers

The book follows the structure of the method itself, moving from the core concepts through each phase of development.

Chapter 1, Introducing Spec Driven Development and BMAD Method, introduces Spec-Driven Development and the BMAD Method. It covers the core idea behind artifact-driven AI development and explains why it produces different outcomes than unstructured prompting.

Chapter 2, Upstream Phase: Analysis, Planning and Solutioning, covers the analysis, planning, and solutioning phases. These are the upstream phases, where the work of defining the product, understanding the domain, and designing the solution happens before any code is written. Each phase has dedicated agents and workflows that guide the process.

Chapter 3, Downstream Phase: Implementing and Sprinting, covers the implementation phase. This is where stories are developed, code is written, tests are generated, and progress is tracked. It is where the artifacts from the upstream phases pay off.

Chapter 4, Applying BMAD to an Existing Project, addresses working with existing applications. Applying BMAD to a greenfield project is different from applying it to an existing codebase. This chapter covers the specific adaptations the method requires when the starting point is not a blank slate.

Chapter 5, Applying BMAD to a New Project, covers working with new applications, from the first brainstorming session through to a working implementation. It follows the recommended flow from end to end, with examples drawn from real project work.

Chapter 6, BMAD in Practice: Answers to Real-World Questions, addresses frequently asked questions and real-world scenarios. It covers the situations that do not fit cleanly into the standard flow: scope changes during implementation, working without a complete set of artifacts, integrating BMAD into team environments, and handling the edge cases that any serious use of the method eventually produces.

The method is learnable. The process is repeatable. That is the claim this book makes, and each chapter is an attempt to demonstrate it.

To get the most out of this book

The examples in this book use Cursor as the primary AI-powered IDE. Cursor was chosen because it offers tight integration between the editor and the model, and because it reflects how many developers are currently working with AI tools in practice. If you prefer a different environment, the method translates directly. VS Code, Windsurf, or any other AI-native editor will work. The BMAD artifacts are plain-text files. The agents are prompts. The process does not depend on any particular tool.

Software engineering experience is helpful but not required. You will encounter code in the implementation chapters, and familiarity with at least one programming language will help you follow along more closely. That said, the core of what BMAD teaches happens before the code is written: how to define the problem, how to structure the solution, and how to give an AI model the context it needs to do useful work. Those skills transfer regardless of your technical background.

Before you start, you will need access to an AI-powered IDE and an active subscription or API key for a capable model, such as Anthropic Claude, OpenAI GPT, or Cursor Composer. The book does not cover model selection in depth, but any model capable of maintaining context and generating code will be sufficient.

Download the example code files

This book includes a complete downloadable code bundle containing all the example projects and files used throughout the chapters. We recommend downloading the bundle so you can follow along smoothly and experiment with the examples.

Use the bundle as a practical starting point. Modify it, extend it, and apply what you learn by creating your own variations as you progress through the chapters.

Get the code bundle

If you bought the book directly from Packt:

1. Go to **packtpub.com**
2. Click your **profile picture** and select **Your Orders**
3. Find this book and click **Download Code**

If you bought this book from Amazon or any other channel partner:

1. Go to `packtpub.com/unlock` or scan the following QR code:
2. Search for this book
3. Sign up or log in to your free Packt account
4. Upload your proof of purchase and download the code bundle locally

Usage note: You're free to use and modify this code for personal learning and non-commercial projects.

Download the color images

Your purchase includes a color, DRM-free PDF copy of this book, ideal for viewing color images, screenshots, and diagrams. Refer to *Free benefits with your book section* at the end of the *Preface* to unlock your PDF copy.

Conventions used

There are a number of text conventions used throughout this book.

`CodeInText`: Indicates code words in text, database table names, folder names, filenames, file extensions, pathnames, dummy URLs, user input, and Twitter handles. For example: "Execute the `/bmad-prd` command:"

Any command-line input or output is written as follows:

```
npx install bmad-method
```

Bold: Indicates a new term, an important word, or words that you see on the screen. For instance, words in menus or dialog boxes appear in the text like this. For example: "Select **BMAD Agile-Driven** from the **Modules** section."

> **Note**
>
> Warnings or important notes appear like this.

> **Tip**
>
> Tips and tricks appear like this.

Get in touch

Feedback from our readers is always welcome.

General feedback: If you have questions about any aspect of this book or have any general feedback, please email us at `customercare@packt.com` and mention the book's title in the subject of your message.

Errata: Although we have taken every care to ensure the accuracy of our content, mistakes do happen. If you have found a mistake in this book, we would be grateful if you reported this to us. Please visit `http://www.packt.com/submit-errata`, click **Submit Errata**, and fill in the form.

Piracy: If you come across any illegal copies of our works in any form on the internet, we would be grateful if you would provide us with the location address or website name. Please contact us at `copyright@packt.com` with a link to the material.

If you are interested in becoming an author: If there is a topic that you have expertise in and you are interested in either writing or contributing to a book, please visit `http://authors.packt.com/`.

Free benefits with your book

This book includes free benefits designed to support your learning and help you apply what you learn effectively. Activate them now for instant access (see the *How to unlock* section for instructions).

Here's a quick overview of what you can instantly unlock with your purchase:

How to unlock

Scan the QR code (or go to `packtpub.com/unlock`). Search for this book by name, confirm the edition, and then follow the steps on the page.

UNLOCK NOW

Note: Have your invoice handy. Purchases made directly from the Packt website don't require an invoice.

Share your thoughts

Once you've read *Spec-Driven Development with BMAD*, we'd love to hear your thoughts! Scan the QR code below to go straight to the Amazon review page for this book and share your feedback.

https://packt.link/r/1808086074

Your review is important to us and the tech community and will help us make sure we're delivering excellent quality content.

1

Introducing Spec-Driven Development and BMAD Method

The way we build software is changing rapidly with the adoption of AI-assisted development tools. However, as many teams are already experiencing, simply prompting **large language models (LLMs)** with vague instructions is not enough to build reliable and scalable systems. As projects grow in complexity, the lack of structured context leads to inconsistent implementations, architectural problems, missing requirements, and significant rework.

In this chapter, we go through spec-driven development as a practical approach to solving those problems and present the BMAD method as a framework for implementing this methodology in real projects. Instead of relying on improvised prompts and reactive development, we will focus on creating structured specifications that provide AI agents with the necessary context to generate higher-quality outputs throughout the software lifecycle.

We will explore the philosophy behind BMAD, understand the difference between upstream and downstream development processes, and learn how specialized AI agents collaborate to support planning, architecture, implementation, and quality assurance. We will also cover the fundamentals of context engineering and understand why defining the who, why, and what of a project is essential before thinking about implementation details.

We will cover the following main topics:

- Why **Spec-Driven Development** (**SDD**) is the future of development
- Introducing the BMAD method
- Understanding the BMAD philosophy
- Understanding the BMAD workflow
- Context engineering: the foundation of good specs

- The three pillars of upstream context
- Building a full feature using the complete BMAD cycle
- Configuring BMAD in the Project
- What is new in v6
- BMAD Agile and TEA workflows
- The importance of `project-context.md`
- Installing v6 and updating from v4
- Recommended workflow for getting started

By the end of this chapter, we will understand the limitations of vibe coding, learn the foundations of spec-driven development, explore the BMAD workflow and its agents, and see how context engineering helps us create clearer and more reliable AI-assisted development processes.

> Note
>
> **Download the code bundle and the PDF version of this book**
>
> Your purchase includes a DRM-free PDF copy of this book, the code bundle, and a range of exclusive benefits. To unlock everything, follow the *Free benefits with your book* section in the *Preface.*

Technical requirements

To get started with BMAD, there are a few essential technical prerequisites you must have installed on your machine. Your environment will need Node.js version 20.12 or higher to run the core framework installer (`npx bmad-method install`), along with Python 3.10 or higher. You'll also need to have `uv` (the fast Python package installer and resolver) installed. Once your local environment meets these requirements, BMAD integrates seamlessly into your workflow via your preferred AI-powered IDE.

> Note
>
> At the time this book is written, the current BMAD version is 6.8.0 and the BMAD Test Architect module is at version 1.19.0.

While Cursor is a popular choice (and our examples in this book will use Cursor), BMAD is highly flexible and can be used with a wide variety of AI IDEs, including Claude Code, Codex, GitHub Copilot, Cline, Gemini, Google Antigravity, Kiro, OpenCode, Windsurf and another 30

tools available in the market, allowing you to build and plan without being locked into a single editor.

Why SDD is the future of development

In this section, we discuss why spec-driven development is the future of AI development and why the current approach of vibe coding creates significant problems in real-world software engineering.

For those familiar with tools such as Cursor and Claude Code, vibe coding is usually described as asking an LLM for what we want and allowing it to generate a solution based on the provided prompt. Most of the time, the generated code is of high quality. However, as the scenarios become more complex, vague prompts no longer provide enough context for the AI assistants to fully understand the problem. Instead of delivering solutions and moving to the next feature, we end up fixing problems introduced by missing context.

This is why specifications as the source of truth become the solution to the vibe coding problem. With AI, we can create highly detailed product and technical specifications. Spec-driven development states that if something is not present in the specifications, the code will not reflect the intended behavior.

This becomes a game changer because development is now driven by specifications. We always have the latest version of what the system needs to do, and the documentation accurately reflects what the code must implement.

This approach addresses one of the most common complaints in software engineering: outdated or missing documentation. By generating specifications from both business and technical perspectives, we can provide AI agents with precise context. The likelihood that they misunderstand requirements or miss important constraints decreases significantly, which reduces the number of errors introduced into the codebase.

Within this approach, we spend much more time sharpening the axe. That means thinking deeply about what we need to deliver instead of immediately jumping into implementation. Many times, teams only discover architectural flaws or design problems after reaching a major milestone, which forces them to rewrite code that was already delivered or nearly completed.

This is an extremely important shift in mindset.

In general, spec-driven development improves both the upstream and downstream process because we think through the entire lifecycle, from ideation to software delivery. We work through every stage intentionally instead of reacting to problems during implementation.

This is where the BMAD method comes into play and why it matters to software developers, engineers, managers, and other technical roles.

Looking at the BMAD method

BMAD known as **Breakthrough Method of Agile AI-Driven Development** or **Build More Architect Dreams** is a framework that implements the spec-driven development approach. Spec-driven development should be viewed as a new programming paradigm in the same way we think about functional programming or **object-oriented programming (OOP)**. It represents a different way of solving problems using technology.

BMAD method was created by Brian Madison as an open-source project (`https://github.com/bmad-code-org/BMAD-METHOD`). The main idea behind the implementation is simulating an agile way of working. Each stage of the process is handled by a specialized AI agent that acts in a specific professional role.

For example:

- A product manager agent
- A software architect agent
- A developer agent

Each agent has its own role and domain knowledge. These agents provide insights and perform specialized work so we can explore problems deeply, provide the necessary context, and receive highly professional outputs that support the development process.

BMAD helps implement spec-driven development because it eliminates inconsistencies in planning and reduces context loss, which is currently one of the main problems when working with large language models.

BMAD can be used inside IDEs/CLIs such as Claude Code, Codex, Cursor, GitHub Copilot, Cline, Gemini, Google Antigravity, Kiro, OpenClaw, OpenCode, Windsurf and another 30 tools available in the market. Let's now dive deep into the BMAD philosophy.

Understanding the BMAD workflows

Despite having specialized agents, BMAD is also structured in different workflows that represent the work each phase should execute during a project, without the need to load an agent definition to execute a specific task, simulating an agile team development process. These are the most important ones:

Figure 1.1 – BMAD workflows

Understanding BMAD modules

BMAD is powerful out of the box, but its true scalability lies in its official add-on modules. Designed to extend beyond the built-in core and BMM (the ones we'll cover in this book), these modules provide specialized agents, workflows, and tasks tailored for specific domains.

Whether you are extending the framework itself, brainstorming new products, developing a video game, or building enterprise-grade testing strategies, there is a dedicated module for the job. Below is a breakdown of the official BMAD modules and when they should be utilized in your projects.

BMAD Builder

BMAD Builder is the meta-module of the ecosystem. It provides guided assistance for creating custom agents, structured workflows, and domain-specific modules. It features interactive setup capabilities using YAML configuration and seamless npm publishing support.

When to use it: You should use the BMAD Builder when you need to extend the BMAD framework itself. If your team requires highly specialized AI agents with custom expertise, bespoke decision-point workflows, or if you want to package and share your own custom module with the wider community, this is your starting point.

Creative Intelligence Suite (CIS)

The **Creative Intelligence Suite** (**CIS**) is a collection of AI-powered tools designed to facilitate structured creativity, ideation, and innovation. It comes equipped with specialized agents like Innovation Strategist, Design Thinking Coach, and Storyteller, employing proven frameworks such as SCAMPER and reverse brainstorming.

When to use it: Deploy CIS during the early stages of product development. It is the ideal module when you are facing complex problem-solving hurdles, need lateral thinking exercises, are drafting narratives and pitches, or require a structured environment to brainstorm and refine abstract ideas.

Game Dev Studio (GDS)

Game Dev Studio (**GDS**) is a highly specialized module providing structured game development workflows adapted for major engines like Unity, Unreal, Godot, and custom builds. It handles everything from rapid prototyping in **Quick Dev mode** to epic-driven production sprints.

When to use it: As the name implies, GDS is designed for game developers. You should use it when you need to generate comprehensive **Game Design Documents** (**GDDs**), establish world-building and character dialog, or need engine-specific architecture guidance across various game types.

Test enterprise architect (TEA)

TEA brings enterprise-grade test strategy, automation guidance, and release gate decision-making to the table. This module goes far beyond standard QA by offering risk-based prioritization, requirements traceability, and nine distinct structured workflows.

When to use it: You should integrate TEA when software quality, test design, and automated testing are paramount. It is built for teams that need strict **non-functional requirement** (**NFR**) assessments, CI setup assistance, **Acceptance Test-Driven Development** (**ATDD**) workflows, and rigorous P0-P3 bug prioritization.

Moving forward: our focus on quality

While BMAD Builder, the CIS, and Game Dev Studio offer incredible value for their respective niches, testing and quality assurance remain the universal bottlenecks for most development teams.

For that reason, we're going to cover TEA in this book, not the others. In the upcoming chapters, we will dive deep into the TEA module and how it is associated in both upstream and downstream phases. We will explore how to collaborate with the TEA agent, set up

requirements traceability, and leverage TEA's structured workflows to ensure your next release is robust, automated, and deployment-ready.

Context engineering: the foundation of good specs

Before moving into practice, we need to understand what makes a good specification. This is where context engineering becomes essential.

The context gap challenge

When working on a project, developers naturally possess the full project context:

- Business goals
- Historical decisions
- Implicit constraints
- Domain knowledge

AI agents do not have this context. LLMs are trained on generic datasets, which means we must explicitly provide the necessary information for them to generate accurate solutions.

Without this bridge, most AI-assisted projects fail. This relates directly to the vibe coding problem we discussed earlier.

Context drift

Providing too much information can also create problems. When context becomes excessively large, AI systems may begin compacting or shrinking previous information. This phenomenon is commonly known as **context drift**.

As new prompts are added, the model continually reprocesses earlier context, which increases the chance of losing important details.

What is context engineering?

Context engineering is the systematic process of structuring information to constrain the AI's creative space before implementation begins. This differs from prompt engineering. Prompt engineering focuses on writing better instructions for a single query or conversation.

Context engineering builds a persistent knowledge base that AI agents consult before processing requests.

This is what enables consistent and reliable output. The purpose of context engineering is to create boundaries of truth that the AI cannot cross.

This becomes the foundation of successful upstream planning.

The three pillars of upstream context

To build effective specifications, we must clearly define:

- Who are we targeting?
- Why are we building the solution?
- What are we building?

The upstream process intentionally ignores the how. Technology decisions are not discussed at this stage.

The architect agent only becomes involved later. The upstream process primarily relies on the analyst and product manager agents because they focus on the following three pillars.

The first pillar: the who

The main question is: *Who is the software for?*

Specificity matters. Saying that we are targeting "users" is vague. Instead, define a persona such as the following:

A senior financial analyst who needs high-contrast data visualization and hates scrolling.

It provides the AI model with meaningful context.

This specificity influences:

- UI density
- Accessibility standards
- Workflow complexity
- UX decisions

When the UX agent receives this information, it can generate significantly better guidance.

The second pillar: the why

The next question is: *Why are we building this?*

Many failed projects originate from poorly defined business value. To answer this correctly, we need to define success metrics. For example:

- Reducing support tickets by 20%
- Enabling checkout completion in under 30 seconds

These metrics influence engineering trade-offs, including the following:

- Performance priorities
- Aesthetic priorities
- MVP scope

They also help AI agents prioritize features during conflicts.

The third pillar: the what

The final question is: *What are we building?*

Equally important is defining what is out of scope. This prevents **scope creep** and unnecessary overengineering.

We must clearly define:

- Required features
- Hard constraints
- Explicit exclusions

Examples include:

- Google authentication
- CSV export
- No social features

This creates negative constraints that help prevent unnecessary complexity. The goal is to deliver software that solves the current business problem while allowing future incremental improvements.

A real-world context example

A vague prompt to any LLM, such as the following: *Build a to-do list app,* will usually produce a generic application using React suitable for no specific audience.

Using BMAD, the existing workflows will guide you to gather more context, and this will become much more precise. Let's look at an engineering context with BMAD:

- **The Who**: Busy freelance designers
- **The Why**: Track billable hours per task to increase revenue
- **The What**: A Kanban board with an integrated timer and no social features

The result becomes a tailored product that is much closer to a market-ready solution.

Building a full feature using the complete BMAD cycle

In this book, we will build a to-do list application. However, the primary goal is not the technology or business complexity. The objective is to understand the BMAD process from upstream planning to downstream implementation.

The same workflow can then be applied to larger projects. BMAD is most useful for medium- to high-complexity tasks. It is not intended to replace UI-oriented prompt tools such as Lovable or V0 for simple implementations. For simpler work, plan modes in Cursor or Claude are often sufficient.

BMAD becomes valuable when:

- The feature has significant business impact
- The implementation complexity is high
- Existing users may be affected
- Architectural thinking is required

Applying the context engineering principles discussed earlier, the project in this book would include the following:

- **The Who**: Busy freelancers
- **The Why**: Track billable hours per task to increase revenue
- **The What**:
    - A Kanban board
    - Integrated timers
    - A web-based application
    - No social features
    - Local storage persistence instead of database complexity

The book compares two versions of the same application using the same PRD:

- A version generated in Lovable, with too much context injected at once and keeping important features out of scope without user consensus. Here is a screenshot of the project:

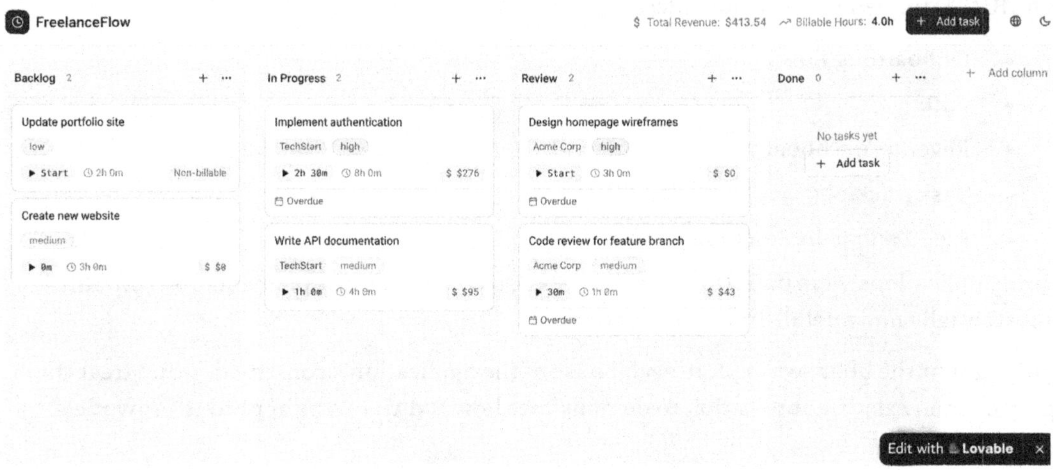

Figure 1.2 – Project built on Lovable

- A version generated using the BMAD method, following all functional and non-functional requirements the user wants. Here is a screenshot of the BMAD version:

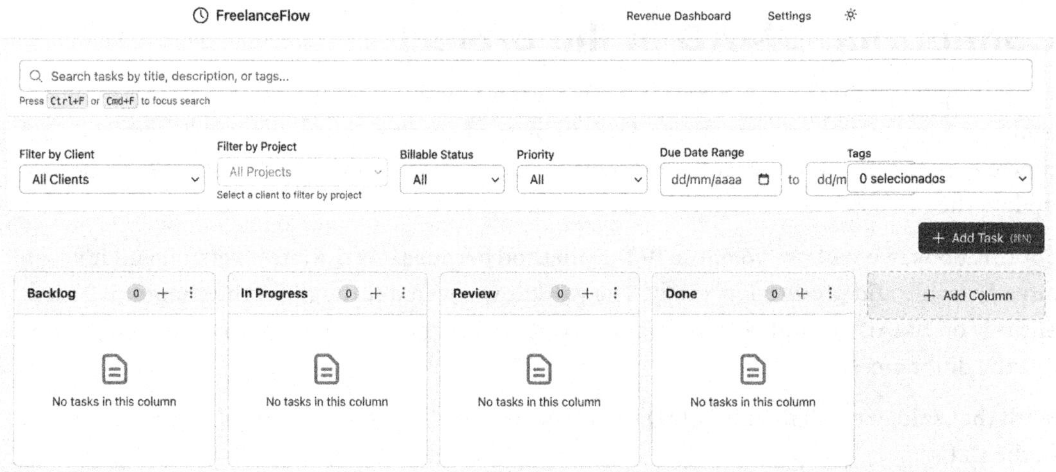

Figure 1.3 – Application built with BMAD

The BMAD implementation includes:

- Onboarding flows
- Filters
- Revenue dashboards
- Task tracking
- Rich Kanban interactions

Both applications were built from the same PRD, but the BMAD implementation contains substantially more detail and product depth.

Throughout the book, we explore each phase of the application's construction and treat the project as an existing application to demonstrate how BMAD can be applied to brownfield projects.

The focus remains on the process itself and how BMAD improves software delivery, accelerates development, and creates higher-quality implementations. We will also see how to apply BMAD to greenfield projects, making sure that our application starts correctly from business, product, and technology perspectives.

Configuring BMAD in the project

Before implementing BMAD in a project, one important consideration is that BMAD is an evolving open-source framework, and this book might contain outdated info depending on the time you're reading it, because Brian Madison and the open-source community continuously update the project.

For this book, we will use v6 of the BMAD method because it is the latest version and it's already stable and production-ready. The workflow covered throughout the chapter is based entirely on BMAD v6, and we'll have some comparisons between v4 and v6 to explicitly point out the differences.

With that said, we will install BMAD in Cursor. To install BMAD, run the following command in the CLI:

```
npx bmad-method install
```

Following is what we get after using the command:

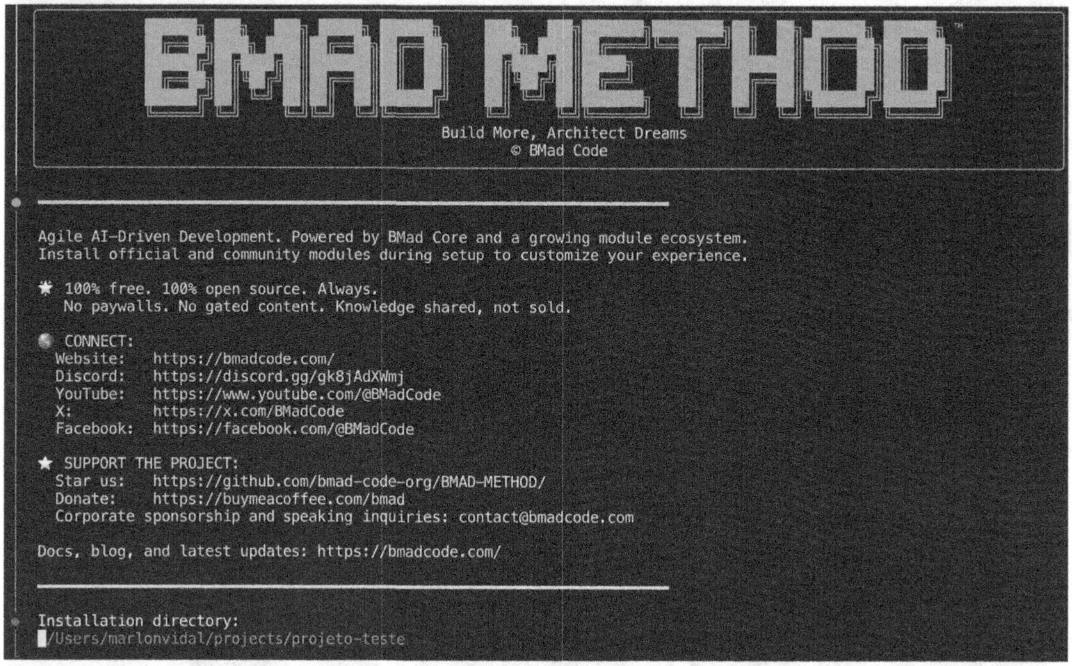

Figure 1.4 – Result of the installation command

During installation, BMAD asks a series of configuration questions. First, we select the installation path for the project.

Tip

You can type `.` for the current directory.

After selecting the installation location, we choose the BMAD modules that will be installed in the same folder. This is where you will select BMAD Method and TEA modules, the ones we'll cover through this book. You can navigate up and down with keyboard arrows and press space to select them. Feel free to select other modules and explore them further, but we'll not focus on them in this book.

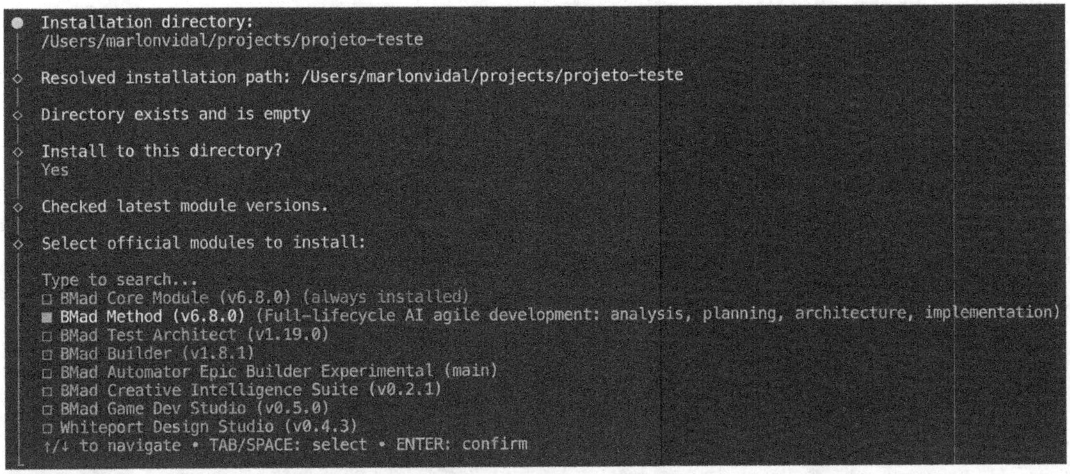

Figure 1.5 – Module selection

Right after, we select the IDE integrations that BMAD should support. BMAD can integrate with multiple tools simultaneously, including Cursor, Claude Code, among others. In this implementation, the workflow focuses on Cursor:

Figure 1.6 – IDE configuration

Then it will ask your name, the project name, which language should agents use when chatting with you and which language the output documents should be written in. Localization for both conversation and output documents was a highly requested feature since v4 to allow people who don't know English to use BMAD at its maximum performance.

To finish, you should select where the output files generated by the method will be placed. I strongly suggest using the default `_bmad-output` folder for organizational purposes.

Concluding the process, lots of files will be created (depending on the IDE you chose) to define how the agents behave, how workflows will execute, and how BMAD interprets the commands throughout the development process.

If multiple IDE integrations are selected during installation, BMAD creates separate folders for each supported tool, since for v6 all workflows and agents are skills for easy maintenance and to adhere to industry standards. For example, the skills can be created in the following folders depending on the IDE you choose:

- `.agents`
- `.claude`
- `.opencode`

> **Note**
>
> From this point forward, we'll learn about the agents and the workflows BMAD offers to us. But in a real-world scenario, most of the time we'll use workflows and not the agents (they are loaded under the scenes when you select a workflow). Use these learnings as references to understand the bigger picture.

The _bmad-output folder

Every artifact produced during the BMAD workflow is written to a dedicated folder at the root of the project: `_bmad-output`. This is where the results of all agent sessions land: brainstorming notes, project context files, planning artifacts, implementation readiness reports, and any other document generated across the workflow phases. Rather than scattering outputs across the project or relying on the user to organize them manually, BMAD writes each artifact to a predictable, consistent location.

The folder uses subfolders to separate artifacts by type, so a brainstorming session lands in `_bmad-output/brainstorming/` while planning documents land in `_bmad-output/planning-artifacts/`. This structure makes it straightforward to locate any artifact at any point in the process. As the project progresses through phases, the `_bmad-output` folder becomes the accumulated record of what the workflow has produced and the foundation from which downstream agents draw their context.

Differences between v4 and v6

As of April 2026, BMAD has reached v6, and the gap between this release and v4 is significant enough to warrant a dedicated review. The most important shift is flexibility: v6 is far less rigid than v4. Until that date, v4 was the latest stable version, and BMAD had increased its popularity.

In v4, working with BMAD requires following a strict methodology and a defined set of workflows to produce specifications and drive implementation. That overhead makes sense for

large, complex projects, but for small projects or simple features, v4 is overkill. V6 changes the underlying model entirely.

The core architectural change is this: in v6, workflows can be run without loading agents. v4 centers on agent interaction, you activate an agent, and from that agent you execute workflows. In v6, workflows are first-class citizens. You can invoke a workflow directly without worrying about which agent to load first. The agent definition is pulled in behind the scenes when needed. This makes it significantly easier to track where you are in the BMAD process and to call the appropriate workflow for the moment.

The architect role has also been relaxed. In v4, creating architecture documents requires filling out a considerable amount of detail, which can be challenging for those without a strong technical background. v6 guides users through the process more naturally, while still supporting the creation of rich, detailed architecture documents for those who want that depth.

Quality assurance has been extracted into its own module, the TEA module, which we will cover in detail later in this book. I consider this one of the most meaningful improvements in v6.

v6 also removes the distinction between greenfield and brownfield workflow commands. In v4, you need to run specific commands depending on whether you are starting fresh or working on an existing codebase. In v6, running the workflow is enough; it automatically detects the project state and proceeds accordingly.

Finally, the file sharding mechanism from v4 is no longer required. As LLMs have matured, a technique called progressive disclosure has emerged that makes sharding unnecessary. We will examine this in the next section.

Progressive disclosure

Progressive disclosure is one of the fundamental changes in how language models process text, and it is the reason file sharding is no longer necessary in BMAD v6. The term originates from UX design, where it describes the principle that users should be able to discover what they need without being confronted with all options at once.

In the context of LLMs, and especially in IDEs like Cursor, progressive disclosure means the model can use grep-style commands to search a file based on intent and keywords, loading only the relevant sections into context rather than ingesting the entire file. The model searches for headers that are relevant to the current task and pulls in just that portion of the document.

In BMAD v4, PRD and architecture files can grow to thousands of lines. The sharding process exists specifically to break those long files into smaller chunks, with an index file BMAD uses to

reference the right context when creating story files. Progressive disclosure replaces that mechanism. We can now maintain very long files and rely on the model to read only the appropriate sections when needed, saving tokens and keeping context focused.

What is new in v6

Beyond the changes described above, v6 introduces several new capabilities worth understanding before starting to work with the framework.

Modular architecture

The most impactful structural change is the reorganization around modules. In v4, BMAD ships as a monolith with a few add-ons like the game development module and the creative suite. In v6, the BMAD core is a standalone module that empowers all the others. Every extension to BMAD's functionality is built on top of that core.

Workflows without agents

As noted earlier, you no longer need to activate an agent to run a workflow. The agent definition is loaded in the background automatically. This is a meaningful quality-of-life improvement; instead of memorizing which agent corresponds to which workflow, you focus on the workflow itself.

QuickSpec workflow

V4 requires passing through all phases of the BMAD process—analysis, planning, solutioning—regardless of the scope of the task. For small, well-understood changes, that overhead is disproportionate. The QuickSpec workflow addresses this. You provide your intent, and BMAD generates a concise specification you can implement, guided by your project conventions. We will see live examples of this workflow later.

This is what makes BMAD v6 applicable to any size of project: small, medium, and large. V4 was effectively a framework for complex projects only.

BMAD Help

One of the friction points in v4 is knowing which workflow to trigger next. You need to understand the agents, their associated workflows, and the correct sequencing. The BMAD Help workflow solves this. Given your current status in the process, it tells you which workflow to run next and answers any questions about the framework.

I used BMAD Help extensively while working on this book. If anything in this material raises a question, BMAD Help is a reliable first reference, and you will likely get a very similar answer.

Party Mode

Party Mode loads all agents simultaneously, giving you multiple perspectives on the discussion you are having with the AI. This is particularly useful when finalizing a product requirements document or working through a broad architectural question. We will use it in specific scenarios throughout the book.

Project context

The project context is a new top-level concept in v6, and it is important enough to warrant its own dedicated section. It is the primary file BMAD loads into every workflow and agent definition, containing the conventions, tech stack, code standards, and product overview that all agents must follow. We will cover it in detail in *The Importance of project-context.md* section.

BMAD Agile and TEA workflows

With the structural changes understood, we can now walk through the full set of workflows v6 proposes. These span the BMAD Agile module and the TEA module. Here are the different phases:

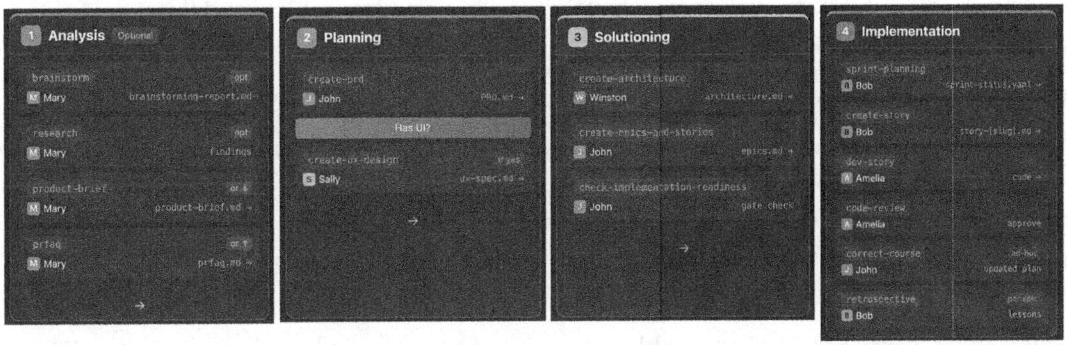

Figure 1.7 – The different phases of BMAD v6

Analysis phase

The analysis phase contains four workflows: Brainstorm, Market Research, Technical Research, and Domain Research. At this stage, we generate ideas through structured guidance to help us extract our best ideas and to make sure we are in the right direction. Each workflow is still associated with an agent; this is the inheritance from v4, but as established earlier, you do not need to activate the agent to run the workflow. You can activate the workflow directly or load the agent and run from there. Both paths are valid.

Planning phase

The planning phase contains two workflows:

- PRD
- UX

This is where we create the PRD, driven by the product manager (John) agent. If we have a new UI component, we can also run the `UX` workflow here; it generates comprehensive UX design specifications that feed into the later phases.

Solutioning phase

The solutioning phase contains three workflows:

- Architecture
- Epics and Stories
- Check Implementation Readiness

This phase introduces an important structural change from v4. Previously, epics, and stories were created inside the PRD workflow itself. The problem was that significant architectural details discovered later were often absent from those epics and stories. In v6, the PRD and the architecture are decoupled. We first run the `create-architecture` workflow to produce the `architecture.md` file, and only after we have the PRD, the architecture, and optionally the UX design do we create the epics and stories. This sequencing ensures implementation artifacts are informed by the full picture.

The solutioning phase ends with the `Check Implementation Readiness` workflow, an optional but strongly encouraged quality gate before moving into implementation. If everything passes, we proceed.

Implementation phase

The implementation phase contains six workflows:

- Sprint planning
- Create story
- Develop story
- Code review
- Correct course
- Retrospective

Tracking story status was difficult in v4. The Sprint Planning workflow addresses this by generating a sprint status file that shows the current state of every epic and story, making it straightforward to see what has been done and what still needs to be implemented.

For each story, the implementation loop works as follows: we draft the story, run the dev story workflow to implement it, then run the code review workflow. In v4, code review is performed by a dedicated quality assurance agent. In v6, the developer agent performs the code review itself. The purpose remains the same, validating acceptance criteria against the delivered code, but the agent responsible has changed.

The `Correct Course` workflow, provided by the product manager agent, handles mid-implementation scope changes. This was a point of confusion in v4, where `Correct Course` existed for both the product manager and the scrum master agent. The key concept here is timing: once implementation is underway, changing the PRD directly can have a disproportionate impact. `Correct Course` provides a controlled mechanism for adjusting a specific story without destabilizing the broader plan.

The implementation phase closes with the `Retrospective` workflow, which collects learning notes written by the developer inside the story files and uses them to improve the project context. This is how continuous improvement is built into the BMAD process.

TEA workflows

The TEA module works alongside the BMAD Agile workflows. Its workflows are organized into two groups: setup and per-story quality loops. Here is a diagram of the workflow:

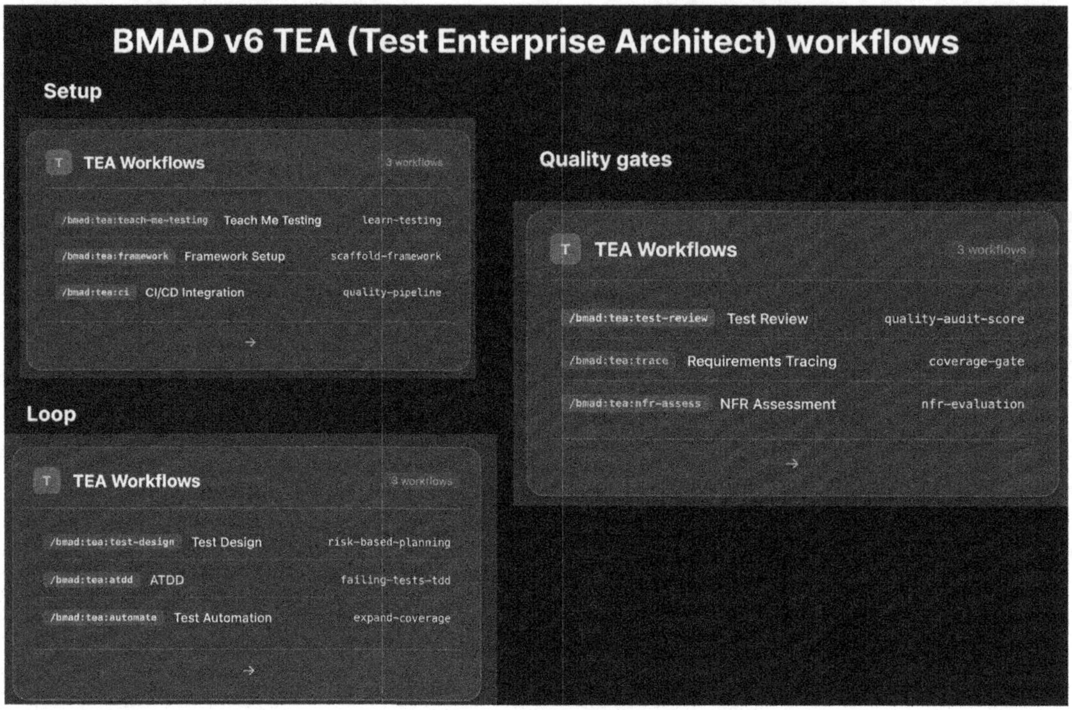

Figure 1.8 – Diagram of TEA workflow

Setup workflows:

- **Teach Me Testing**: if automated testing is new territory, this is the recommended starting point. We will cover it to a degree in this book, but I recommend spending additional time with this workflow.
- **Framework**: reads the repository and scaffolds the testing framework configuration that the TEA module will use going forward.
- **CI/CD Integration**: integrates testing into the pipeline so that pushing to core branches triggers the test suite automatically

Per-story quality workflows (run alongside the dev story loop):

- **Test Design**: evaluates which test scenarios should exist based on a priority scale, applicable at either the project or feature level.

- **ATDD**: produces test-driven development steps following the red-green approach. All unit tests are written to fail first, and the code is written to make them pass. This ensures AI-generated code satisfies all acceptance criteria and that the tests themselves serve as a guide for how the code should be structured. This is particularly powerful in agentic development.
- **Automate**: expands coverage after the unit tests pass. It creates end-to-end test features to guard against regression and verify that unit tests continue to hold

Quality gate workflows:

- **Test Reveal**: verifies that all tests suggested by the framework are covered in the implementation, evaluated at a broad scope
- **Trace**: similar to Test Reveal but focused on the feature level
- **NFR Assess**: a dedicated workflow for validating non-functional requirements against their expected behavior

We will learn how to combine Agile and TEA workflows in practice throughout the rest of this book.

The importance of project-context.md

The project context is the heart of BMAD. It represents the link between the business, the product, and the technology. This file defines the conventions, the tech stack, the code standards, and the product overview for a given project, and it is the source that most workflows load when the product manager, architect, and developer agents are summoned.

Without this file, the major rules your project requires will not be taken into consideration by any of the agents. For existing projects, generating the project context should be the first action you take when onboarding BMAD. For new projects, it should be the immediate next step after creating the architecture document.

We will walk through the steps required to activate the workflow that generates this file. The workflow handles the heavy lifting; your job is to provide the input it needs.

It is worth clarifying the relationship between the project context and other rule files you may already be using. Files like `agents.md`, `claude.md`, and `.cursorrules` are always loaded by the language model regardless of what you are doing; they store general rules and standards the agent should follow universally. The project context is different. It applies only within BMAD workflows and can coexist with those files without conflict.

The project context is most consequential during the implementation phase. When the developer agent is invoked by the dev story workflow, it reads this file and uses it to ensure

implementation details are followed precisely. This is what prevents agents from drifting from the established conventions and from hallucinating decisions that should already be settled.

Installing v6 and updating from v4

We will now look at how to install BMAD v6 and, if applicable, upgrade from v4. The examples here use Cursor, but the same process applies to other IDEs. VS Code works as well, and if you are using Claude Code, you can run everything from the terminal.

Prerequisites

Here are the prerequisites:

- Cursor (or another supported IDE such as VS Code, or Claude Code via terminal)
- Node.js version 20 or higher

Fresh installation

To install the latest version of BMAD (currently v6):

```
npx bmad-method install
```

This installs v6 with whatever patches and upgrades have been deployed. BMAD releases updates weekly, so the installed build will always reflect the latest stable state.

To install v4 specifically (the latest stable v4 build at the time of recording):

```
npx bmad-method@v4.44.2 install
```

Upgrading from v4 to v6

Running `npx bmad-method install` from a repository that already has v4 will automatically detect the existing installation and walk you through the upgrade steps. The core change is architectural: in v6, everything is a skill, which means the framework is no longer tied to any specific vendor. The previous version stored configuration inside cursor rules or `.claude/commands` depending on the IDE — those files need to be removed before proceeding.

My strong recommendation: do not upgrade mid-work. If there is work in progress, finish it first. Upgrading while stories are active or workflows are partially complete is likely to break the current logic. Finish the current workflow, remove the old files, install v6, and then continue.

We will explore the practical usage of these commands in more depth when we get to the hands-on exercises later in the chapter.

Recommended workflow for getting started

Before jumping into the practice exercises, here are the module installation recommendations depending on your situation.

New projects

For projects starting from scratch, I recommend installing all three of the following:

- **Core** — mandatory. Everything else depends on it.
- **Agile** — for the full development workflow.
- **TEA** — especially if you are a technical practitioner and want quality to be a first-class concern in your solution.

Existing projects

For existing codebases, install at a minimum:

- **Core** — mandatory
- **Agile** — to generate the project context, produce project documentation, and use the quick flows for smaller features

The TEA module is optional for existing projects, with one caveat: it uses Playwright and Cypress as its primary test tooling, covering unit tests, integration tests, and end-to-end tests. If your existing project uses a different testing framework, I have not personally worked through the TEA module with tools other than those two, so proceed with that in mind and evaluate whether it fits your setup.

With that, we are ready to move from theory into practice. The next section puts all of this to work.

Summary

In this chapter, we explored why spec-driven development is becoming essential for AI-assisted software engineering and how the BMAD method provides a structured, practical approach to implementing it. We discussed the limitations of vibe coding, the importance of upstream thinking and context engineering, and the role of BMAD agents throughout the software development lifecycle. We also examined the key improvements introduced in BMAD v6, including independent workflows, a modular architecture, progressive disclosure, and the project context file, which provides a shared set of conventions for all workflows and agents. With the core, Agile, and TEA modules installed and configured, you now have a solid foundation for applying BMAD to real-world projects.

In the next chapter, we will learn about the analysis phase.

2

Upstream Phase: Analysis, Planning and Solutioning

In this chapter, we are going to explore the complete upstream phase of the BMAD method, starting from product discovery and brainstorming sessions all the way to creating **Product Requirements Documents (PRDs)**, UX specifications and architecture documents. We will learn about BMAD agents and workflows to understand how they collaborate to structure product ideas, validate technical decisions, generate implementation guidance, and prepare projects for downstream development workflows.

This chapter establishes the planning and architectural foundation that the downstream development workflows will rely on later. Everything we create here, including the PRD, architecture documents, UX specifications, and shared technical standards, becomes the source of truth for the implementation process that follows in the next chapters.

We will cover the following main topics:

- The analysis phase
- The planning phase
- The solution phase

By the end of this chapter, we will understand how to use the BMAD upstream process to create structured project documentation, evaluate architectural decisions, organize requirements into epics and stories, and generate technical foundations that can guide consistent AI-assisted development. We will also learn how to set up the `project-context.md` file, so downstream agents and workflows can work with a much more focused implementation context.

The analysis phase

The analysis phase is the starting point of the BMAD workflow. Before any requirements are written, any architecture is designed, or any code is generated, BMAD provides a structured space for exploring the idea itself.

Mary is the business analyst agent in BMAD. She brings expertise in market research, competitive analysis, requirements elicitation, and domain knowledge. Her role is to translate vague ideas into structured artifacts that the rest of the workflow can build on.

To invoke Mary, trigger `/bmad-agent-analyst` or type:

```
Talk to Mary
```

You can see the response we get from Mary in the following image:

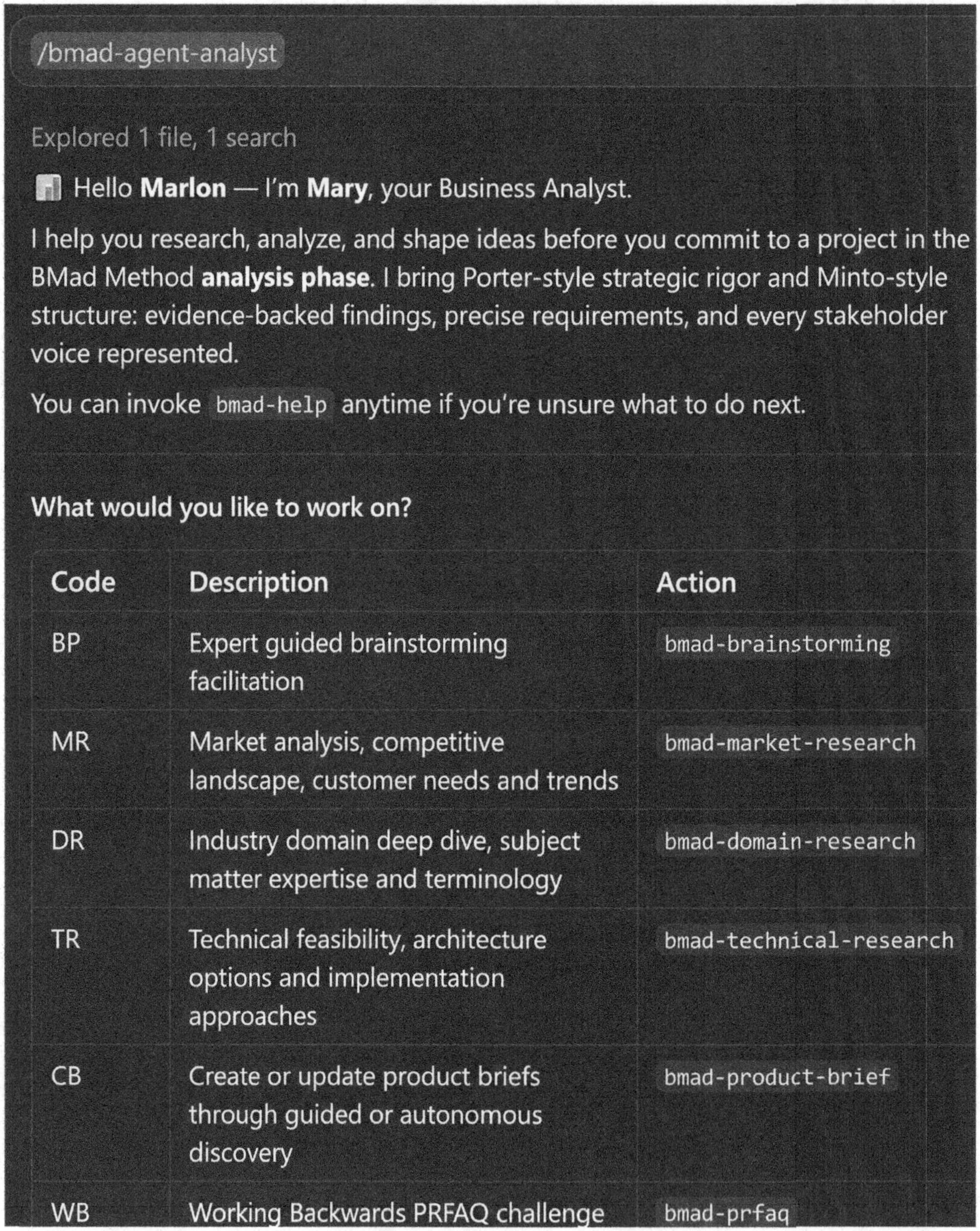

/bmad-agent-analyst

Explored 1 file, 1 search

Hello **Marlon** — I'm **Mary**, your Business Analyst.

I help you research, analyze, and shape ideas before you commit to a project in the BMad Method **analysis phase**. I bring Porter-style strategic rigor and Minto-style structure: evidence-backed findings, precise requirements, and every stakeholder voice represented.

You can invoke `bmad-help` anytime if you're unsure what to do next.

What would you like to work on?

Code	Description	Action
BP	Expert guided brainstorming facilitation	`bmad-brainstorming`
MR	Market analysis, competitive landscape, customer needs and trends	`bmad-market-research`
DR	Industry domain deep dive, subject matter expertise and terminology	`bmad-domain-research`
TR	Technical feasibility, architecture options and implementation approaches	`bmad-technical-research`
CB	Create or update product briefs through guided or autonomous discovery	`bmad-product-brief`
WB	Working Backwards PRFAQ challenge	`bmad-prfaq`

Figure 2.1 – Response from Mary, the business analyst agent

Once loaded, Mary introduces herself and presents her available workflows as a menu of trigger codes. Each code maps to a specific analysis workflow:

- `BP` or `/bmad-brainstorming` - Collaborative brainstorming
- `MR` or `/bmad-market-research` - Market research
- `DR` or `/bmad-domain-research` - Domain research
- `TR` or `/bmad-technical-research` - Technical research
- `CB` or `/bmad-product-brief` - Product brief
- `WB` or `/bmad-prfaq` - Working Backward / PRFAQ

All of these workflows are optional. A project can move directly into the PM phase without passing through the analysis phase at all. However, we recommend using at least the brainstorming workflow before moving forward. The context accumulated during the analysis phase carries into every downstream agent, reducing repetition and improving the quality of what those agents produce.

None of the analysis workflows strictly require the others. They are designed to be composable. A project may run only the product brief, or only the PRFAQ, depending on what the team needs. At the same time, when run together in sequence, they build on each other naturally, each session enriching the context available to the next.

Brainstorming the product idea

The brainstorming workflow is the natural entry point when a product idea exists but its shape is still unclear. It uses guided facilitation techniques to explore and refine the idea before any formal documents are created. To start a brainstorming session, use `BP` code from Mary's menu and describe the idea, or call `/bmad-brainstorming` workflow:

```
/bmad-brainstorming a to-do list app for busy freelancers
```

Following is the response we get:

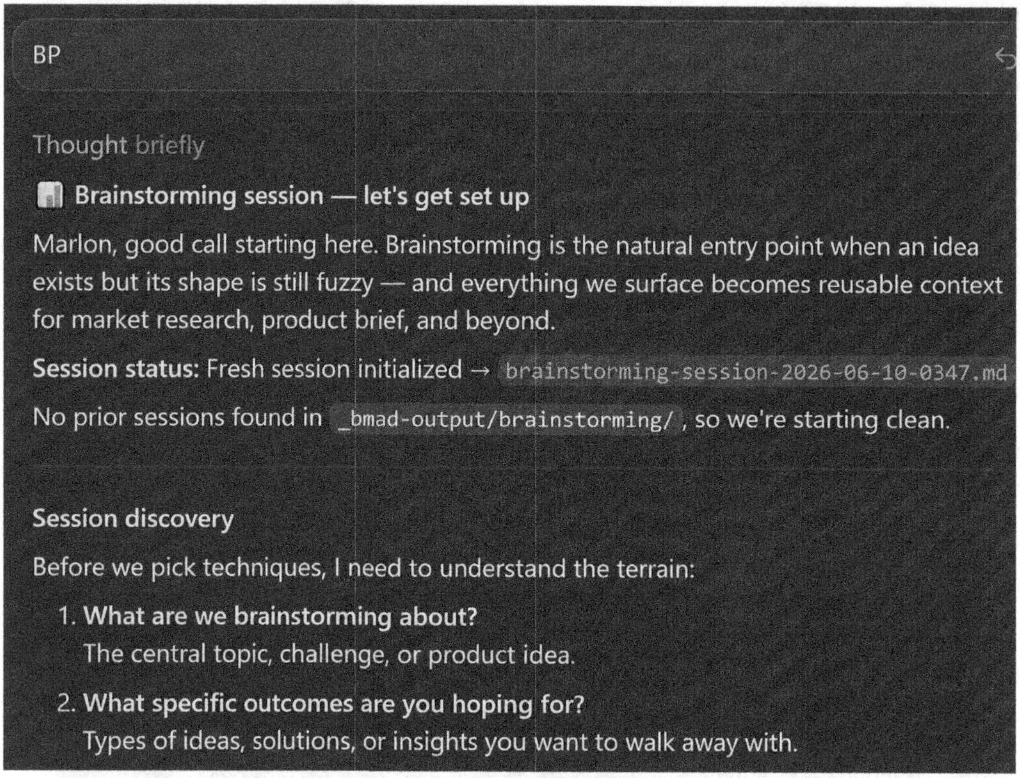

Figure 2.2 – Brainstorming session start

Mary begins by asking a sequence of structured questions to establish context:

- What are we brainstorming about?
- Are there any constraints or parameters?
- Is the goal broad exploration or focused ideation?
- Should a structured document be generated for later reference?

Note

Please note that due to the non-deterministic characteristics of LLMs, the screenshot might differ from your output.

These questions are the mechanism through which the session becomes relevant to the actual problem rather than remaining a generic exploration. The goal at this stage is to define the audience, the problem, the business objective, and the constraints before any techniques are introduced.

Once the initial context is established, Mary proposes a set of brainstorming techniques. BMAD contains more than 50 different techniques to explore your ideas. These may include:

- Role-playing
- Five Whys
- SCAMPER
- Assumption Reversal
- Six Thinking Hats

The ideal techniques vary depending on the product type and goals described during setup. Rather than selecting a technique at random, we would recommend letting Mary choose based on the context already provided. Because the agent already understands the idea, goals, and constraints, it can usually propose more appropriate techniques for the scenario.

Context read: To-do apps are a crowded, well-understood space. The risk is listing obvious features (due dates, tags, reminders). We need techniques that force **freelancer-specific** thinking and **deliberate differentiation**.

Recommended technique sequence

Phase 1: Foundation — Role Playing *(Collaborative · ~15 min · Medium energy)*

- **Why this fits:** Freelancers aren't one persona — they're designers juggling client feedback, developers context-switching between projects, consultants tracking billable work. Role-playing surfaces features generic task apps miss because they optimize for a single "user," not a **multi-hat operator**.
- **Expected outcome:** A grounded map of freelancer workflows, pain points, and feature gaps from 3–4 stakeholder lenses.

Phase 2: Idea generation — Reverse Brainstorming *(Creative · ~15 min · High energy)*

- **Why this builds on Phase 1:** Once we know the workflow, we flip the lens — "*How could a to-do app make a freelancer's day worse?*" Sabotage reveals hidden assumptions and turns anti-patterns into feature opportunities.
- **Expected outcome:** 20–30 feature ideas born from real failure modes, not feature-parity copying.

Figure 2.3 – Brainstorming technique suggestions

Once a technique is selected, the session becomes more exploratory. For role-playing, Mary creates a scenario where the user acts as a representative of the target audience, navigating real workflow situations. This approach is valuable because it forces the problem to be examined from a specific operational perspective rather than in abstract terms.

The session progressively refines the problem space. Mary introduces follow-up questions to surface edge cases, expose assumptions, and expand areas that initially appear straightforward. Rather than generating a feature list, the goal is to force deliberate thinking about user behavior, workflow constraints, and product boundaries.

At the end of the session, Mary generates a structured document: `brainstorming-report.md`. This document contains:

- Executive summary
- Constraints defined during the session
- Brainstorming techniques applied
- Ideas generated
- Problem assumptions
- Proposed solution directions

The purpose of the brainstorming workflow is to create structured context that becomes reusable throughout the remaining upstream phases. That generated context then becomes the foundation for the next analyst workflow: market research.

Performing market research

Once brainstorming is complete, the next step is market research. This workflow is especially useful when the product will face competition, when the target customer segment is unclear, or when assumptions about the market need to be validated before planning begins.

To start the market research session, use the MR code from Mary's menu, or invoke the `/bmad-market-research` workflow:

```
MR
```

The workflow begins by defining the scope of the research:

- Research objectives
- Methodology
- Competitive landscape
- Market size and growth potential

- Customer pain points
- Product positioning opportunities

Mary also proposes a research rationale and identifies primary data sources, analysis frameworks, and known limitations before proceeding.

At this stage, BMAD introduces one of its most useful concepts: elicitations. **Elicitations** are structured reasoning methods that challenge assumptions and evaluate the product from different perspectives. One particularly valuable elicitation during market research is the critical perspective review. This approach intentionally critiques the product assumptions rather than supporting them.

When the critical perspective elicitation is applied, the session may surface issues such as:

- The concept is product-focused rather than market-focused
- There is no clear differentiation strategy
- The proposed solution addresses a personal workflow problem rather than a broader market need

This is where market research becomes more than a research exercise. It becomes a stress-test of the idea before any commitment to planning is made. If the research surfaces that the product is intended as an internal tool rather than a commercial one, the research direction can be adjusted accordingly, shifting focus away from pricing and go-to-market strategy and toward workflow comparisons and existing tool analysis.

This demonstrates one of the most important characteristics of the BMAD workflow: the quality of every output depends directly on the clarity and accuracy of the context provided throughout the session.

At the end of the session, Mary generates a comprehensive market research document containing:

- Research methodology and objectives
- Market overview
- Competitor analysis
- Customer segment findings
- Strategic positioning recommendations
- Risks and open questions

This document becomes input for both the product brief and, later, the PRD.

> **Note**
>
> You can also run `/bmad-domain-research` and `/bmad-technical-research` to enhance your research phase.

Creating the product brief

After brainstorming and market research are complete, the next workflow is the product brief. The product brief is best used when the product concept is already clear and needs to be formalized before writing a full PRD. It produces a concise document that captures strategic intent, target users, key differentiators, and success criteria.

To create the product brief, use the `CB` code from Mary's menu, or invoke the `/bmad-product-brief` workflow:

```
CB
```

At this stage, the earlier brainstorming and market research sessions become extremely important. The product brief workflow does not start from scratch. Instead, Mary uses all the reasoning already established in the session, the brainstorming discussions, the constraints, the research findings, and the assumptions explored to progressively assemble the brief section by section.

At each stage, validate the generated content carefully to confirm it accurately reflects the product direction established during the earlier sessions. Once all sections are validated, a `product-brief.md` file will be created containing the following content:

- Product vision
- Problem statement
- Target users
- Key differentiators
- Success criteria
- MVP scope
- Constraints and risks

The brief acts as an upstream document for the PRD. When the PM agent later creates the PRD, it can extract the brief as a source of context, reducing re-explanation and keeping the two documents aligned. Neither requires the other; a project can begin directly with the PRD if the product direction is already well understood. However, when the brief exists, the PRD workflow produces better results because the foundational thinking has already been done

and documented. Another good example of creating the product brief first is that it does not include any technical information, making it perfect for stakeholder back and forth validation.

Working backwards with PRFAQ

The PRFAQ workflow applies the Amazon Working Backward method, a product development process where teams start the innovation cycle by defining the final customer experience. Rather than starting from requirements, it starts from the customer outcome, writing the press release and FAQ as if the product had already shipped successfully. This forces clarity on customer value and business case before any planning begins.

The PRFAQ workflow is especially useful when:

- The product idea needs to be validated before committing to planning
- The team is misaligned on what success looks like
- Customer benefit needs to be articulated before requirements are written

To start the PRFAQ session, use the `WB` code from Mary's menu, or invoke `/bmad-prfaq workflow`:

```
WB
```

The workflow proceeds in two stages. In the first stage, Mary facilitates writing the press release: a short, customer-facing announcement describing what the product does, who it is for, and why it matters, written as if it already exists in the market. In the second stage, the FAQ is written, covering anticipated customer questions and internal questions about implementation, scalability, and risk.

Once both are drafted, Mary applies critique to stress-test the assumptions embedded in each document. This is where the method reveals gaps in the product concept that might otherwise remain hidden until much later in the process.

The output of the session is `prfaq-{project}.md`, which contains:

- The press release
- The customer FAQ
- The internal FAQ

This document becomes the north star for everything that follows. It can inform or replace the product brief, and it provides the "why" context that the PRD builds on. Rather than jumping directly into features and requirements, the PRFAQ ensures that the problem and the customer benefit are clearly articulated before any formal planning begins.

At this point, the analysis phase is complete. The artifacts generated—the brainstorming report, market research findings, product brief and PRFAQ—form the foundation of context that the PM agent will draw on when creating the PRD. The amount of thinking invested here directly affects the quality of everything that follows.

The planning phase

The planning phase is where the product idea becomes a concrete specification. The analysis phase produced a body of context: brainstorming findings, market research, a product brief, or a PRFAQ. The planning phase consumes that context and transforms it into two categories of artifacts: requirements and experience design. Two agents own this phase: John, the product manager, and Sally, the UX designer.

A small project with a clear scope and no user-facing interface might skip the planning phase and move directly into architecture and implementation. However, for most projects, skipping the PRD means the architecture and implementation agents are working from unvalidated assumptions. The planning phase is where those assumptions are made explicit and stress-tested before any technical decisions are made, and this is where BMAD shines.

Working with John, the product manager

John is the product manager agent in BMAD. He drives requirements discovery through structured interviews, stakeholder alignment, and incremental validation, translating the product vision into a documented set of requirements that development can act on.

To invoke John, trigger `/bmad-agent-pm` or type:

```
Talk to John
```

This is the response we get:

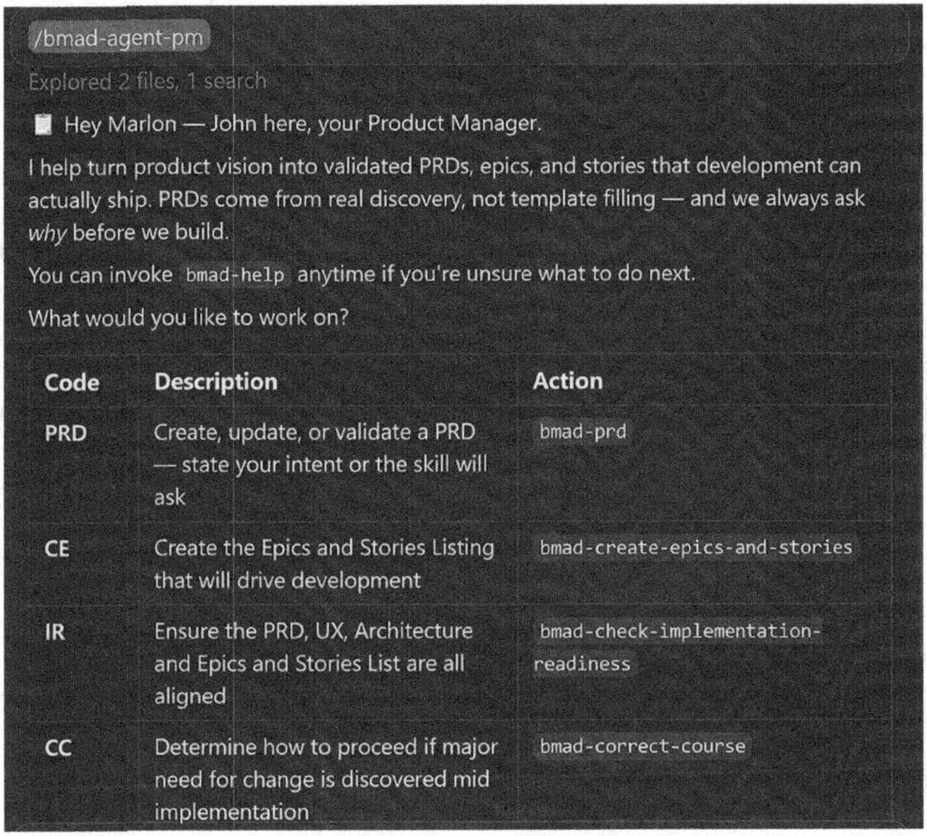

Figure 2.4 – Response from the agent

Once loaded, John introduces himself and presents his available workflows as a menu of trigger codes:

- `PRD` or `/bmad-prd` — Create, update, or validate a PRD
- `CE` or `/bmad-create-epics-and-stories` — Create epics and stories
- `IR` or `/bmad-check-implementation-readiness` — Check implementation readiness
- `CC` or `/bmad-correct-course` — Correct course mid-sprint

The `PRD` workflow is the primary activity in the planning phase. The remaining three workflows belong to the solutioning and implementation phases and will be covered in those chapters.

Creating the PRD

The PRD is the central planning artifact of BMAD Method. It defines what the product does, who it is for, what success looks like, and what constraints the implementation must operate within. Everything that follows in the BMAD workflow—the UX design, the architecture, the epics, and every individual story—is derived from the PRD.

To start the PRD creation workflow, use the `PRD` trigger from John's menu or invoke `/bmad-prd`:

```
PRD
```

This is the response we get:

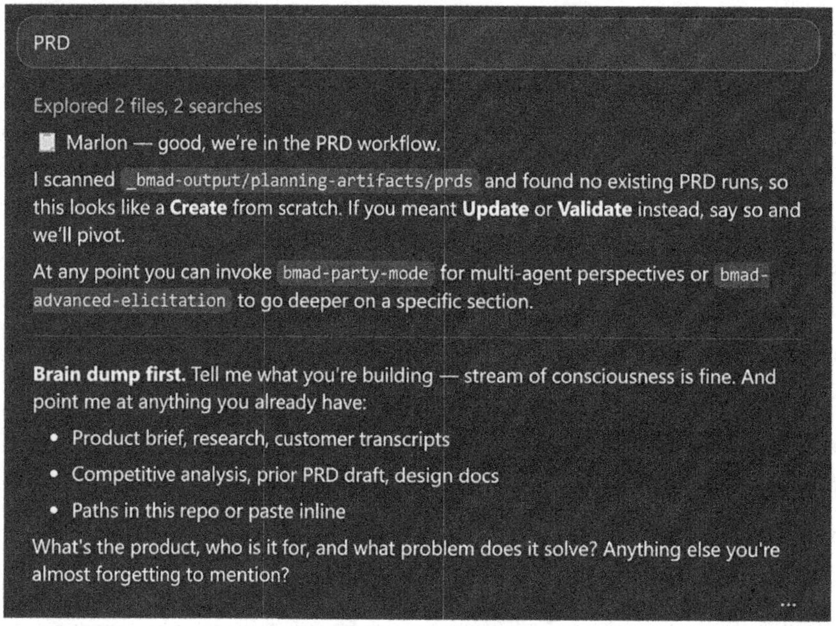

Figure 2.5 – Creating a new PRD

> **Note**
>
> On v6.8.0, `/bmad-prd workflow` was consolidated into one single slash command. For previous versions, you might find it through `/bmad-create-prd`, `/bmad-edit-prd`, or `/bmad-validate-prd`.

John begins the session with a structured discovery interview. The questions surface:

- Product goals and success criteria
- Target users and their core needs
- Key features and functional requirements
- Non-functional requirements and constraints
- Known risks and open questions

At this stage, any artifacts from the analysis phase—a product brief, a PRFAQ or market research findings—can become John's starting context. The more thorough the analysis phase was, the less ground needs to be covered here.

Rather than filling out a form, the session is conversational. John asks one question at a time, explores responses, and progressively builds understanding before moving to the next area. The result is a PRD that reflects real thinking rather than a template filled in under pressure.

Once discovery is complete, John assembles the PRD section by section. Review each section before confirming it; inconsistencies caught here are far cheaper than ones caught after architecture begins. When all sections are confirmed, a `prd.md` file will be created containing:

- Product overview and vision
- Target users and personas
- Goals and success criteria
- Functional requirements
- Non-functional requirements
- Constraints and assumptions
- Open questions and risks

Two companion files might also be generated alongside the PRD:

- The `addendum.md` captures decisions that are known to matter but were not resolved in this session
- The `decision-log.md` records the reasoning behind key choices made during the interview, so future sessions can understand why the PRD contains what it contains

Updating and validating the PRD

The PRD workflow supports three distinct intents: create, update, and validate. Creation is the starting point. But a PRD is a living document, and BMAD provides structured ways to maintain it throughout the project.

When the project scope changes, use the update intent to reconcile the existing PRD with the new direction. Rather than editing the document directly, the update intent surfaces conflicts between the change and the existing requirements before applying anything. This prevents silent inconsistencies from propagating into architecture and stories.

The validate intent produces a structured review of the PRD against a configurable checklist. It surfaces gaps, ambiguities, and internal inconsistencies before architecture begins. The output is a `validation-report.md` and a companion `.html` report, each containing a list of findings categorized by severity.

I would recommend running the validate intent at least once before handing the PRD to the architect, even though it's an optional step. The architecture decisions made in the next phase are difficult to reverse, and gaps in the requirements tend to become expensive problems once design is underway.

At this point, the requirements are documented and validated. The next step depends on whether the product has a user-facing interface. If it does, the workflow moves to Sally.

Working with Sally, the UX designer

Sally is the UX designer agent in BMAD. She translates user needs into interaction design and UX specifications, balancing empathy with edge-case rigor, and feeding both architecture and implementation with clear, opinionated design intent.

Sally is an optional agent. Projects without a user-facing interface can proceed directly from the PRD to the architect. However, for any product where users will interact directly with a screen, Sally's output significantly improves the quality of both the architecture and the implementation. Without a design specification, implementation agents make assumptions about layout, behavior, and edge cases that are often wrong and expensive to revisit later.

To invoke Sally, trigger `/bmad-agent-ux-designer` or type:

```
Talk to Sally
```

The response should be similar to the following:

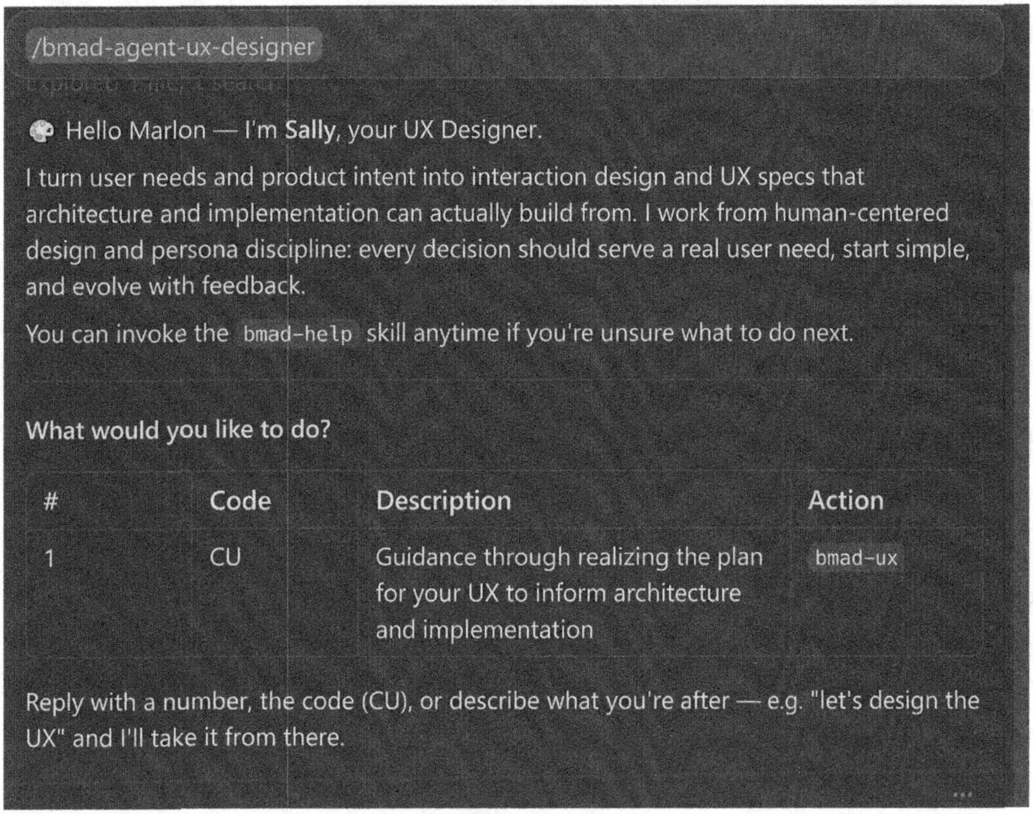

Figure 2.6 – Sally's response

Once loaded, Sally presents her available workflow:

- `CU` or `/bmad-ux – Create UX design`

Creating the UX design

The UX workflow produces two specification files that together define both what the product looks like and how it behaves. Sally calls this pair the spine.

To start the UX workflow, use the `CU` trigger from Sally's menu:

```
CU
```

This is the response we get:

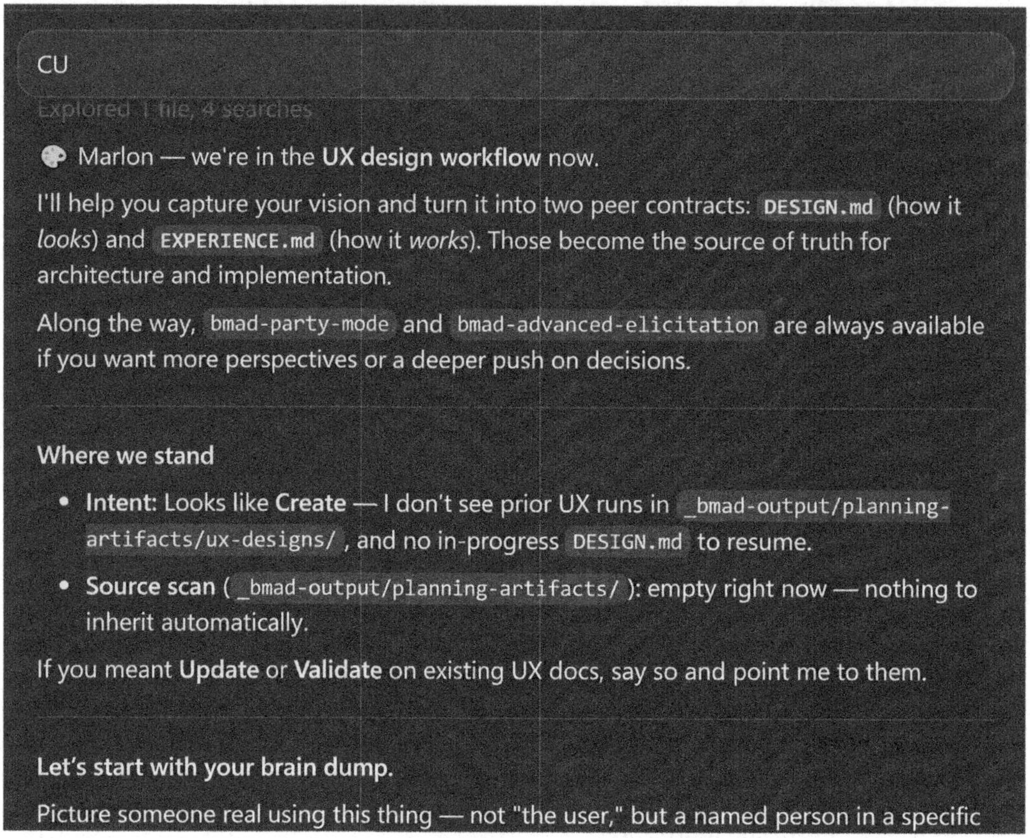

Figure 2.7 – UX Design workflow

> **Note**
>
> For previous versions, the command is called `/bmad-create-ux-design`.

Before starting the session, bring Sally the materials she needs to produce a design grounded in the actual product requirements:

- The `prd.md` from John
- Examples, inspirations, and references
- Branding guidelines, if any exist

At this stage, the PRD becomes Sally's primary input. The feature scope defined in the PRD determines what Sally needs to design. Rather than exploring the product concept from scratch, Sally enters the session with the requirements already understood and focuses immediately on design decisions.

The session proceeds through two design layers. The first is visual design: how the product looks, what components it uses, how the layout is organized, and how visual hierarchy guides the user's attention. The second is behavioral design: how the product responds to user actions, how it handles states and transitions, and what happens at the edges: error states, empty states, and edge cases.

Sally does not simply accept the first reasonable design direction. She proposes options, explains the trade-offs, and asks about constraints that might affect the choice. This is especially useful when the product has competing design priorities, for example, when simplicity for new users conflicts with efficiency for experienced ones.

Once both design layers are explored and validated, the workflow produces two files:

- `DESIGN.md`: The visual design specification:
    - Layout and component structure
    - Visual hierarchy
    - Branding alignment
    - Component library mappings
- `EXPERIENCE.md`: The behavioral design specification:
    - User flows and journeys
    - State transitions
    - Edge cases and error handling
    - Interaction patterns

A `.decision-log.md` is also generated, capturing the reasoning behind key design choices in the same way John's PRD workflow tracks requirement decisions.

These two files are not wireframes or mockups. They are written specifications. This is intentional. Written specifications are directly consumable by both the architect and the implementation agents. They can be referenced, diffed, and kept in version control alongside the code they describe.

This is where the connection between the planning phase and the next phase becomes concrete. The architect receives both the `prd.md` from John and the `DESIGN.md` plus `EXPERIENCE.md` from Sally. Together, these three documents define what the system must do and how users will experience doing it. The architecture decisions that follow are grounded in both the requirements and the design intent, rather than being made in isolation from either.

At this point, the planning phase is complete. The PRD defines the requirements. The UX design defines the experience. These artifacts are the direct inputs to the solutioning phase, where Winston, the architect, takes over.

The solution phase

The solutioning phase is where decisions become binding. The planning phase produced a PRD that defines what the system must do and, optionally, a UX design that defines how users will experience doing it. The solutioning phase takes those artifacts and answers the next set of questions: how the system will be built, what risks exist in building it, and what work the implementation team will need to execute. Four workflows drive this phase: architecture design, test strategy, epic and story creation, and an implementation readiness gate.

Three agents operate in this phase. Winston, the system architect, owns the technical direction. Murat, the test engineering architect, owns the quality strategy. John, the product manager from the planning phase, returns to decompose requirements into implementable work items. The phase ends only when all three are done and the readiness gate clears.

Working with Winston, the architect

Winston is the system architect agent in BMAD. He turns product requirements and UX specifications into technical architecture, makes technology stack choices, defines system boundaries, documents integration patterns, and records the reasoning behind major trade-offs.

To invoke Winston, invoke `/bmad-agent-architect` or type:

```
Talk to Winston
```

You should get a similar response:

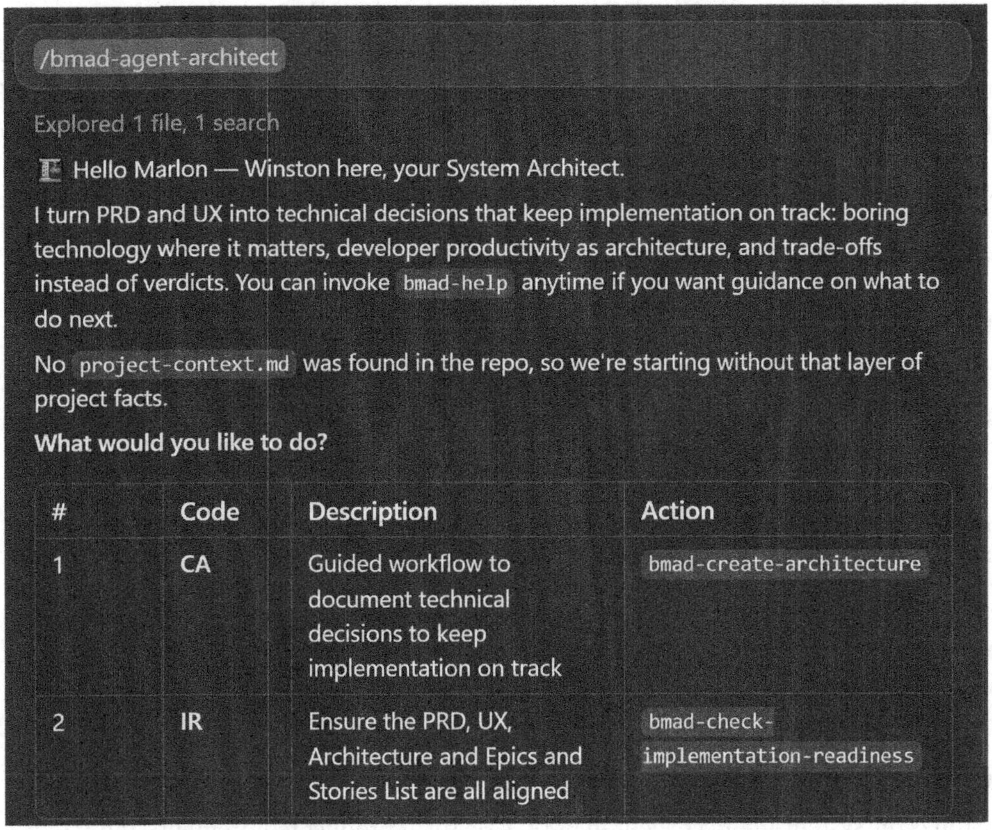

Figure 2.8 – Winston presentation and available workflows

Once loaded, Winston introduces himself and presents his available workflows as a menu of trigger codes:

- `CA` or `/bmad-create-architecture`: Create architecture
- `IR` or `/bmad-check-implementation-readiness`: Check implementation readiness

The `CA` workflow is the primary activity at this stage. The `IR` workflow is the gate check at the end of the solutioning phase and will be covered later in this chapter.

Creating the architecture

The architecture document is the technical counterpart to the PRD. Where the PRD defines what the system must do, the architecture document defines how the system will do it. It captures technology stack decisions, system component breakdown, integration patterns, non-functional requirements approach, and the **Architecture Decision Records (ADRs)** that explain why each major trade-off was made the way it was.

To start the architecture workflow, use the `CA` trigger from Winston's menu:

```
CA
```

Here is the response I got:

Figure 2.9 – Create architecture workflow

Before starting, bring Winston the artifacts from the planning phase:

- The `prd.md` from John
- The `DESIGN.md` and `EXPERIENCE.md` from Sally, if UX design was performed

At this stage, the PRD becomes Winston's primary input. The functional requirements, non-functional requirements, and constraints documented by John determine the technical boundaries within which Winston works. Rather than designing in isolation, Winston grounds every decision in requirements that have already been validated.

Winston does not produce a single recommendation. For each major decision, he presents options, explains the trade-offs, and asks about constraints that might affect the choice. This is especially useful when non-functional requirements create tension. For example, when a performance target conflicts with a preferred technology choice or when a security constraint rules out an otherwise obvious integration pattern.

Once all decisions are explored and confirmed, the architecture document `architecture.md` is created and it contains:

- Technology stack choices with rationale
- System component breakdown
- Integration patterns
- Non-functional requirements approach (performance, security, observability)
- Architecture Decision Records for each major trade-off

Generating project context

After the architecture document is written, one additional step prepares the environment for all downstream agents. The `/bmad-generate-project-context` workflow produces a `project-context.md`, a constitution for the project that every AI agent will use as baseline context during implementation.

```
/bmad-generate-project-context
```

Here is the response:

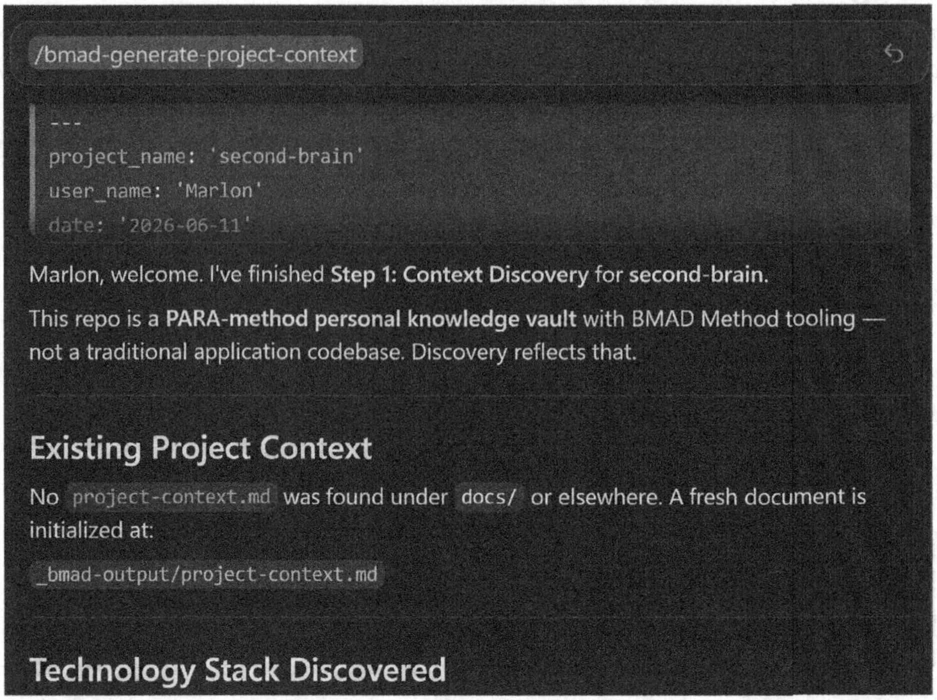

Figure 2.10 – Generating project context workflow

This document serves as the technical rule set for the project. When Amelia, the development agent, implements stories later in the process, she reads this file first. It ensures consistent technology choices, naming conventions, and architectural patterns across every implementation session, regardless of when the session happens or what scope is in focus.

This is where the planning and solutioning phases connect concretely. The `prd.md`, the UX design files, and the `architecture.md` together define the full shape of the system. The `project-context.md` distills the architecture decisions into a portable context that survives across sessions.

> **Note**
>
> Note that `/bmad-generate-project-context` is not owned by any agent. Workflows are a major change in v6, and they can be invoked without loading the agent first. This makes the comprehension of the framework easier for newcomers to Spec Driven Development.

Working with Murat, the test architect

Once the architecture is documented, the next step is test design. Murat is the Test Engineering Architect agent in BMAD, part of the TEA module, which is installed alongside the core BMAD Method. He brings risk-based testing strategy, automation expertise, and release gate authority, covering the full testing lifecycle from design through the CI pipeline to coverage traceability.

To invoke Murat, use `/bmad-tea` or type:

```
Talk to Murat
```

This is the response:

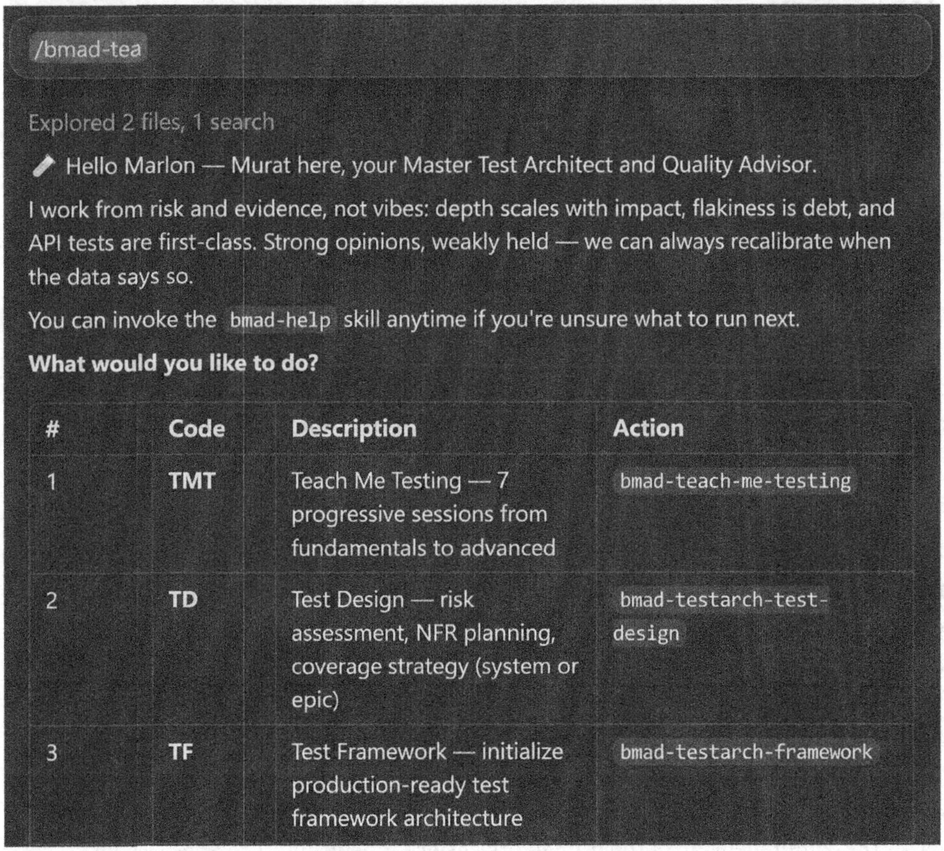

Figure 2.11 – Test Architect presentation and available workflows

Once loaded, Murat presents his full workflow menu. His trigger set spans the solutioning and implementation phases:

- `TD` or `/bmad-testarch-test-design`: Risk-based test planning (system or epic level)
- `TF` or `/bmad-testarch-framework`: Scaffold test framework
- `CI` or `/bmad-testarch-ci`: Set up CI/CD quality pipeline
- `AT` or `/bmad-testarch-atdd`: Generate red-phase acceptance test scaffolds
- `TA` or `/bmad-testarch-automate`: Expand automation coverage for existing features
- `RV` or `/bmad-testarch-test-review`: Quality audit with objective scoring
- `TR` or `/bmad-testarch-trace`: Coverage traceability and go/no-go gate decision
- `NR` or `/bmad-testarch-nfr`: Non-functional evidence audit
- `TMT` or `/bmad-teach-me-testing`: Structured testing course (7 sessions)
- `GATE`: Guide through the release gate sequence

In the solutioning phase, the relevant trigger is `TD`. The remaining workflows belong to the implementation phase and will be covered in that chapter.

Designing the test strategy

The **TD** workflow operates in two modes: system-level and epic-level. In the solutioning phase, we run it at the system level. The goal is not to write tests, it is to define what must be tested, at what thresholds, and with what tools, before a single line of implementation code is written. This shifts testing concerns left, surfacing testability gaps in the architecture before they become expensive implementation problems.

To start the system-level test design workflow, use the `TD` trigger from Murat's menu:

```
TD
```

Here is the response:

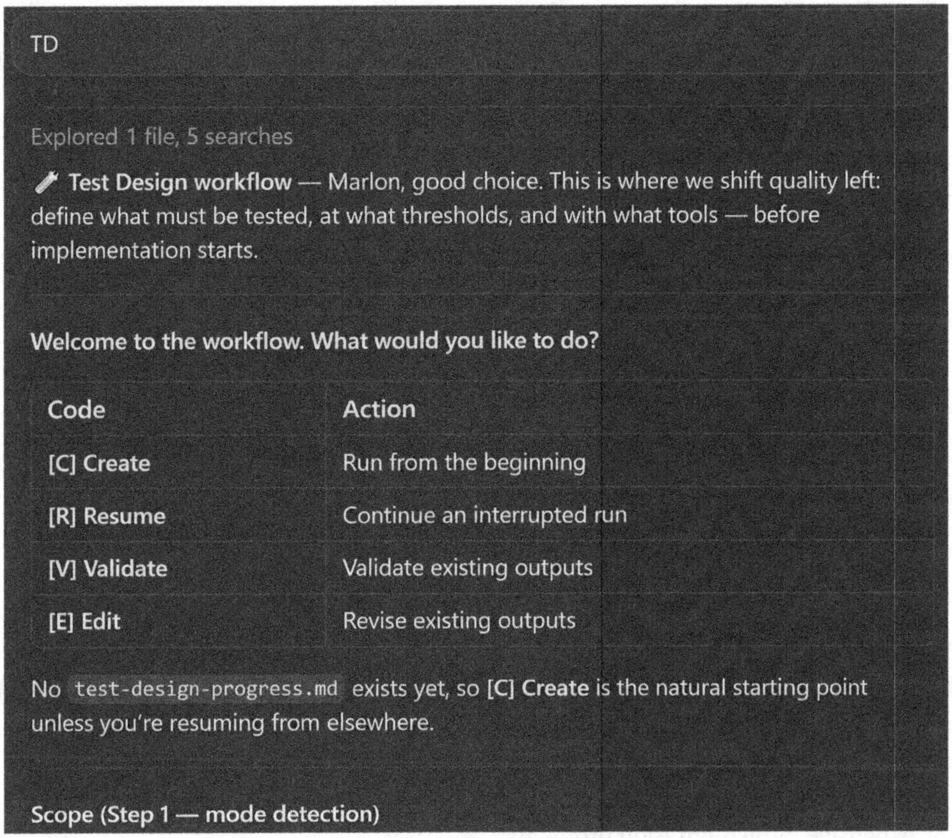

Figure 2.12 – Test design workflow

Bring Murat the architecture document and the PRD. The architecture gives him the system structure and ADRs to review for testability gaps. The PRD provides the non-functional requirements, like performance targets, SLO/SLA commitments and compliance requirements that become the thresholds he defines.

Murat works through the architecture layer by layer, scoring risk using a probability-times-impact model. Each area of the system receives a P0 through P3 priority designation. P0 areas are critical path and must be covered. P3 areas are low risk and optional. The test design defines coverage targets and planned validation tools for each priority level.

> **Note**
>
> The thresholds and coverage strategies defined by Murat become the hard constraints for the "Plan" pillar. These artifacts dictate the **Arrange, Act, Assert (AAA)** validation boundaries that Amelia (the Developer agent) must satisfy during implementation.

Once the analysis is complete, the workflow produces two documents:

- `test-design-architecture.md`: for architecture and development teams:
    - Quick guide with blocker, high priority, and info-only findings
    - Risk assessment with P0–P3 scoring
    - NFR testability requirements: thresholds, unknowns, architecture gaps, planned evidence
    - ADR gaps and assumptions surfaced during review
- `test-design-qa.md`: for QA teams:
    - Test coverage plan with P0/P1/P2/P3 scenarios as checkboxes
    - NFR test coverage: planned validation tools and evidence artifacts
    - Sprint 0 setup requirements — blockers, environments, and infrastructure needs

I would recommend reviewing the blockers section of `test-design-architecture.md` before moving forward. A blocker at this stage means the architecture is missing a decision that testing depends on. It is significantly cheaper to resolve that gap now than to discover it after implementation has started.

At this point, the architecture is designed and the test strategy is defined. The next step is translating the requirements and architecture into a structured backlog.

Creating epics and stories

With the architecture in place, John returns to the solutioning phase to decompose the PRD into implementable work. The `CE` workflow breaks requirements into epics, a collection of related user stories, sized and sequenced for sprint execution. John does this work informed by both the PRD and the architecture, so the epic boundaries reflect the technical structure of the system.

At this point, you can trigger `/bmad-create-epics-and-stories` without the need to invoke the John agent definition:

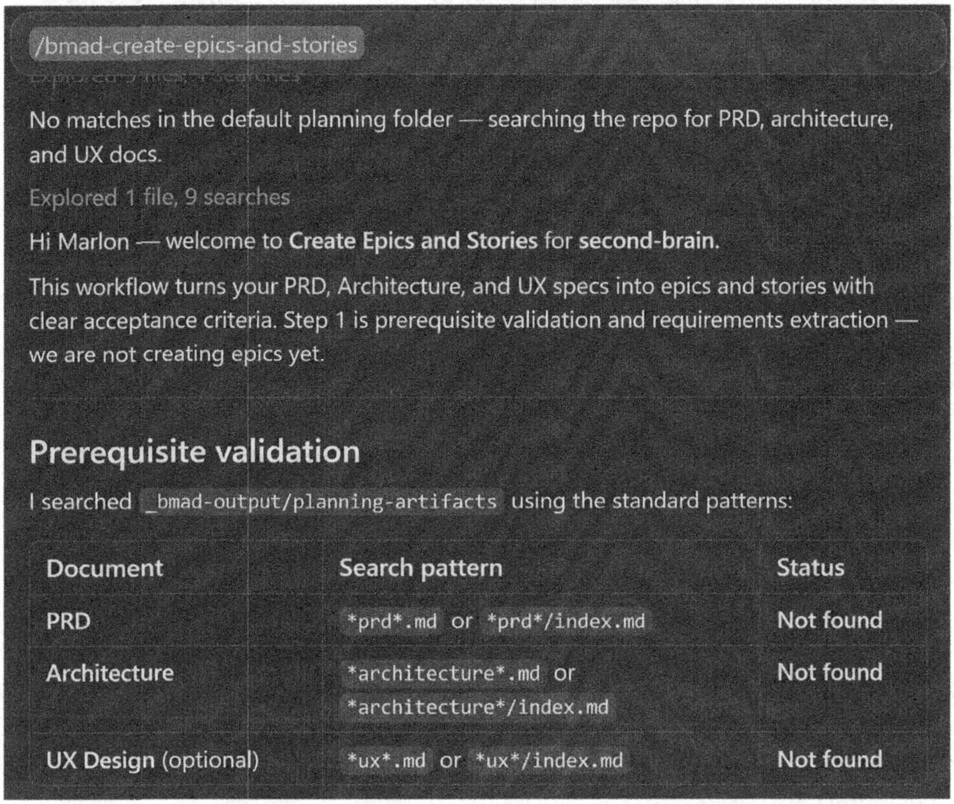

Figure 2.13 – Creating epics and stories workflow

After the workflow is loaded, bring the `prd.md` and the `architecture.md` if they are not identified automatically. The PRD defines the features to decompose. The architecture defines the technical boundaries that should inform how epics are grouped; for example, a feature that spans two distinct system components may become two epics, not one, if the implementation dependencies require it.

The workflow will propose an epic structure and sequence the stories within each epic. Each story is sized to be implementable in one focused session by the development agent. Stories are the unit of context for implementation: self-contained, with all acceptance criteria and references to relevant PRD sections and architecture decisions built in.

Once the epic structure is confirmed, an `epics.md` file is generated and contains:

- Epics goal and scope
- User stories with acceptance criteria
- Story dependencies and sequencing hints
- References to relevant PRD sections and architecture decisions

This epic file becomes the direct input for sprint planning and, ultimately, for the individual story files that the development agent will execute.

Checking implementation readiness

The solutioning phase ends with a gate check. The `/bmad-check-implementation-readiness` workflow validates that all planning and solutioning artifacts are complete, consistent, and ready to hand off to the implementation team. Notice that it is available from both Winston's and John's menus, and it checks across every artifact produced so far: the PRD, the UX design, the architecture, and the epics, but as we learned, we're going to invoke the workflow directly.

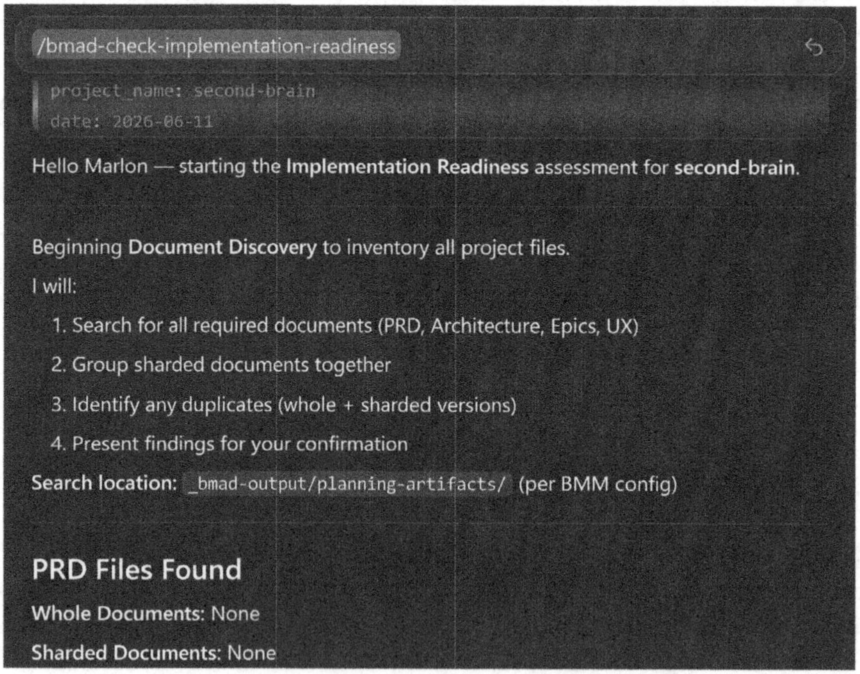

Figure 2.14 – Check implementation readiness workflow

The workflow checks:

- PRD completeness and internal consistency
- UX design coverage, if applicable
- Architecture decisions and ADR coverage
- Test design evaluation
- Epic and story granularity and completeness
- Cross-artifact consistency: PRD ↔ architecture ↔ epics

The output is one of three decisions:

- **PASS** — implementation can begin
- **CONCERNS** — issues found but not blockers; proceed with awareness
- **FAIL** — gaps must be addressed before implementation

A FAIL decision means one or more of the artifacts has a gap that would leave the implementation team without the information they need. Rather than treating this as a setback, treat it as the system doing its job. The gap exists now, in a document, where it is fixable in minutes. If it surfaced during implementation, fixing it would require stopping work, re-entering a planning or architecture session, and reconciling changes with work already in progress.

I would recommend running the gate check on every medium and large project. For small, well-scoped projects with a single developer, it is optional. But for anything with more than one implementation agent, more than two epics, or any non-functional requirements that carry real risk, the gate check is worth the time.

At this point, the solutioning phase is complete. The architecture is designed. The test strategy is defined. The epics and stories are structured and validated. The next phase is implementation, where Amelia, the development agent, begins executing the work.

Summary

In this chapter, we explored the complete BMAD upstream workflow, starting from brainstorming and market research all the way to creating PRDs, UX specifications, test architecture design and architecture documents. We worked with multiple BMAD agents to understand how they help structure requirements, validate assumptions, organize implementation workflows, and generate technical guidance for both greenfield and brownfield projects. By the end of the chapter, we established the technical and product foundations that will guide the development process in the following chapters.

3

Downstream Phase: Implementing and Sprinting

In this chapter, we move into the downstream phase of the BMAD workflow: the implementation sprint. With the PRD, architecture, and UX specification files in place from the upstream process, we now have everything needed to start building.

We will work through the full downstream loop: sprint planning and implementing each story with the Developer Agent, and validating the output with the QA Agent. By the end, the mechanics of how these two agents collaborate, and how to manage the back-and-forth between them until a quality gate passes, should be clear enough to apply to any project.

Beyond the workflow itself, we will also look at how the application evolves story by story across epics, which makes it easier to see why the level of context BMAD provides at each step matters. This is the phase where the upstream investment pays off.

We will cover the following main topics:

- Working with the Dev agent
- Working with the QA agent
- Iterating and performing the next task

Note

Download the code bundle and the PDF version of this book

Your purchase includes a DRM-free PDF copy of this book, the code bundle, and a range of exclusive benefits. To unlock everything, follow the *Free benefits with your book* section in the *Preface*.

The implementation phase

The implementation phase is where the system gets built. The solutioning phase produced everything the implementation team needs: a validated PRD, an architecture document, a test strategy, a structured backlog of epics and stories, and a `project-context.md` that carries the project's technical rules across sessions. The implementation phase consumes all of it, story by story, until the software is done.

Two agents drive this phase. Amelia, the senior software engineer, owns the development cycle: she reads stories, writes code, and runs the review loop until every acceptance criterion passes. Murat, the Test Engineering Architect, owns the quality layer: he scaffolds the test framework, generates test cases before and after implementation, audits quality, and makes the evidence-backed gate decision at the end of each epic. Their loops interlock at every story boundary.

Working with Amelia, the developer

Amelia is the development agent in BMAD. She implements stories using test-first discipline — red, green, refactor — verifying every acceptance criterion before marking a story done. File paths and AC IDs are her primary vocabulary. She does not speculate about scope or make architectural decisions independently: she follows the `project-context.md` and the story file.

To invoke Amelia, trigger `/bmad-agent-dev` or type:

```
Talk to Amelia
```

This is the response we get:

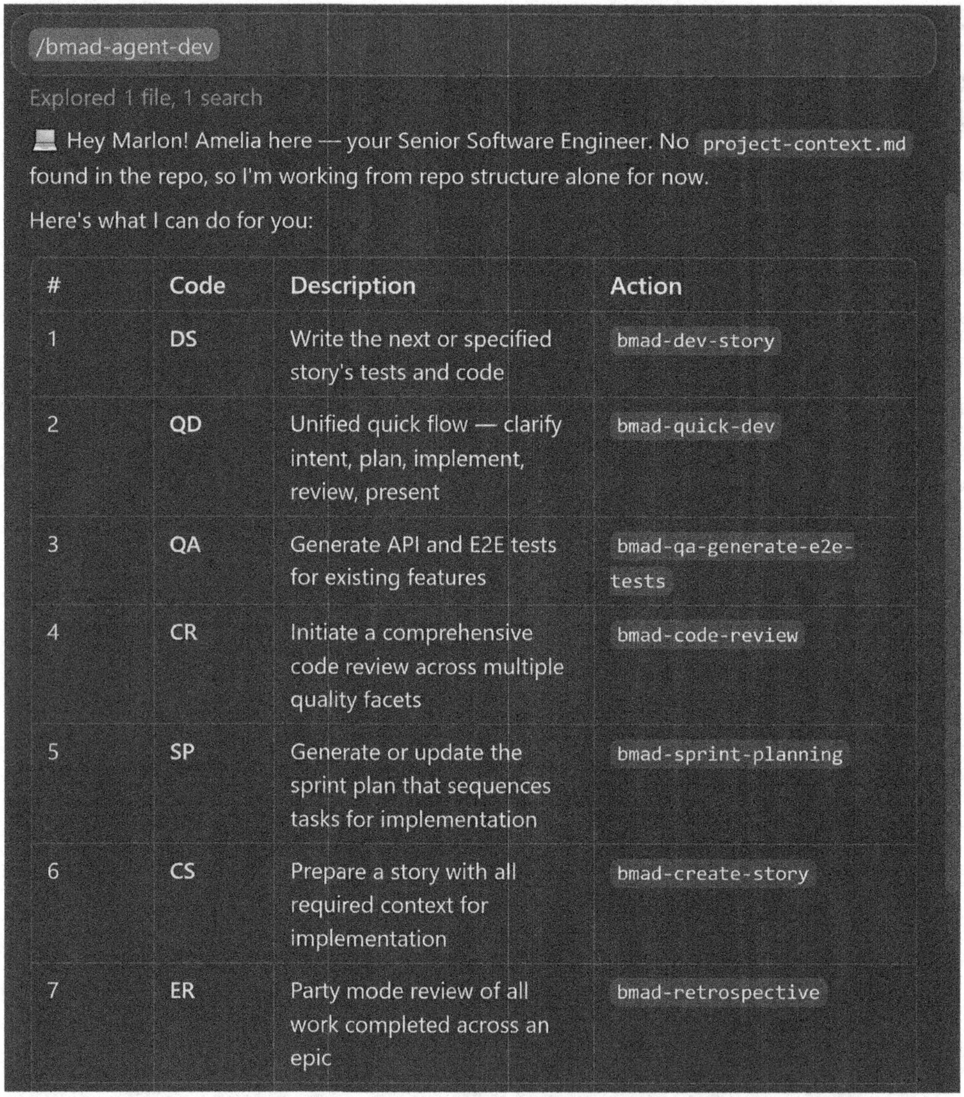

/bmad-agent-dev

Explored 1 file, 1 search

💻 Hey Marlon! Amelia here — your Senior Software Engineer. No `project-context.md` found in the repo, so I'm working from repo structure alone for now.

Here's what I can do for you:

#	Code	Description	Action
1	DS	Write the next or specified story's tests and code	`bmad-dev-story`
2	QD	Unified quick flow — clarify intent, plan, implement, review, present	`bmad-quick-dev`
3	QA	Generate API and E2E tests for existing features	`bmad-qa-generate-e2e-tests`
4	CR	Initiate a comprehensive code review across multiple quality facets	`bmad-code-review`
5	SP	Generate or update the sprint plan that sequences tasks for implementation	`bmad-sprint-planning`
6	CS	Prepare a story with all required context for implementation	`bmad-create-story`
7	ER	Party mode review of all work completed across an epic	`bmad-retrospective`

Figure 3.1 – Response from Amelia

Once loaded, Amelia presents her available workflows as a menu of trigger codes:

- `DS` or `/bmad-dev-story`: Implement a story
- `QD` or `/bmad-quick-dev`: Quick dev, skipping the planning phases
- `CR` or `/bmad-code-review`: Code review
- `SP` or `/bmad-sprint-planning`: Sprint planning
- `CS` or `/bmad-create-story`: Create a story
- `ER` or `/bmad-retrospective`: Epic retrospective
- `IN` or `/bmad-investigate`: Forensic investigation

The `/bmad-sprint-planning` workflow is the starting point for the phase. The `/bmad-create-story`, `/bmad-dev-story`, and `/bmad-code-review` workflows form the repeating story loop that drives all implementation work. The remaining workflows serve specific moments in the cycle and will be covered as they arise.

Initializing the sprint plan

Before the first story is picked up, the sprint plan needs to be initialized. The `/bmad-sprint-planning` workflow reads the `epics.md` from the solutioning phase and transforms the epic and story structure into a machine-readable tracking file.

To start sprint planning, invoke `/bmad-sprint-planning`:

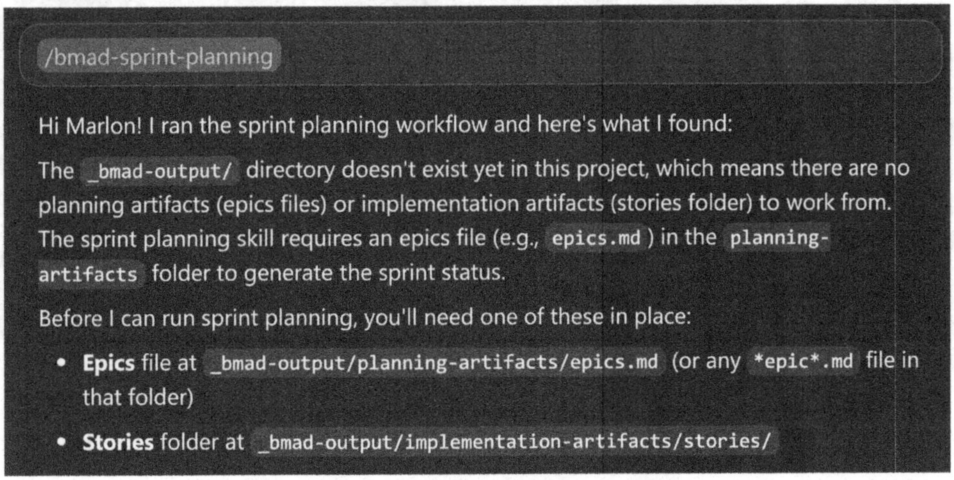

Figure 3.2 – Result of running sprint planning

Bring the `epics.md` from the solutioning phase. Amelia will read the story structure, confirm the sequencing, and generate a `sprint-status.yaml` file. This file is the authoritative record of implementation progress throughout the phase. Every story has a status, and that status is updated as stories move from pending to in-progress to done.

The sprint plan is initialized once per project. After this step, every implementation session starts by checking the sprint status and picking up the next story in sequence.

The development cycle

The core of the implementation phase is a three-step loop that repeats: create a story, implement it, and review it. This loop runs for every story in the sprint plan, in sequence. At this stage, the earlier solutioning work becomes extremely important. Each story file is built from those artifacts, so the quality of what was produced in the solutioning phase directly shapes the quality of what Amelia has to work from.

> **Note**
>
> The complete development cycle uses Developer and QA agent workflows together. We'll learn one by one now, then connect everything together later.

Creating a story

Before implementation begins, the story must be drafted as a self-contained file. The `CS` workflow picks the next story from the sprint plan and produces a story file with everything Amelia needs to implement it in one focused session: the goal, the acceptance criteria with AC IDs, technical implementation notes, test requirements, and references to the relevant architecture decisions.

To draft the next story, invoke `/bmad-create-story`:

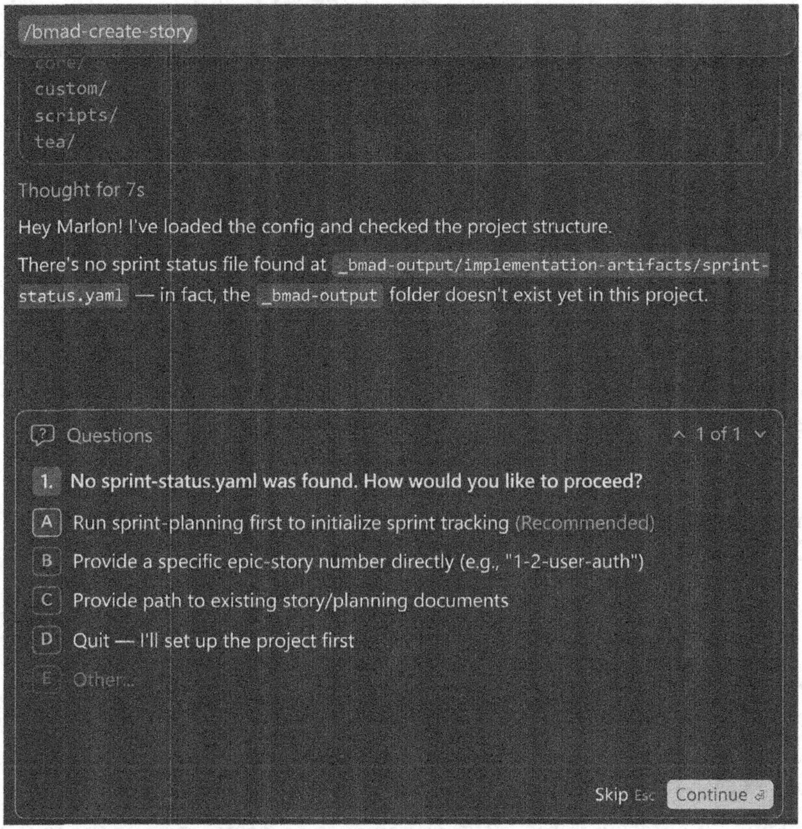

Figure 3.3 – Create story workflow response

Bring the `sprint-status.yaml` and the `epics.md`. Amelia identifies the next pending story, pulls its requirements from the epic file, cross-references the relevant architecture sections, and drafts a `story-[slug].md` file. Review the acceptance criteria before moving forward: the story file is the contract between the planning and the implementation, and AC IDs established here are the IDs that the review layer will verify against.

The completed story file contains:

- Story goal and user value
- Acceptance criteria with unique AC IDs
- Technical implementation notes
- Test requirements

- References to relevant architecture decisions
- Definition of done

Once the story file is confirmed, it becomes the primary input for both the testing scaffold and the implementation itself.

Implementing the story

With the story file in place, the DS workflow implements it. Amelia reads the story, works through each acceptance criterion in order using test-first discipline, and verifies every AC ID before marking the story done. The red-green-refactor cycle is the unit of progress: write a failing test, write the minimum code to pass it, clean up without breaking it.

To start the implementation, invoke `/bmad-dev-story`:

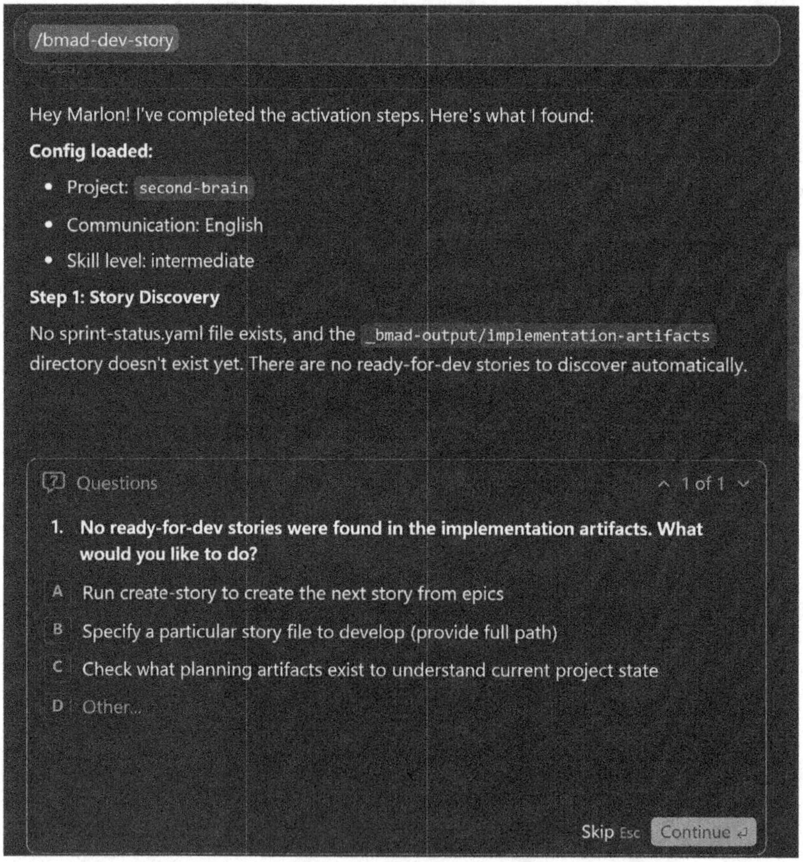

Figure 3.4 – Dev story response

Bring the story file and `project-context.md` will be loaded as part of the development context. The `project-context.md` is the technical constitution established in the solutioning phase. Amelia reads it at the start of every implementation session to ensure that naming conventions, technology choices, and architectural patterns remain consistent across all sessions, regardless of how far apart they happen.

Rather than implementing the entire story at once, Amelia works one acceptance criterion at a time. This is especially useful when a story contains mixed concerns, for example, when a backend endpoint and a UI component are both in scope. The AC-by-AC sequence ensures that each unit of work is independently verifiable before the next begins.

At this stage, the test scaffolds generated by Murat become the guide for implementation. If the `/bmad-testarch-atdd` workflow was run before `/bmad-dev-story`, each acceptance criterion already has a `test.skip()` scaffold waiting. Removing the skip activates the red phase: the test fails because the feature does not exist yet. Implementation proceeds until the test passes, then refactoring begins.

Once all acceptance criteria pass, the story implementation is complete and the output is working code with passing tests for every AC.

Reviewing the Code

Once implementation is done, the `/bmad-code-review` workflow validates the result. Code review in BMAD is adversarial and multi-layered. It does not simply check whether the code compiles. It checks whether the code is correct, whether edge cases are handled, and whether every acceptance criterion from the story file is demonstrably satisfied.

To start the review, invoke `/bmad-code-review`:

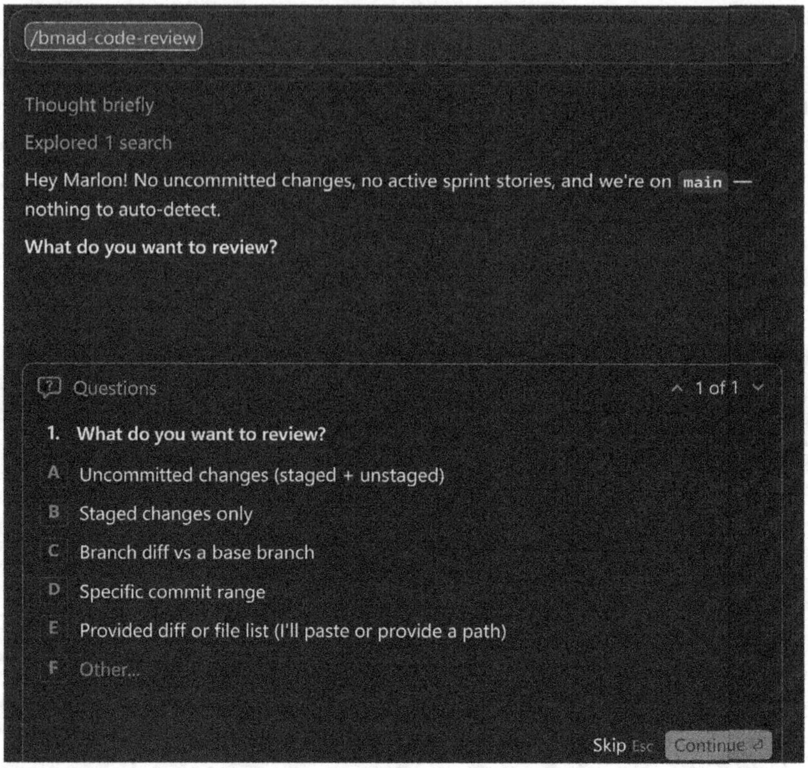

Figure 3.5 – Code review workflow

The review runs three passes in sequence:

- **Blind Hunter**: logic errors, incorrect assumptions, silent failures
- **Edge Case Hunter**: boundary conditions, unhandled inputs, race conditions
- **Acceptance Auditor**: every AC ID from the story file verified against the implementation

The output is a structured decision: **Approved** or **Changes Requested**. An Approved decision means the story is done. A Changes Requested decision includes a triage list of findings. Amelia implements the fixes, then the loop closes with another review pass.

This demonstrates a key property of the development cycle: the review layer is not a formality. It is a deliberate adversarial check designed to catch what the implementation session misses. Running it on every story, rather than at the end of the epic, means that issues are isolated to the story that introduced them rather than compounding across multiple sessions.

The quick dev workflow

Not every task justifies the full development cycle. Bug fixes, small self-contained features, and changes with a small scope do not need a PRD, an architecture document, or a sprint plan. For this category of work, Amelia provides the `/bmad-quick-dev` workflow, a parallel track that collapses intent, planning, implementation, review, and presentation into a single continuous session.

To start a quick dev session, use the QD trigger from Amelia's menu or invoke `/bmad-quick-dev`:

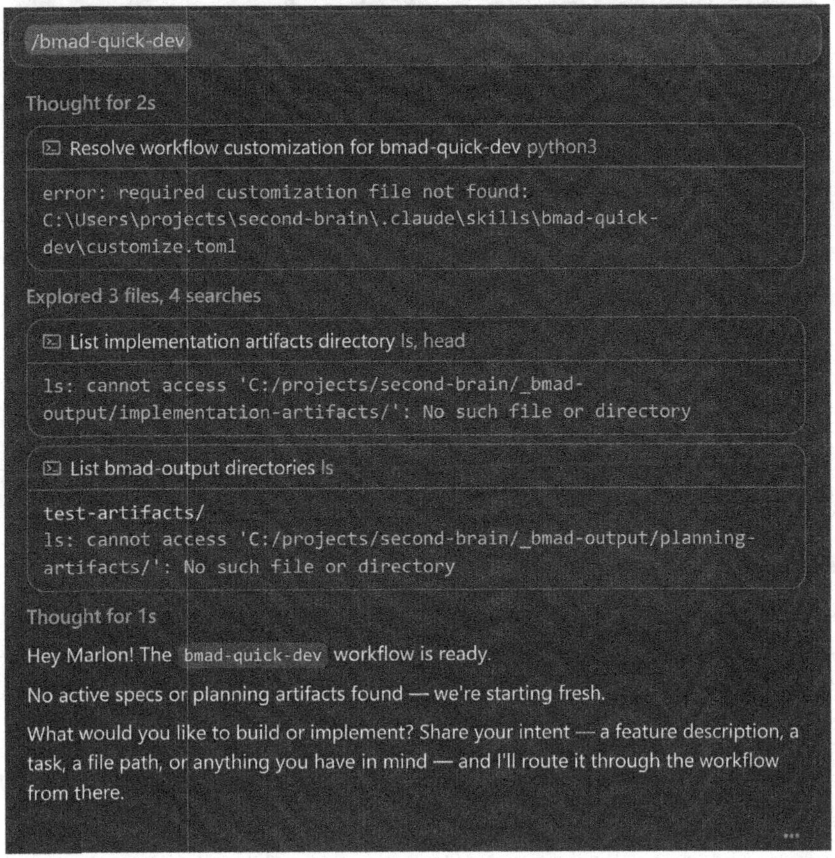

Figure 3.6 – Quick dev workflow response

Once loaded, Amelia runs a five-step sequence without stopping for external artifacts:

1. **Clarify intent**: Amelia asks questions to establish what the task requires and what done looks like
2. **Produce a lightweight spec**: A `spec-*.md` file is written. This replaces the story file for quick dev work and holds the same function: a contract between what was agreed and what will be built.
3. **Implement the code**: Amelia writes the implementation against the spec
4. **Self-review**: The same adversarial review discipline from the `CR` workflow runs internally
5. **Present the result**: Amelia presents the finished work with a summary of what was built and any decisions made during implementation

> **Note**
>
> `/bmad-quick-dev` can sometimes skip the spec file creation due to a routing logic built into this workflow. To avoid this behavior, explicitly ask to create the spec.

The `quick dev` workflow is appropriate when three conditions hold: the scope is small and well understood, no stakeholder alignment is needed, and the work does not raise architecture-level questions. When any of these conditions is absent, the full development cycle is the right path. Work that seems small at the start sometimes reveals architectural constraints mid-session. At that point, the CC workflow handles the course correction, or the session is parked and restarted as a full cycle.

This is especially useful when iterating on an existing feature, like adding a field, fixing a regression, or adjusting behavior in a single path. In those situations, the project context and architecture decisions are already established, the spec writes quickly, and the implementation can complete in a single focused session.

Handling Mid-Sprint changes

Occasionally, a story surfaces a discovery that invalidates previous plans. A technical constraint turns out to be different from what the architecture assumed. A scope element turns out to be larger than the epic structure anticipated. These situations require the `/bmad-correct-course` workflow, handled by John, the product manager from the planning phase.

This workflow is not for routine implementation decisions. It is for changes significant enough to affect other stories or the sprint plan. To use it, trigger `/bmad-correct-course`:

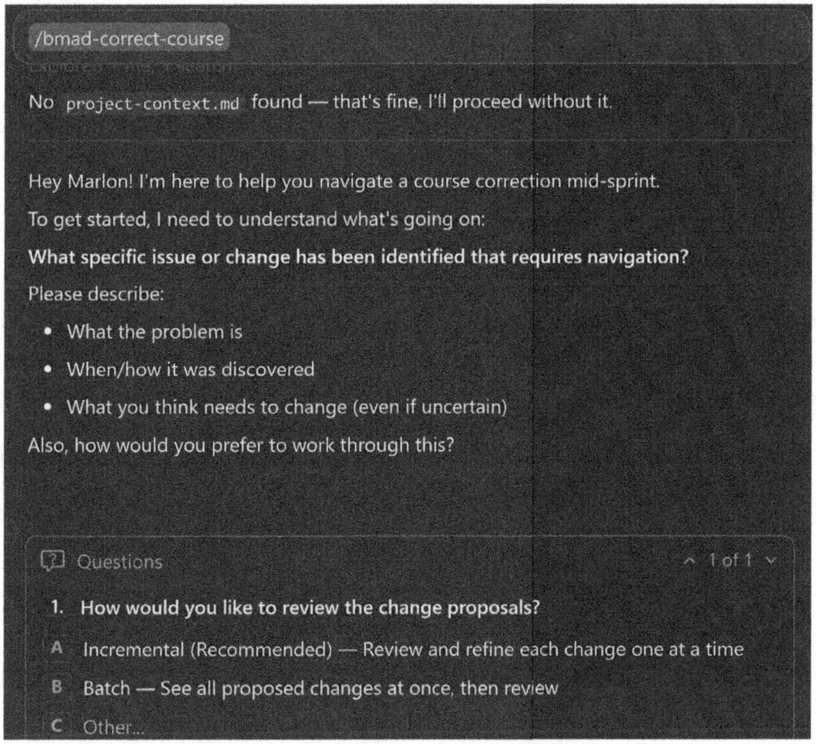

Figure 3.7 – Correct course workflow

John reviews the discovery, assesses the impact on the remaining stories and the epic structure, and produces an updated plan. The `sprint-status.yaml` is updated to reflect the change, and any affected story files are flagged for revision. This is the same pattern as the `/bmad-prd update` intent covered in the planning phase chapter: rather than making changes in isolation, the workflow surfaces conflicts and reconciles them explicitly before anything propagates.

The testing cycle

Murat's testing workflows run alongside and between each development loop iteration. The testing cycle should be an integrated discipline that shapes what development produces. Two workflows run once per project to establish the infrastructure. The remaining workflows interlock with every story.

Setting up the test framework

The first time Murat's workflows are needed in a new project, the test framework needs to be scaffolded. The `/bmad-testarch-framework` workflow produces the directory structure, configuration files, sample specs, and environment template aligned with the project's technology stack.

To scaffold the test framework, invoke `/bmad-testarch-framework`:

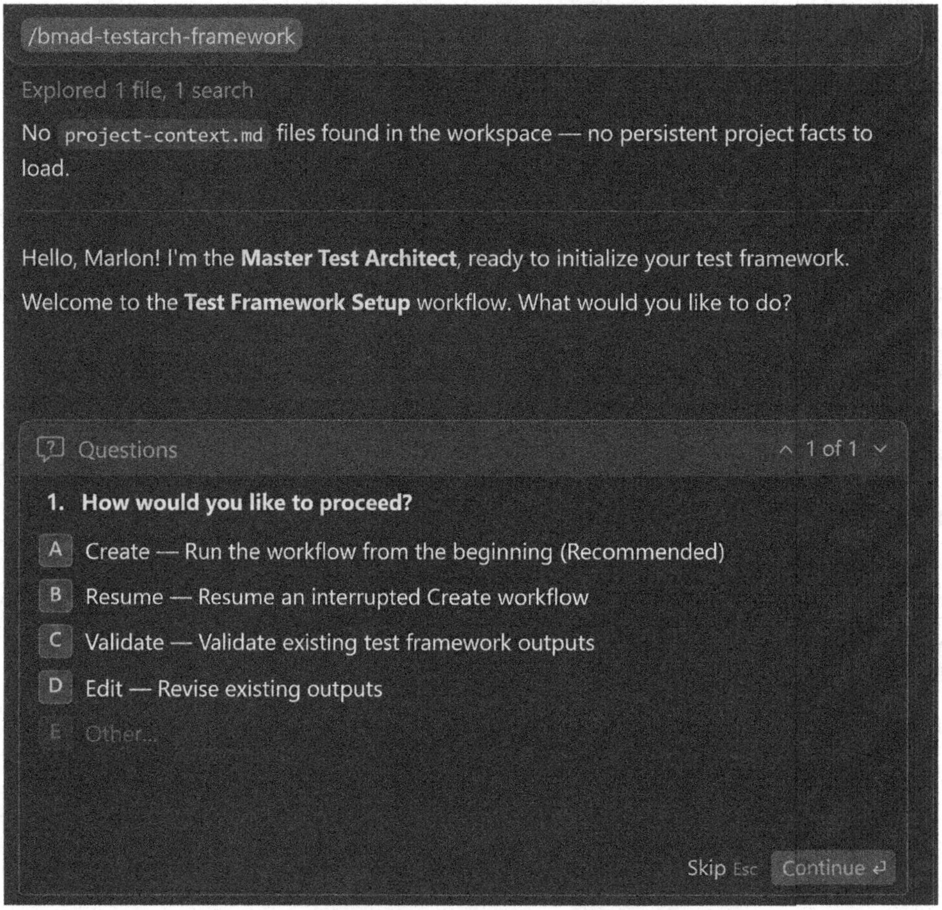

Figure 3.8 – Test framework workflow response

Based on `architecture.md`, Murat reads the technology stack decisions and selects the appropriate testing tools. For a Node.js fullstack project, the options include Playwright and Cypress. For a Python backend, pytest or Playwright for Python. For a .NET service, xUnit or Playwright for .NET.

The scaffolded framework produces a `tests/` directory with this structure:

```
tests/
├── e2e/
│   ├── example.spec.ts
│   └── fixtures/
├── integration/
├── unit/
├── playwright.config.ts
└── README.md
```

Additional files generated alongside the test directory include a `.env.example` for environment variables, a version file aligned with the project's runtime, and updates to the project `README` with testing instructions.

This workflow runs once per repository. After the framework is in place, the next step is the CI pipeline.

Configuring the CI pipeline

The `/bmad-testarch-ci` workflow configures a production-ready CI/CD pipeline that runs the test framework on every pull request. The goal is PR feedback in under five minutes, achieved through parallel test sharding, selective testing based on changed files, and burn-in loops for flakiness detection.

To configure the pipeline, invoke `/bmad-testarch-ci`:

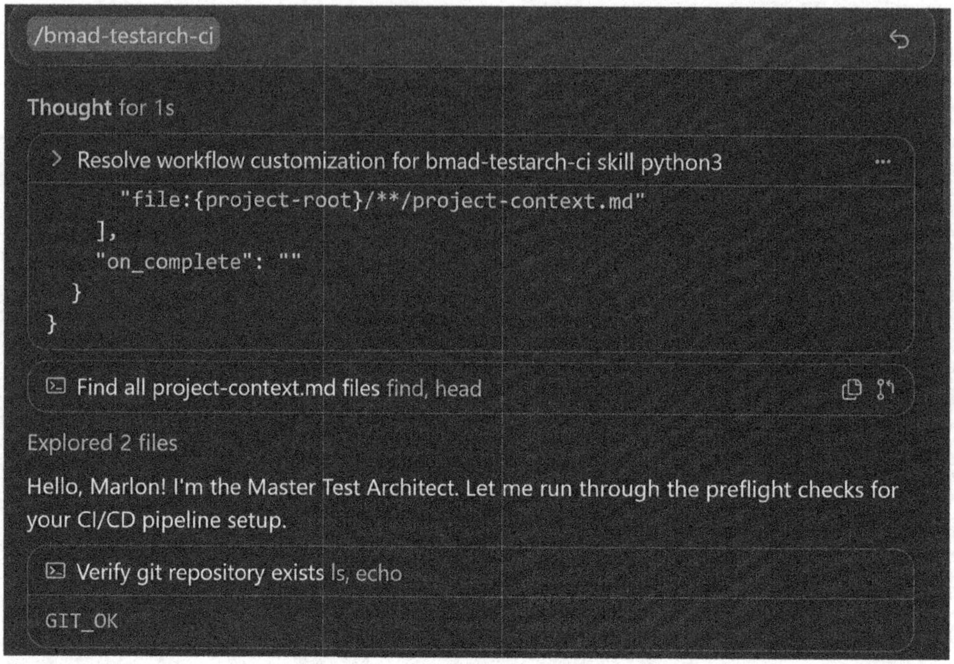

Figure 3.9 – Testarch CI workflow response

Murat generates a platform-specific pipeline configuration file. GitHub Actions, GitLab CI, Jenkins, Azure DevOps, and CircleCI are all supported. The generated pipeline includes:

- Parallel sharding across N workers for faster execution
- Selective testing on PRs — only tests affected by changed files run
- Full suite on the main branch
- Artifact collection: test results, screenshots and videos on failure, Playwright trace files for debugging

I would recommend adopting the pipeline incrementally rather than activating all capabilities at once. Especially on existing projects that might have complex CI pipelines, I would recommend a careful approach here; otherwise, you might introduce problems that you don't know how to fix later.

Once the framework and pipeline are in place, the per-story testing loop begins.

Generating test scaffolds before implementation

When practicing test-driven development, the `/bmad-testarch-atdd` workflow runs before each story implementation. It generates red-phase acceptance test scaffolds based on the story's acceptance criteria. Each scaffold is a `test.skip()` that names a specific AC: the skip

must be removed before writing any implementation code, and the test must fail before implementation begins.

To generate test scaffolds for a story, invoke `/bmad-testarch-atdd`:

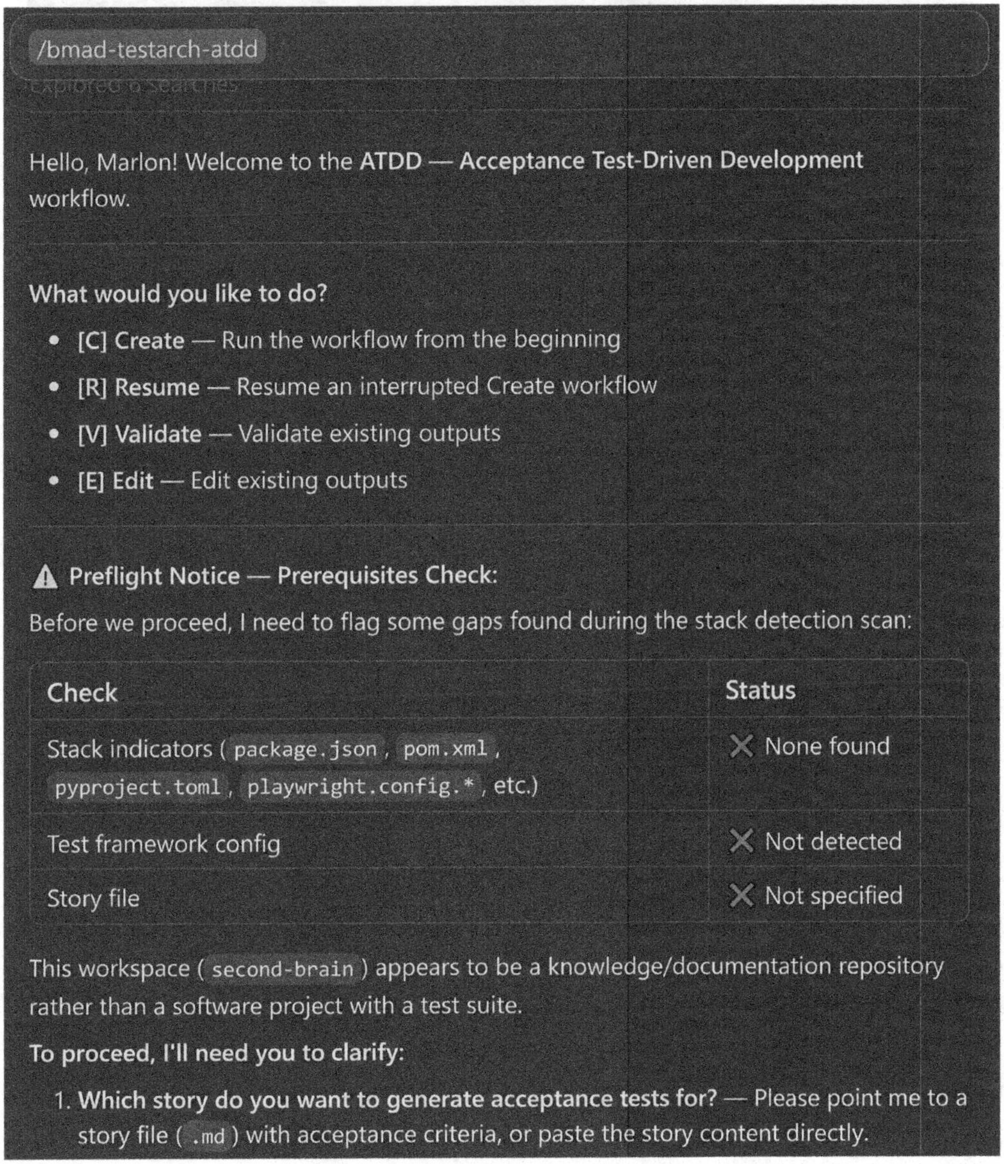

Figure 3.10 – Testarch ATDD workflow response

Bring the story file and, if available, the `test-design-epic-N.md` from the solutioning phase. Murat uses the test design priorities to focus scaffold generation on P0 and P1 scenarios first, avoiding generating scaffolds for low-risk paths when the critical path is not yet covered.

The workflow generates scaffolds across three test levels:

- **API tests**: Backend endpoints, validated first because they provide the fastest feedback loop
- **E2E tests**: Full user journeys from the browser
- **Component tests**: UI components in isolation

Alongside the scaffolds, Murat produces an implementation checklist: backend tasks, frontend tasks, and the test activation sequence. Rather than leaving the developer to decide what to build in what order, the checklist maps directly to the AC IDs in the story file.

The TDD cycle per story then follows this sequence:

1. Generate `test.skip()` scaffolds with ATDD
2. Review scaffolds and confirm AC coverage
3. Remove `test.skip()` from the first task — the test fails (red)
4. Implement the minimum code to pass it (green)
5. Refactor without breaking the test
6. Repeat per task until all ACs are covered

This is where the connection between the solutioning and implementation phases is most concrete. The test design produced by Murat during the solutioning phase defines the priorities and thresholds. The ATDD scaffolds operationalize those priorities into the specific failing tests that guide each story.

Expanding coverage after implementation

Once a story is implemented and reviewed, the `/bmad-testarch-automate` workflow expands test coverage beyond what the TDD cycle produced. Unlike `/bmad-testarch-atdd`, which generates failing scaffolds before the feature exists, `/bmad-testarch-automate` generates passing tests for features that already work. It covers acceptance criteria, edge cases, and error scenarios that the implementation checklist did not prioritize.

To expand coverage after a story is done, invoke `/bmad-testarch-automate`:

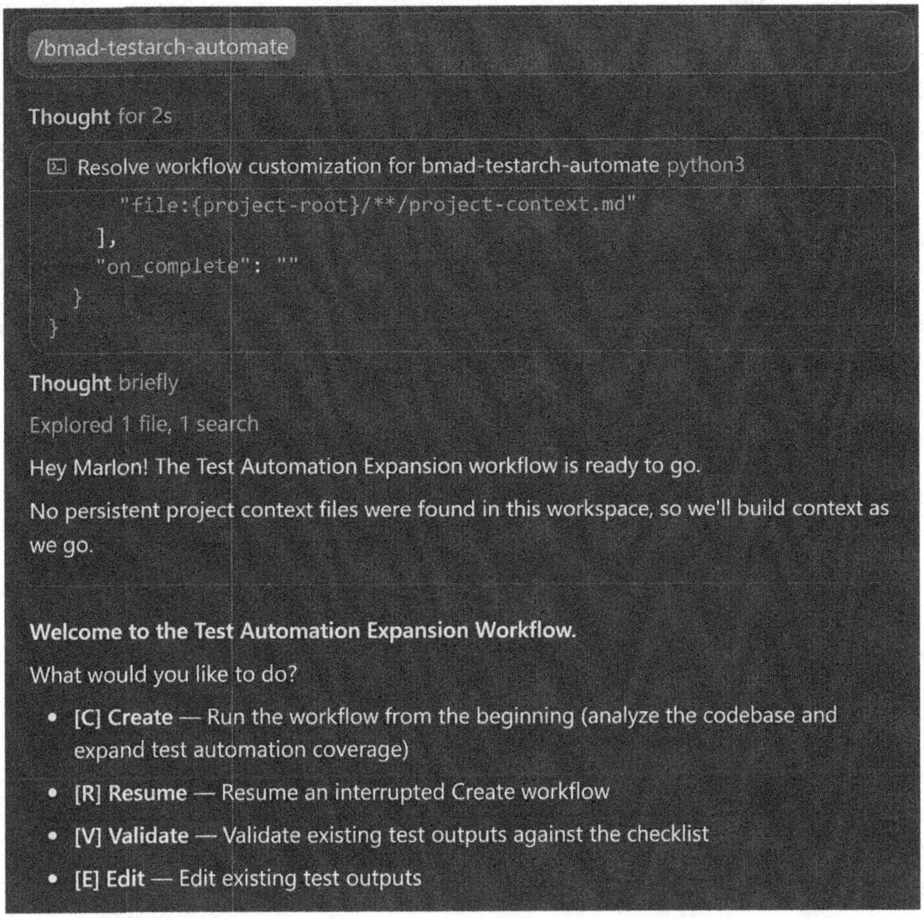

Figure 3.11 – Testarch automated workflow response

Bring the story file, the `test-design-epic-N.md`, and the list of existing tests to avoid duplication. Murat runs in BMAD-integrated mode by default: he reads the story's AC, the test design priorities, and the existing test files, then generates tests that fill the gaps without duplicating what is already there.

The coverage scope generated by `/bmad-testarch-automate` follows the same P0–P3 priority model from the test design:

- P0 critical path is mandatory
- P1 validation and error scenarios are included by default

- P2 edge cases are generated on request
- P3 low-risk scenarios are optional

This workflow runs after `bmad-code-review` for each story, before the per-epic coverage gate.

The coverage gate

At the end of each epic, the `/bmad-testarch-trace` workflow makes the go/no-go decision. This is the evidence-backed coverage gate. It runs in two phases: Phase 1 maps requirements to implemented tests and produces a traceability matrix with gap analysis; Phase 2 evaluates the matrix against the thresholds defined in the `test-design-architecture.md` and issues a verdict.

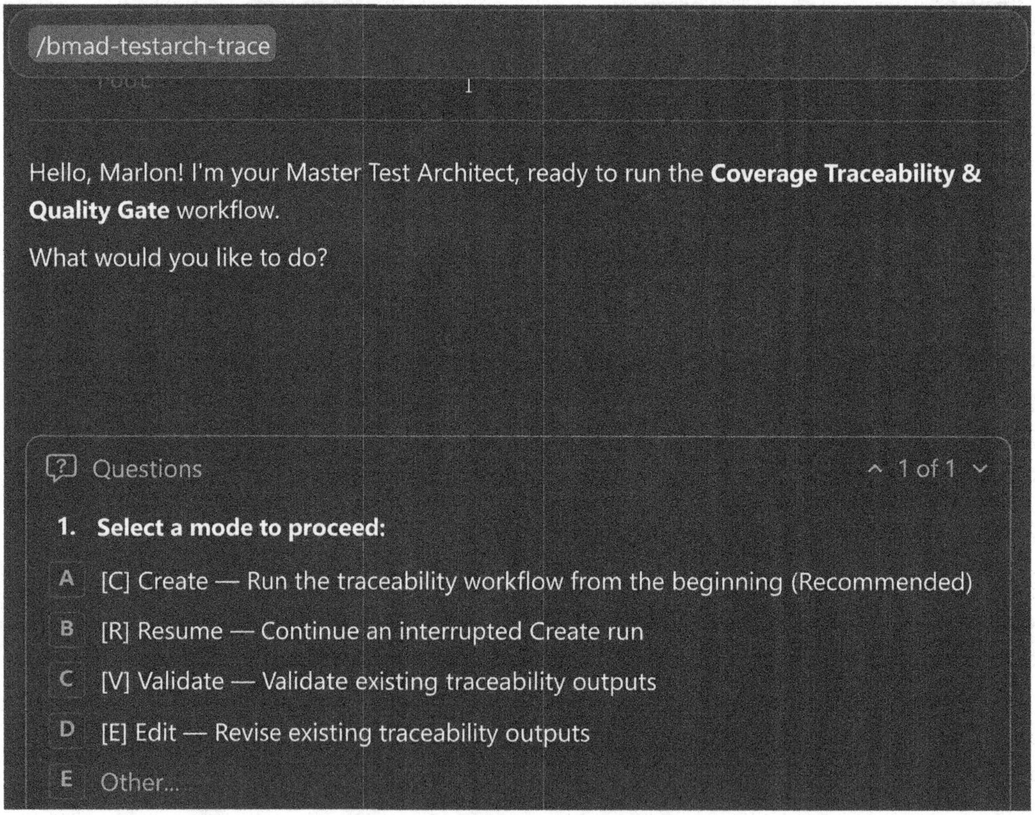

Figure 3.12 – Testarch trace workflow

Bring the coverage oracle for the current scope. For an epic-level gate, the `test-design-epic-N.md` is the oracle. For a release gate, the `prd.md` covers the full system. Murat resolves the oracle automatically if the artifacts are in the `_bmad-output` folder.

Phase 1 produces a `trace-coverage.md` containing the full traceability matrix, coverage gaps classified by P0–P3 priority, and a prioritized list of missing tests. Review the gaps before moving to Phase 2. If P0 or P1 gaps exist, the TEA workflow fills them, and Phase 1 runs again with the updated test suite.

Phase 2 evaluates the Phase 1 matrix against the coverage thresholds:

Priority	Threshold	Gate impact
P0	100%	FAIL if any P0 is uncovered
P1	≥ 80%	CONCERNS if below
P2	≥ 50%	Advisory
P3	No threshold	Informational

Table 3.1 – Coverage thresholds

The output is one of four decisions: **PASS**, **CONCERNS**, **FAIL**, or **WAIVED**. PASS means coverage thresholds are met and the epic can close. CONCERNS means gaps exist but are not blocking; you can proceed with awareness. FAIL means the coverage gaps must be resolved before the epic closes. WAIVED is a business-approved exception, documented with rationale.

The epic retrospective

Once all stories in an epic are done and the coverage gate passes, the `/bmad-retrospective` workflow closes the epic with a structured retrospective. This is not an optional ceremony. The lessons captured here feed directly back into the `project-context.md`, so the next epic starts with an improved set of conventions and a record of what did and did not work.

To run the epic retrospective, invoke `/bmad-retrospective`:

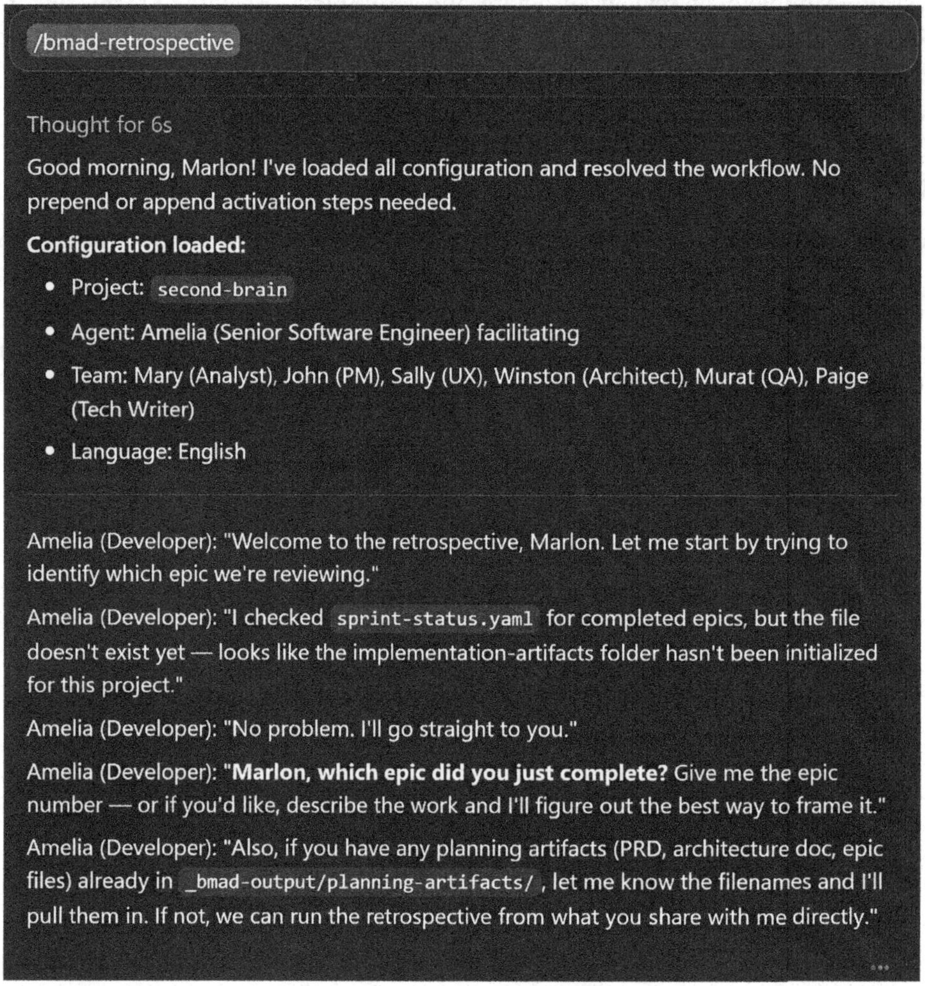

Figure 3.13 – Retrospective workflow response

After the retrospective session is complete, run `/bmad-generate-project-context` to update the `project-context.md` with the lessons learned.

This step ensures that the accumulated knowledge from the epic is available to every subsequent implementation session. Rather than letting insights drift, the `project-context.md` becomes the living record of how the project has learned to build itself.

The loop then resets. The `sprint-status.yaml` is updated, the next epic begins with `/bmad-create-story`, and the development cycle runs again.

At this point, the pattern of the implementation phase is complete. Stories move through create, scaffold, implement, review, automate, and gate. Epics close with retrospectives that improve the next cycle. The system is built incrementally, with quality verified at every boundary rather than assessed at the end. When the last epic closes and the release gate passes, the implementation phase is done.

Summary

In this chapter we covered the full downstream phase of the BMAD workflow. The Developer Agent planned the sprint and executed each approved story sequentially, and the QA Agent validated the output through quality gate decisions. The back-and-forth between the Developer and QA agents mirrors a real-world development cycle, the rule being not to proceed until the gate passes.

4

Applying BMAD to an Existing Project

In the previous chapter, we explored the fundamentals of the BMAD methodology and its AI-driven workflows. In this chapter, we move from theory to practice by applying BMAD to an existing software project. You'll learn how to document a brownfield application, generate project context, introduce new features, fix bugs, and establish a comprehensive testing strategy using the **Test Enterprise Architecture** (**TEA**) module. We'll also explore when to use lightweight workflows such as **Quick Dev** and when to adopt the complete BMAD planning process, including PRD creation, story generation, sprint planning, implementation, code reviews, retrospectives, and course correction.

By working through a realistic project, you'll gain practical experience applying BMAD workflows throughout the entire software development lifecycle. Rather than focusing on isolated features, you'll see how planning, implementation, testing, validation, and continuous improvement work together to produce production-ready software with AI agents. You'll also learn best practices for maintaining project context, preventing hallucinations, integrating automated testing, and managing evolving requirements in existing applications.

Specifically, we will cover the following topics:

- Knowing the project and installing dependencies
- Knowing the problems and installing BMAD v6
- Running the TEA framework
- Documenting the project
- Creating the project context
- Adding new customers via quick spec

- Using TEA automate to create E2E tests
- Adding new tags via quick spec and using TEA ATDD
- Using TEA ATDD to generate tests before implementing
- Adding new tags via quick spec and using TEA ATDD
- Using TEA ATDD to generate tests before implementing
- Wrapping up implementation and using TEA automate
- Validating tests and real-world scenarios
- Recommended workflow for quick spec
- Creating a dashboard through PRD
- Creating epics and stories
- Validating implementation readiness
- Sprint planning
- Creating test scenarios
- Creating the story
- Creating tests using ATDD
- Developing the story
- Reviewing the code
- Automating tests
- Wrapping up the entire workflow
- Correcting the course during the sprint
- Performing the retrospective

By the end of this chapter, you'll be able to confidently use BMAD to modernize existing applications, select the appropriate workflow for tasks of varying complexity, generate and maintain project documentation, create high-quality specifications, implement features using AI-assisted development, automate testing with the TEA framework, and manage the complete delivery process from planning through retrospective while maintaining quality and architectural consistency.

> **Note**
>
> Whenever we are going to run a workflow, we need to open a new chat. This is extremely important. BMAD will load a significant amount of information before running a specific workflow or loading an agent definition, and if we do not clean the current context, we will reach the total number of available tokens, which will cause workflow performance to degrade over time.

> In BMAD v6, every workflow tracks its own step. No matter how much conversation has accumulated in a session, if the context window fills up, we can always start fresh, restart the workflow, and continue from where we left off. We will see this in practice in this chapter.

Technical requirements

To work with this project, you will need an internet connection and Git installed on your computer (`https://git-scm.com/install`). You should already have Node v20+ installed from previous chapters.

Knowing the project and installing dependencies

To make it easier to learn all the concepts across the BMAD version stack, we are going to apply BMAD to both a new and an existing project. The first task is to update an existing application. We will create a project context, fix some bugs, and implement a new feature, so we can see all the steps BMAD can provide in action.

We are also going to create the same application from scratch, focusing on the process. We will use BMAD for major and high-complexity projects. For simpler purposes we can use tools like Lovable, V0, Bolt and similar, especially when creating working prototypes to share with stakeholders.

Here is the Kanban application we will use throughout this chapter:

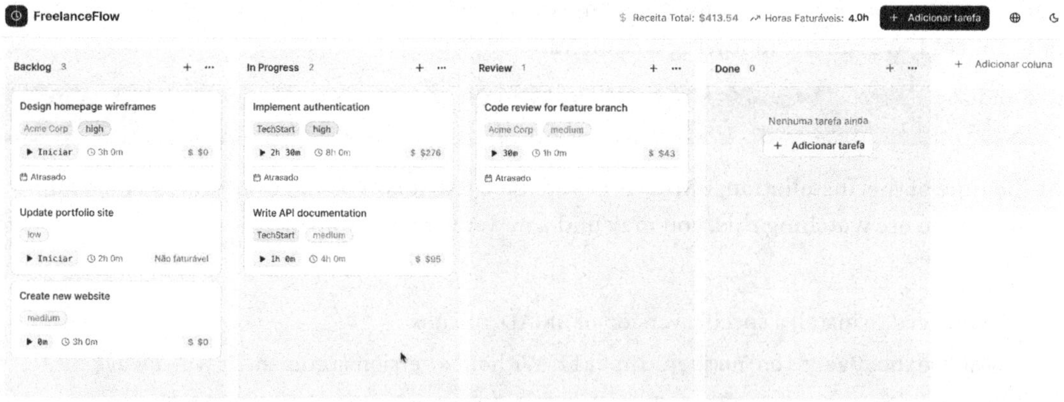

Figure 4.1 – Kanban application showing task cards organized by lane with light/dark mode toggle

The application we are working with is a simple Kanban task tracker for freelance work provided to customers. We can change cards from lane to lane, add new tasks, and toggle

between light and dark mode. Currently, there is no dashboard or any analysis of earnings across different customers.

To access the project, follow the steps in the *Download the example code files* section in the *Preface*. If you are not a technical person, you can access the link, click on **Code**, and download the ZIP. Otherwise, we can git clone and start working directly.

After cloning the repository, open it in Cursor and run `npm install` to install all dependencies. Once that completes, run `npm run dev` to confirm the application is running locally.

We are all set to begin now.

Knowing the problems and installing BMAD v6

Now that we have the project installed, we need to understand which problems we are going to resolve using BMAD:

- There are no tests of any kind implemented in the application. Most of the time you will open a project that has no tests at all. We will see how the Test Enterprise Architecture module helps us overcome this.
- There is no way to add new customers. Since this is a freelancer tracking tool, we need to constantly add new customers to see how much we are earning from them.

There are no tags to categorize tasks. There is no dashboard for more elaborate analysis. We need to implement charts in the application.

Setting up BMAD

Let's open Cursor again. To set up BMAD inside the project, after downloading and running `npm install`, we run the following command:

```
npx bmad-method install
```

At the time of this installation, BMAD is at version 6.8.0. It is evolving over time, so depending on when you are watching this, you may find a newer version available.

> **Note**
>
> If you need to install a specific version of BMAD, run `npx bmad-method@version-number install`. Without a version argument, it will always install the latest version. Check the full version reference here: `https://github.com/bmad-code-org/BMAD-METHOD/releases`.

The installer will ask several questions. For the installation directory, we use the default, which corresponds to the current working directory. It then confirms the directory exists and asks for approval.

We already covered installation and options in *Chapter 1*, at this point we just need to make sure we will install BMAD Agile-AI Driven development and Test Enterprise Architect modules.

Once installation is complete, let's walk through what was created.

Understanding the installed folder structure

The first folder is `_bmad`. This is where all BMAD configurations live inside the project. BMAD is a collection of files and folders that instruct how the LLM will perform tasks and workflows. Inside the `_config` directory, there are CSV files representing the skills and files BMAD uses, allowing it to quickly identify workflows and understand the purpose of each file in the process.

One change introduced in newer versions of version 6 is that all modules now have empty folders. Starting around version 6.2, everything became a skill inside BMAD. If we open the `.agents` folder, we can see all agent definitions and all workflow definitions under the `skills` folder. Whenever we want to understand how something works or how it is structured, go to the `SKILL.md` file in the `.agents/skills` folder.

The `agent` folder is the new industry standard for storing agent-related files. Most IDEs selected during setup will create and read skills from this folder. At the time of recording, selecting Claude Code installs files under the `.claude` folder. BMAD automatically discovers which folder to create based on the tool selected.

Finally, the `_bmad-output` folder is our working workspace, as we presented in *Chapter 1* as well. During the planning phase, while interacting with analyst, product manager, and architect agents or workflows, all artifacts are created inside the `planning-artifacts` subfolder. Once we move to implementation, files are written to implementation-artifacts. The Test Enterprise Architecture module places its outputs in the `test-artifacts` folder. When finished with a set of tasks, we can move the contents of BMAD output into an archive folder, and we will see examples of this pattern in the coming sections.

Running the TEA framework

Now that BMAD is installed, we will create the BMAD test structure by running the `/bmad-test-arch-framework` workflow. This workflow is responsible for creating the basic structure needed to start writing unit tests.

> **Note**
>
> From this point forward, it is a good practice to always commit your work to Git after every presented workflow, to keep track of changes and follow software engineering best practices!

As noted earlier, this project has no tests at all — no unit tests, no end-to-end tests. This is where the Test Enterprise Architecture module shines, because it provides the framework scaffolding to start creating this kind of test coverage.

To invoke any workflow or agent in BMAD, we open the agent panel in Cursor and type a forward slash. This loads all the skills from the folders shown earlier.

> **Note**
>
> To open the agent panel, press *Ctrl* + *L* (in Windows/Linux), or *Command* + *L* (in Mac).

We type framework and select the `/bmad-test-arch-framework` workflow. One thing to note: especially for upstream phases involving project definitions and heavy architectural lifting, the model we use can influence the output. Prioritize better models at this phase to produce better output documents.

> **Note**
>
> LLMs are non-deterministic, so the exact output on your machine may differ from what is shown here.

After the workflow loads, it greets us using the username entered during BMAD installation and asks whether we want to create, resume, or validate an existing test framework:

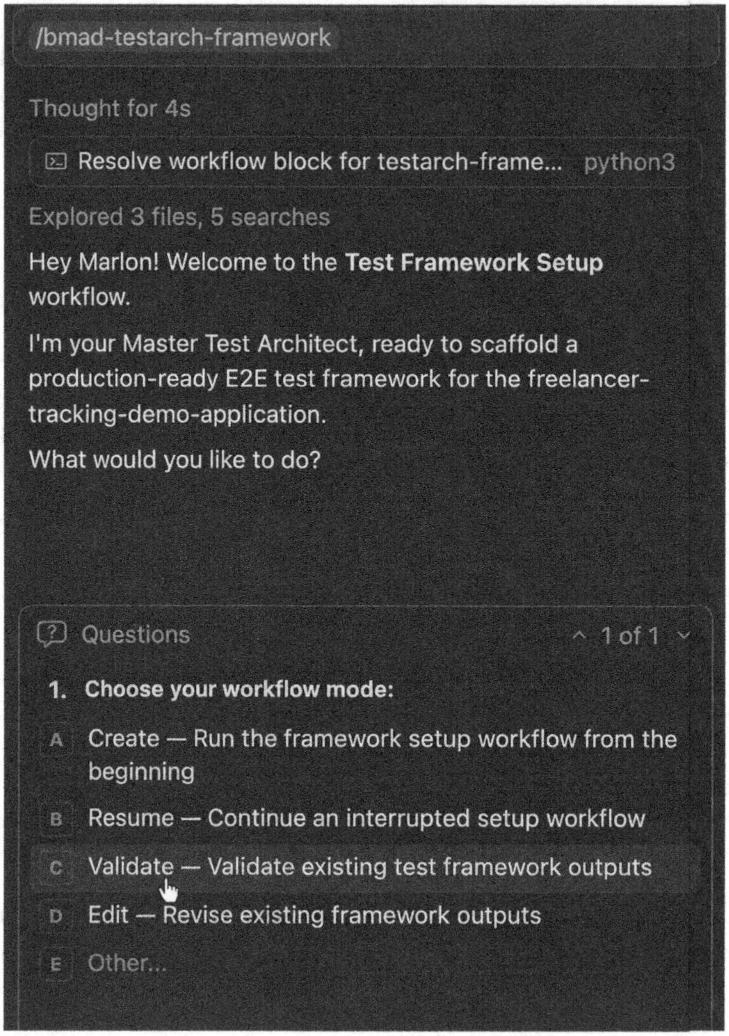

Figure 4.2 – Choosing the workflow mode

Since we are starting from scratch, we select the create workflow.

The reason to run this as the first step in the application is to ensure that every implementation we deliver going forward can start to be covered with test scenarios, which is how we guarantee quality from the beginning.

By default, this framework workflow works with Cypress and Playwright. If working on a legacy application that uses a different framework, the `validate` option can be used, and the workflow will attempt to understand the current scenario and propose alternatives compatible with the Test Enterprise Architecture module.

Before proceeding, let's look at what the workflow reads during load. It searches files inside the `/bmad-test-arch-framework`, including `package.json`, `playwright.config`, and `cypress.config`. These are the files it uses to detect the existing testing landscape.

Step one runs and identifies key files inside the project. Since we have no architecture document yet — we will cover that in the next section — it determines that we have no end-to-end framework, but we have a unit test framework set up via Vite, even though no tests have been written. It then moves to step two.

Step two is framework selection. Since we have no end-to-end framework, Playwright is suggested as the default recommendation with supporting rationale. Because the test framework configuration is set to auto and Playwright is the default recommendation, the workflow does not ask for any input at step two and moves forward automatically.

The workflow identifies domain context, creates fixtures, sample test scenarios, and the necessary dependencies and configuration. After completion, we can see all the steps and outputs inside the BMAD output folder under test-artifacts, in a file called `framework-setup-progress`.

All workflows in this version track steps completed, so this file records exactly which step was performed and what comes next. If a conversation becomes too large, this is where we resume. Step one, step two, step three, and what was accomplished at each are all recorded here. The workflow also confirms no conflicts in the stack were identified, the framework was selected, the directory structure was created, environment files and fixture helpers were generated, and everything needed to run tests is now in place.

Playwright is set up for end-to-end tests, and Vite is already in the application for unit tests. We will see both in practice shortly.

Documenting the project

In this section, we run the BMAD document project workflow. This workflow facilitates PRD creation by generating documentation when starting a project, especially when nothing exists yet. It helps not just from a technical perspective but also provides an overview of what the project should do.

As always, before running a new workflow, we open a fresh agent session by clicking on the + button. We run the `/bmad-document-project` workflow.

The workflow loads the base configuration and identifies that there is no existing documentation. We are starting from scratch. It automatically identifies 12 types of projects and acts as a scan guide. BMAD is not tied to any technology or language — it can be applied to any kind of project.

The following are the available scan options and their purposes:

1. **Quick Scan (2–5 minutes) [DEFAULT]**
    - Pattern-based analysis without reading source files
    - **Scans**: Config files, package manifests, directory structure
    - **Best for**: Quick project overview, initial understanding
    - **File reading**: Minimal (configs, README, `package.json`, etc.)
2. **Deep Scan (10–30 minutes)**
    - Reads files in critical directories based on project type
    - **Scans**: All critical paths from documentation requirements
    - **Best for**: Comprehensive documentation for brownfield PRD
    - **File reading**: Selective (key files in critical directories)
3. **Exhaustive Scan (30–120 minutes)**
    - Reads ALL source files in the project
    - **Scans**: Every source file (excluding `node_modules`, `dist`, `build`)
    - **Best for**: Complete analysis, migration planning, detailed audit
    - **File reading**: Complete (all source files)

Token usage scales similarly. An exhaustive scan will spend significantly more tokens than a quick scan, but the focus should not be on token cost — it should be on the level of documentation produced, which will make everything easier going forward.

There is also a sequencing consideration here. The reason we ran the TEA framework workflow in the previous section before running this documentation workflow is that creating a test infrastructure represents a major architectural change.

This workflow should be called whenever there is a significant product requirement or architectural change. If we had run it first, created documentation, then added the test framework, we would have needed to run it again. Running the framework first and then documenting saves tokens without sacrificing quality.

For this demonstration, we use the quick scan. The recommendation remains to run at least a deep scan on real projects.

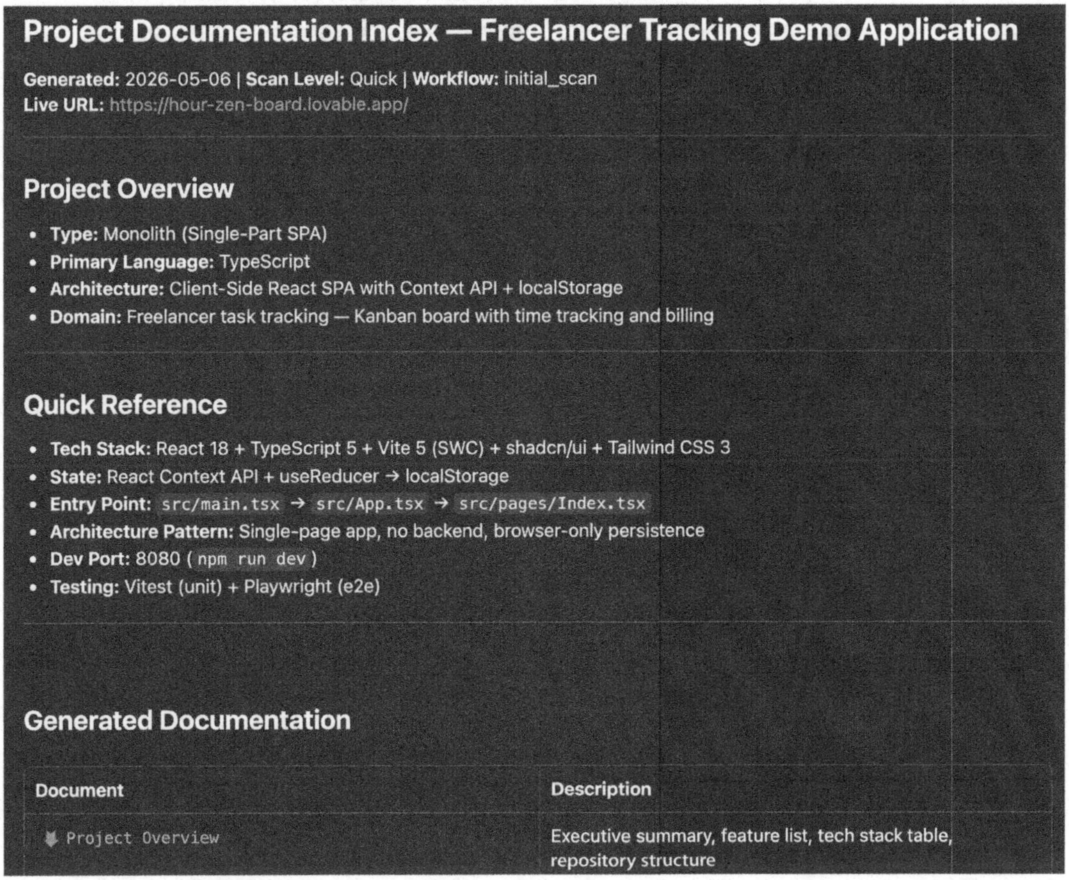

Project Documentation Index — Freelancer Tracking Demo Application

Generated: 2026-05-06 | **Scan Level:** Quick | **Workflow:** initial_scan
Live URL: https://hour-zen-board.lovable.app/

Project Overview

- **Type:** Monolith (Single-Part SPA)
- **Primary Language:** TypeScript
- **Architecture:** Client-Side React SPA with Context API + localStorage
- **Domain:** Freelancer task tracking — Kanban board with time tracking and billing

Quick Reference

- **Tech Stack:** React 18 + TypeScript 5 + Vite 5 (SWC) + shadcn/ui + Tailwind CSS 3
- **State:** React Context API + useReducer → localStorage
- **Entry Point:** `src/main.tsx` → `src/App.tsx` → `src/pages/Index.tsx`
- **Architecture Pattern:** Single-page app, no backend, browser-only persistence
- **Dev Port:** 8080 (`npm run dev`)
- **Testing:** Vitest (unit) + Playwright (e2e)

Generated Documentation

Document	Description
Project Overview	Executive summary, feature list, tech stack table, repository structure

Figure 4.3 – Output of quick scan

After a few minutes, the files are created inside the `docs` folder:

Figure 4.4 – Files inside the docs folder

The `index` file points to the application-level information needed for context. More detailed files are available for deeper reference. The `architecture` file describes the entire architecture, technology stack, state management approach, and other technical details that will serve as the foundation for all subsequent work. The `architecture.md` file replaces the `create-architecture` workflow mentioned elsewhere in the documentation — more on that difference later.

We also have data models describing entities and interfaces, a `dev-workflow` file describing the development environment and build commands, a source-tree analysis of how the architecture is distributed across files and folders, and a `project scan report` with the most important findings from the workflow execution.

With this workflow complete, we are ready to create the project context.

Creating the project context

In this section we run the `/bmad-generate-project-context` workflow. A quick reminder about the difference between this workflow and the one in the previous section: the document project workflow is for documenting the project, especially after major architectural changes. The project context file generated here is what gets loaded by most BMAD workflows going forward. It contains the technical patterns, gotchas, and learnings from the application that prevent the agent from hallucinating.

We open a new chat and run the `/bmad-generate-project-context` workflow. It reads several files and performs several searches to locate all critical documentation in the project and presents its findings.

From the architecture document, it discovers the technology stack and identifies implementation patterns, coding conventions, critical rules, and several key areas for context rules — TypeScript configuration patterns, state management conventions, data model creation conventions, and others.

> **Tip**
>
> Since we created the `architecture.md` document after `/bmad-testarch-framework`, it should contain a section to handle tests in the application. If Playwright was the chosen framework, after `project-context.md` generation, make sure we have a section to address Playwright Clean Code best practices for better output, following these guidelines:
>
> - Web-First Assertions (e.g., `expect(locator).toBeVisible()`)

- Explicit Locators (e.g., `getByRole`, `getByTestId`)
- No Static Waits (e.g., `no page.waitForTimeout()`)
- Strict **AAA (Arrange, Act, Assert)**: Pattern separation

Unlike `AGENTS.md`, `CLAUDE.MD` or similar files, the project context file is loaded only by BMAD agents and workflows. If these files exist in the project, they can enhance how models execute BMAD workflows. The recommendation is to use those files for company-level information and use the project context file for project-specific information.

The `/bmad-generate-project-context` workflow runs through multiple steps and will ask for confirmation at each category. The first category is the technology stack and versions — we evaluate and confirm. The second is language-specific rules — we evaluate and continue. After several steps and a few minutes, the workflow completes.

The output file is located at `bmad-output/project-context.md`. It contains all the rules this application should follow when loaded by BMAD workflows. These numbers can grow over time as the application evolves and as we run retrospectives.

The architecture document should be updated only on major architectural changes. The project context file is a living document and should be updated at least once per sprint, as a best practice, after the implementation phase completes. We will see specific examples of when and where to update this file and when to call this workflow again.

> **Note**
>
> Don't forget: the `project-context.md` file is the primary mechanism to prevent "LLM context drift" and "vibe coding" during the downstream phase. It acts as the immutable technical law that constrains the Developer agent's execution.

The project context file always lives inside the BMAD output folder because it is a critical input for many workflows. Searching for references to the `project-context.md` file in the codebase, we can find 18 workflows and files that reference it:

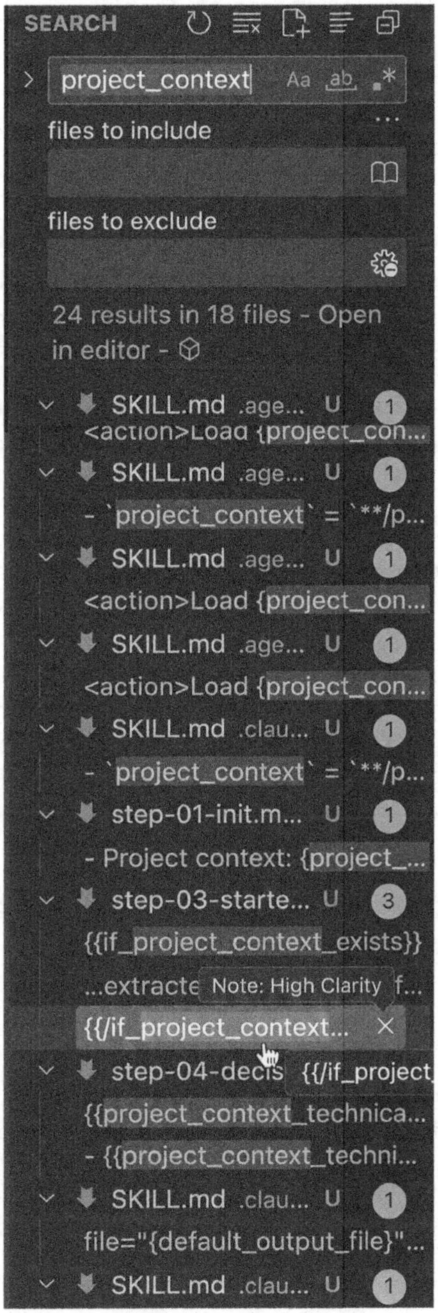

Figure 4.5 – Project content files

This is why keeping this file accurate and up to date directly affects the quality of everything the agents deliver.

Adding new customers via QuickSpec

With the boilerplate workflows complete — project documentation and project context — we are ready to start implementing new features. The first feature is the ability to add new customers. Currently we can create new tasks but not new customers, and that is what we are going to implement now.

We will use the `/bmad-quick-dev` workflow. This is a new workflow in version 6 that enables implementing simpler features and less complex tasks without going through all the stages BMAD normally requires.

We open a new agent session, call the `/bmad-quick-dev` workflow, and press *Enter*. The workflow loads successfully and asks what we want to build, fix, or change.

> **Note**
>
> One practice note before proceeding: this application is not being version controlled here. It is best practice to commit changes before running any significant improvement so the evolution of the project is trackable. Since this is not a Git course, we will skip that step.

We paste the following prompt:

```
I need to follow the inclusion of new clients in the system so that I can select
them when starting a task
```

After a few minutes, BMAD starts reading the source code to identify where changes should be made. Before approving anything, let's look at what happens inside the quick-dev skill definition, because there is an important behavior to understand here.

Understanding the Clarify-and-Route step

An important gotcha about quick-dev workflow: Opening the `bmad-quick-dev` skill file — located under `.agents` or the `.claude` folder depending on the IDE — we can see the clarify-and-route step at the top. This step is responsible for identifying the intent of the implementation. The spec-driven development principle requires that all code changes be performed based on a specification.

If BMAD determines a zero blast radius — meaning no possible path by which the change causes unintended side effects elsewhere — it has a clear intent with no architecture decisions, and it may load a one-shot step and implement changes directly without creating a specification first. This can cause confusion if this is the first time you're working with this workflow.

For anything beyond a truly trivial, contained change, request an explicit spec even if the workflow proposes skipping it, especially for traceability purposes. So when the workflow starts implementing without creating a spec, we stop it and explicitly ask:

```
Before the implementation, create the specification following the workflow rules
```

After the execution, inside the `bmad-output` folder under implementation-artifacts, the specification file is created following the `spec-[intent].md` convention. This is the file to always read before starting implementation. It states the intent, the rules that will be followed, and the scenarios to be implemented. Only after approving this specification does the agent begin the actual implementation.

Before approving, we switch to the terminal and run the application to confirm the current state — we can add tasks by clicking on **Add task** but not customers. We then approve the specification. The status changes from draft to `ready-for-dev`:

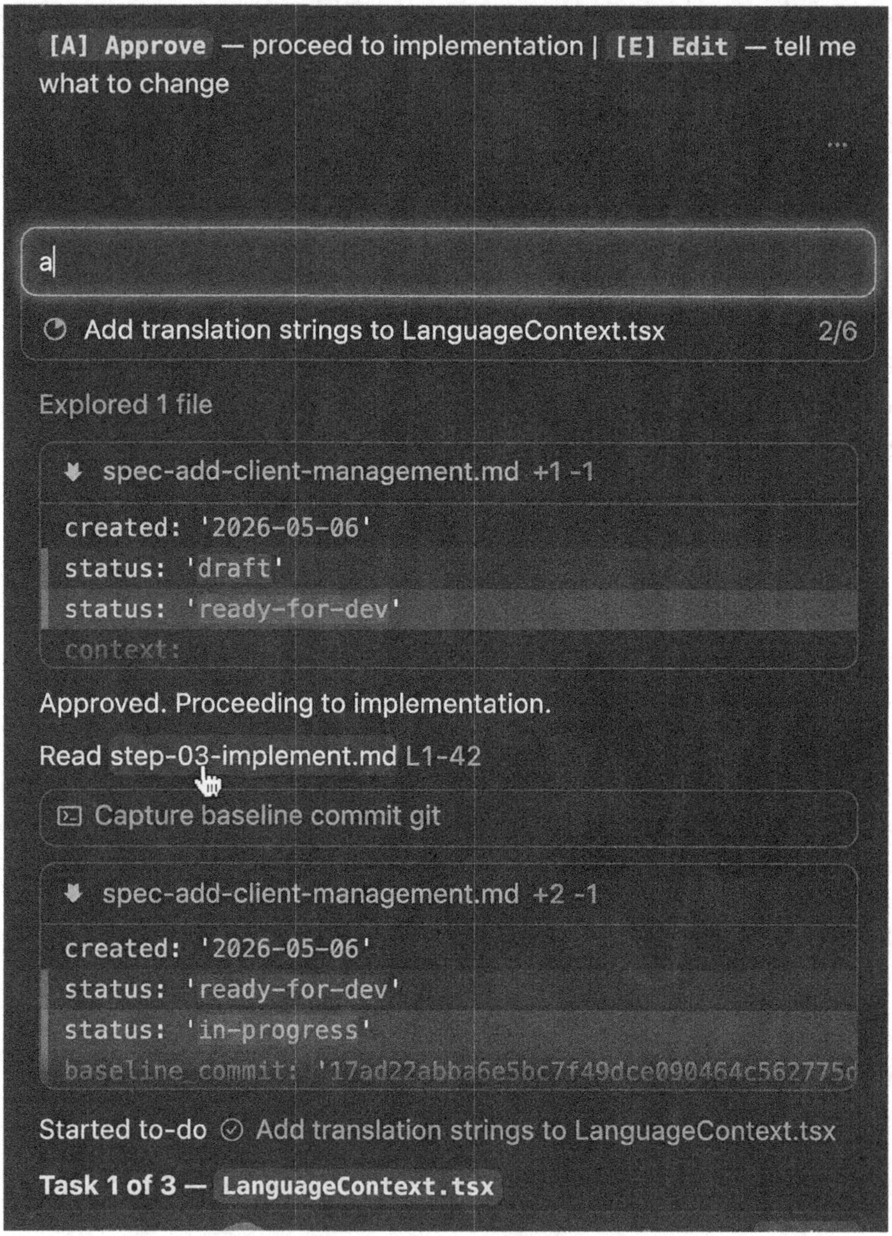

Figure 4.6 – Status changed to ready-for-dev

With approval, the agent begins implementation. After a few minutes it completes. Back in the application, a new button is now visible in the navigation bar:

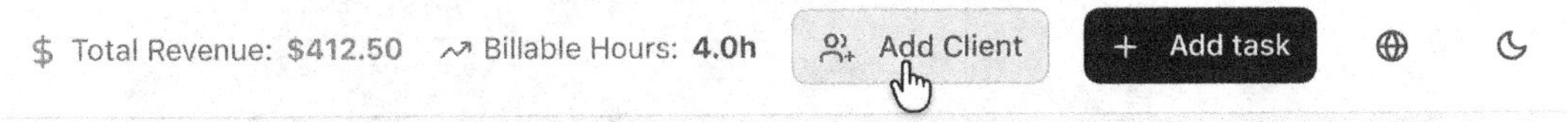

Figure 4.7 – Add client button

We can enter a customer name and hourly rate, create the client, and then select that new client when adding a task.

The `quick-dev` workflow is an excellent approach for bug fixes and small features. Looking at the specification file after implementation, the status is now done. This file serves as a traceable record of what was implemented and why.

The one thing still missing is tests. This is exactly why we included the Test Enterprise Architecture module — and that is what we will address in the next section.

Using TEA automate to create E2E tests

Why is it important to always have a specification even for a small change? Because as we just saw, we implemented the new feature but there are no tests associated with it. And as a rule of thumb, whenever running a new BMAD workflow, we start a fresh session.

We call the `/bmad-testarch-automate` workflow from the Test Architecture module and point it to the specification we just created, which is `spec-add-client-management.md`. This is the workflow to use when creating tests after a feature is already complete. If we want to create tests for existing features, this is the workflow to call.

> **Tip**
>
> As a good practice, always point the workflow to the specification. If working with an existing feature that has no specification, create a minimal one describing what it does—the quality of the output from this workflow is significantly better with that context.

After a few minutes, the workflow completes:

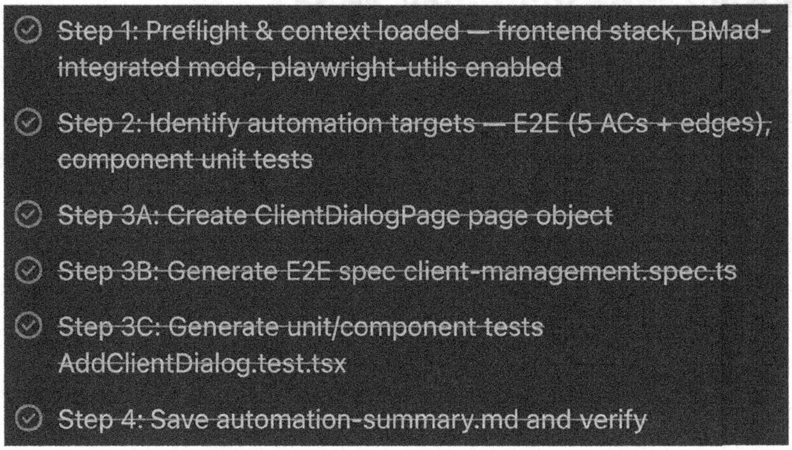

Figure 4.8 – Completed workflow

Its steps are:

1. **Pre-flight and context load**: reads documentation and test setup information about the application
2. **Target identification**: determines what should be automated. This is why the specification matters—without it, there is no structured information to ensure we are creating tests appropriate for the new feature.
3. **Test file creation**: creates end-to-end and unit/component test files
4. **Automation summary**: saves a summary file

Inside `bmad-output/test-artifacts` we can see the automation summary with all files changed and all steps the workflow performed. Under the playwright folder in end-to-end, we now have a client-management test file covering the new feature. Under the `src/tests` folder, unit tests have been written for this feature. This is how we build quality into the application — every new implementation has corresponding unit tests and end-to-end tests using TEA workflows.

Adding new tags via quick spec

We continue fixing bugs. The next issue is tags. There is code in the application to categorize tasks by tags, but the tags are not displaying in the UI:

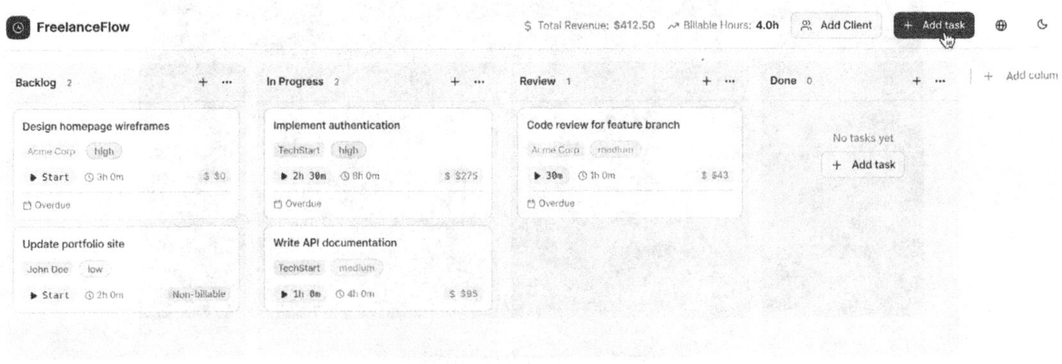

Figure 4.9 – Absence of tags in the UI

To fix this, we run the `/bmad-quick-dev` workflow with the following prompt:

```
/bmad-quick-dev I need to choose an display tags for tasks to make it easier to
classify and organize activities
```

As noted in the previous section, BMAD may try to determine on its own whether a specification should be created or whether it should change the code directly. Rather than relying on that determination, we make it explicit and add the following to the existing prompt:

```
Explicitly create a spec for this
```

The reason it is so important to always have a specification — especially for this bug — is that we are going to use the Test Enterprise Architect the right way this time: with the ATDD workflow, run before implementation starts. The TEA framework will create all tests before the implementation is ready, ensuring that the behavior we want in the application is defined upfront.

In practice, this is implementing TDD to guide the behavior of the implementation rather than adapting tests to fit finished code. This makes a significant difference in the quality of code delivered by the agent. And we can only run the ATDD workflow if we can point it to a specification from a previous workflow.

After the quick-dev workflow finishes, the specification is created and in draft status. It describes that the problem exists — there is code to store and manage tags per task, but no UI code to display them. This is a small change, and we are creating a spec specifically because we want tests in place before the implementation begins. This ensures the functionality is covered regardless of future code changes.

Before approving, we open a new session, run the `/bmad-testarch-atdd` workflow pointing to the `spec-task-tags.md` file, and let it generate the tests.

Using TEA ATDD to generate tests before implementation

After a few minutes, the ATDD workflow completes. What happened behind the scenes: it read the specification, inspected the acceptance criteria from the story, and based on that created all the tests necessary to verify the implementation will pass. These tests represent the red phase of TDD.

The red-green phase is especially important in AI development. All tests intended to cover the desired behavior are created before any code is generated. If tests are created after implementation, we are not necessarily covering all scenarios to verify the implementation works correctly. Even if some code changes are correct, bugs can still be introduced. But if tests are written before implementation, the behavior is defined upfront, and the implementation then makes those tests pass.

Here are the test files created:

Figure 4.10 – Test files generated by the ATDD workflow

The workflow created unit test files for storage-task, task-card, task-detail, and task-dialog — all components that need to change to implement this feature. It also created end-to-end tests.

For end-to-end tests specifically, since they require an actual implementation to run, the tests are marked with a skip command. Running the end-to-end suite now will execute these tests but skip them, so no failures occur before the implementation is ready.

Finally, the workflow produces a checklist artifact that confirms all behaviors from the specification are covered during the test phase.

Now we can implement the feature. We open a new agent, run `/bmad-quick-dev` again, and point to the `spec-tasks-tags.md` specification file. The workflow will not only implement the feature but also take into consideration the tests created during the ATDD phase, adapting the implementation to make all tests pass.

Wrapping up implementation and using TEA automate

After a few minutes, the implementation completes. Back in the application, tags are now visible on each task card, and when adding a new task, the tag selector is also available:

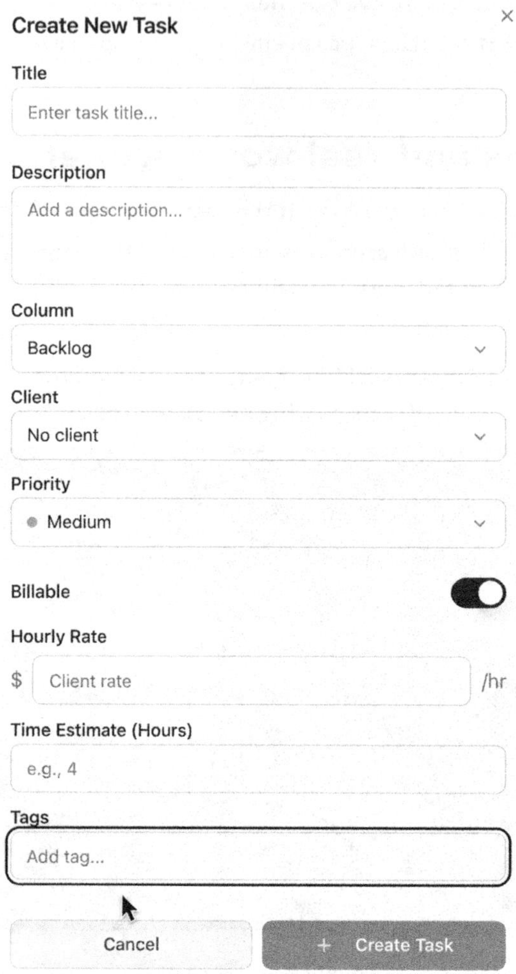

Figure 4.11 – Presence of Tags option

One interesting behavior from this workflow run: it spawned three separate agents to verify edge cases, audit for blind spots, and validate that the acceptance criteria were met after implementation. It surfaced a few things to consider.

For example, it can identify a potential layout issue: if a task has many tags, the card could become crowded. The suggestion is to cap display at three tags. Your decision could be to show all tags rather than capping at three, because hiding tags could lead to incorrect conclusions when reviewing tasks. The right call will vary by scenario, but this illustrates that the Quick Dev workflow does not just follow the project context — it also takes a fine-grained look at how the application should behave in practice.

With the implementation complete, we call the `/bmad-testarch-automate` workflow one more time, pointing to the `spec-task-tags.md` specification. We open a new agent, run automate, and proceed.

Validating tests and real-world scenarios

While the automation is running, let's look at the `test-artifacts` folder and the checklist created during the ATDD phase. All scenarios are recorded there from the red-green phase described earlier. The automated workflow will now ensure all those tests are implemented and passing.

After a few minutes, the automate workflow completes. All workflows and tests are marked as done. The task checklist shows all tests passing and all end-to-end scenarios active:

```
| Test ID | AC | Scenario | Level | Priority | File | Status |
|---|---|---|---|---|---|---|
| UNIT-01 | AC7 | `loadState` normalizes task missing `tags` ~ `tags: []` | Unit | P0 | `storage-task-tags.test.ts` | ✅ PASS |
| UNIT-02 | AC7 | `loadState` preserves existing `tags` on stored tasks | Unit | P0 | `storage-task-tags.test.ts` | ✅ PASS |
| UNIT-03 | AC7 | Mix of tagged + untagged tasks normalized correctly | Unit | P1 | `storage-task-tags.test.ts` | ✅ PASS |
| UNIT-04 | AC7 | Empty tasks array does not crash `loadState` | Unit | P1 | `storage-task-tags.test.ts` | ✅ PASS|
| COMP-01 | AC1 | Enter commits tag chip in AddTaskDialog | Component | P0 | `AddTaskDialog.tags.test.tsx` | ✅ PASS |
| COMP-02 | AC2 | Comma commits tag chip (comma stripped) | Component | P0 | `AddTaskDialog.tags.test.tsx` | ✅ PASS |
| COMP-03 | - | Duplicate tag (case-insensitive) silently dropped | Component | P2 | `AddTaskDialog.tags.test.tsx` | ✅ PASS |
| COMP-04 | - | Whitespace-only input ignored | Component | P0 | `AddTaskDialog.tags.test.tsx` | ✅ PASS |
| COMP-05 | - | × button removes chip from AddTaskDialog | Component | P2 | `AddTaskDialog.tags.test.tsx` | ✅ PASS |
| COMP-06 | AC1 | Tags flow into ADD_TASK dispatch payload | Component | P0 | `AddTaskDialog.tags.test.tsx` | ✅ PASS |
| COMP-07 | AC3 | Existing tags render as chips in TaskDetailPanel | Component | P1 | `TaskDetailPanel.tags.test.tsx` | ✅ PASS |
| COMP-08 | AC4 | Remove chip - UPDATE_TASK dispatched immediately | Component | P0 | `TaskDetailPanel.tags.test.tsx` | ✅ PASS |
| COMP-09 | - | Enter adds tag in panel - UPDATE_TASK dispatched | Component | P1 | `TaskDetailPanel.tags.test.tsx` | ✅ PASS |
| COMP-10 | AC5 | Task with tags shows badge row on TaskCard | Component | P1 | `TaskCard.tags.test.tsx` | ✅ PASS |
| COMP-11 | AC6 | Task with empty tags renders no badge section | Component | P1 | `TaskCard.tags.test.tsx` | ✅ PASS |
| E2E-01 | AC1+AC5 | Add tag in dialog - badge visible on card | E2E | P1 | `task-tags.spec.ts` | ● ACTIVE |
| E2E-01b | AC2 | Comme-typed tag committed as chip, comma stripped | E2E | P2 | `task-tags.spec.ts` | ● ACTIVE |
| E2E-01c | AC6 | Untagged task has no badge row on card | E2E | P1 | `task-tags.spec.ts` | ● ACTIVE |
| E2E-02 | AC7 | Legacy task without `tags` key loads without crash | E2E | P1 | `task-tags.spec.ts` | ● ACTIVE |
| E2E-04 | AC7+AC5 | Tags persist across page reload (localStorage) | E2E | P2 | `task-tags.spec.ts` | ● ACTIVE |

|| E2E-04 | AC3+AC4+AC5 | Remove tag via detail panel → card + localStorage updated | E2E | P1 | `task-tags.spec.ts` | ● ACTIVE (expansion) |

**Total tests: 23 across 5 files** (20 baseline activated + 3 expansion tests added)
```

Figure 4.12 – Task checklist

The results state that unit tests passed and end-to-end tests are ready to run. This is where real-world validation comes in. From this point forward, it is the developer's responsibility to run the application and verify that everything works as expected.

The takeaway: it is always our responsibility to verify that the proposed scenarios are valid for both unit and end-to-end tests. After each scenario is enabled, we run them, and confirm they pass under the test pipeline. Otherwise, tests will break and will not provide the behavior guarantees they are meant to give.

Recommended workflow for quick spec

To summarize the process we just worked through: after the ATDD workflow is executed pointing to the specification file, we run quick-dev to ensure tests pass. Then we run the `/bmad-test-arch-automate` workflow to confirm that both unit tests and end-to-end tests are running and enabled. If any issues are found, we run the workflow again.

In general, for every quick-dev workflow execution:

1. Run quick-dev and explicitly ask it to create a specification
2. Run ATDD, pointing to the specification file
3. Run quick-dev again, pointing to the specification and explicitly ask to make the tests pass
4. Run automate to confirm end-to-end tests are enabled and working

Here is the diagram of the workflow:

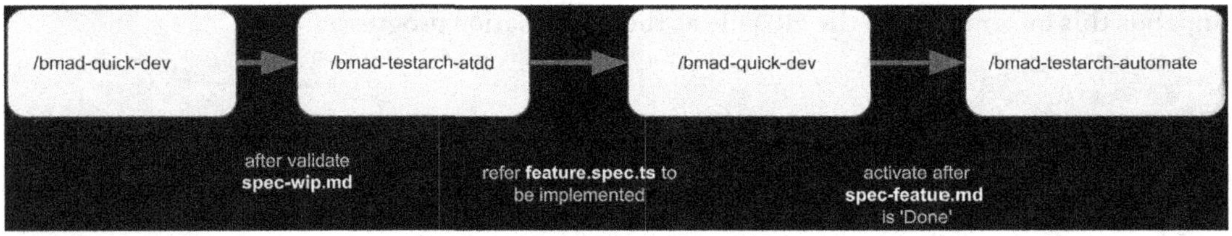

Figure 4.13 – Recommended workflow

This may seem like a lot at first, but this is what makes the application robust and following quality standards — especially for small or simple features. Following this process ensures everything is covered and the feature is production-ready.

Creating a dashboard through a PRD

For the next feature, we are going to create a dashboard. Because a dashboard can have many uncovered details and requires significant design thinking, we are going to run the `/bmad-prd` workflow. At a high level, the intent is to create a new section to display charts indicating earnings by client, project, and tag.

Running the full PRD workflow is necessary here because the workflow guides us through evaluating all the steps and confirming the direction is correct before any code is written.

We open a new tab, type `/bmad-prd`, and summon the workflow. It loads the project context — as stated, this is loaded for the most important BMAD workflows — and also discovers the documentation under the docs folder. It identifies this as a brownfield project, meaning we are enhancing an existing system.

At this point, in the `planning-artifacts` folder, a PRD file has already been created. We are only at the first step out of eleven. If context runs out, we can pause, start a new session, restart the workflow, and point to the file to resume.

We proceed by pasting the prompt describing what we want to build:

```
I need to create a new section to display charts in a dashboard detailing earnings
by client, project and tag
```

The workflow identifies the intent and moves through the process. At step two out of eleven, it classifies the project type, domain, complexity, and brownfield status, asking for confirmation. It identifies the feature as a web app, general domain, low complexity, brownfield—and appends this information to the PRD file as the conversation progresses.

> **Note**
>
> In order to BMAD ask you all questions, please prioritize using better models, like Sonnet 5 or ChatGPT 5.5 with reasoning turned on. The quality of the model will produce better outputs at this stage.

At step three it asks several questions about what we want to achieve:

- How do we want to delight the user?
- What is the differentiation of this feature in the application?
- What is the real problem we are trying to solve?
- What should be in scope to avoid scope creep?

We answer: we want to see the most profitable clients; we want more clarity on the clients driving the most revenue; we want business clarity; and we want more interactivity. All four dimensions are equally important.

Advanced elicitation

Before moving to the next step, let's look at an optional capability in this workflow. Typing the letter A activates the advanced elicitation method. This provides additional perspectives and points of view, so we can challenge our answers and think more carefully about the outcomes we want to achieve.

In our scenario, the workflow proposes five different elicitation methods to sharpen the product vision:

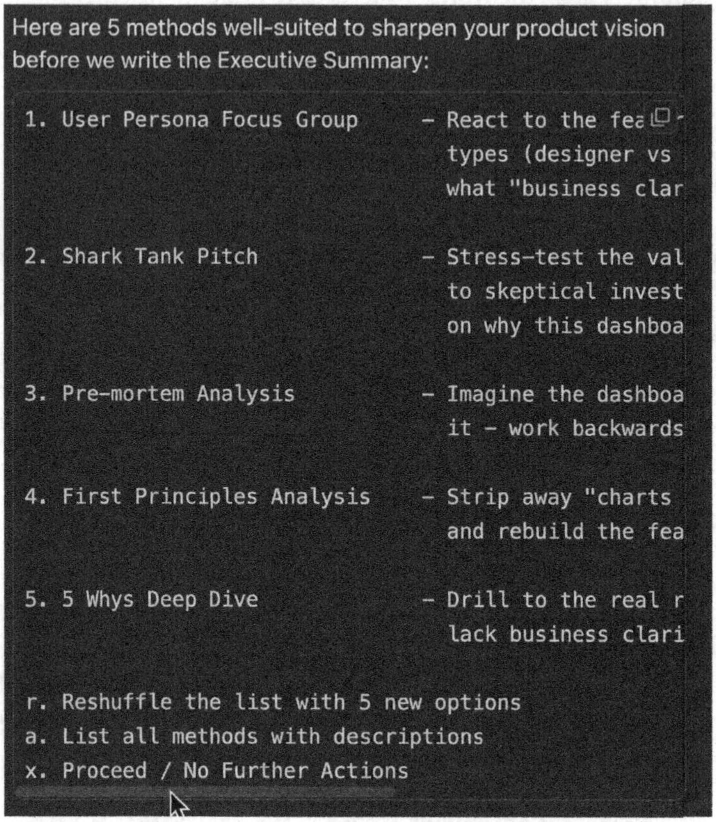

Figure 4.14 – Suggested methods

One of them is a user persona focus group — the model reacts to the feature from different freelancer perspectives (designer, developer, consultant) to validate what business clarity means across personas. Another is a shark tank pitch — the model stress-tests the value proposition as if pitching to skeptical investors, forcing sharper clarity on why this dashboard actually matters.

I am not going to apply these elicitation methods in detail here — the goal is to show that this option exists so we can use it to think more carefully about the PRDs we create. We continue forward without applying any of them.

Party mode

At the executive summary step, the workflow asks us to evaluate whether the summary correctly reflects our proposal. This is a good moment to invoke party mode. We type the letter p and hit *Enter*:

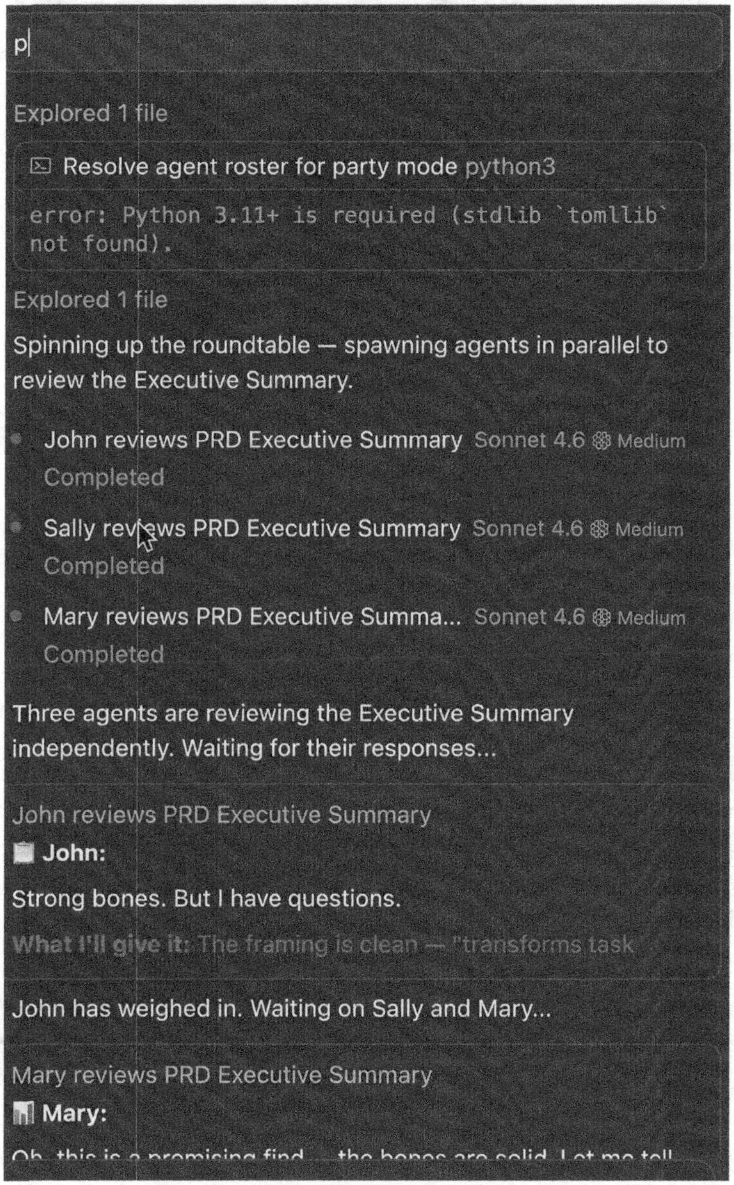

Figure 4.15 – Result of invoking party mode

When party mode is invoked, BMAD spins up a round table of all agents it considers relevant for this subject, as we learned in *Chapter 1*. Each agent reads the PRD file produced so far and provides their analysis — think of it as a group conversation among different specialists. In this context, John, the product manager agent, Mary, the business analyst, and Sally, the UX specialist, each contribute with their own views. If the subject is more technical, Winston, the architect, and Murat, the Test Architect, might join the discussion. The workflow then synthesizes the key points from all of these into a consolidated set of questions and observations.

From the party mode output: the executive summary is missing success criteria and outcomes. The equal weighting of client, project, and tag needs justification — it is not clear from the document why all three are weighted the same. These are the kinds of gaps that can be surfaced and addressed before any implementation starts.

From this point, I continue the workflow through the remaining steps. After several rounds of interaction, the PRD is complete, all steps are done, and the file is fully populated.

The PRD template provided by this workflow guides us through the executive summary, success criteria from user, business, and technical perspectives, measurable outcomes, product scope, user journeys, technical requirements, functional requirements, and non-functional requirements.

As I stated before, this workflow is for medium and high-complexity tasks or systems, because it forces us to think through all the scenarios involved. Since we do not have any working code yet for this feature, we can present this to stakeholders and have back-and-forth conversations until the direction is clear. That is exactly what this workflow is designed to support.

Creating epics and stories

With the PRD and architecture files in place, we are ready to create epics and stories. In this workflow, we point to the `architecture.md` file from the `docs` folder. If starting from scratch, the workflow would load it from the `/implementation-artifacts` folder by default. Using both files, BMAD creates the epics and stories that will drive implementation in the next phase.

We open a new chat and type `/bmad-create-epics-and-stories`. The workflow finds the PRD document under planning-artifacts and the architecture under docs. Since we did not create a UX design file, it notes this as not found—it is optional. With both primary files available, we proceed.

The workflow identifies that previous specifications were created using quick-dev workflows, but since these represent smaller features, they should not factor into the epic and story definitions here. We confirm and proceed using only the PRD and architecture documents.

Based on the functional and non-functional requirements, and after evaluating the architecture file for requirements not explicitly stated in the PRD, the workflow creates an epics.md file. It is our job to verify that all listed requirements are correctly represented.

After agreeing with the epic list, the workflow proposes stories per epic, each with its own acceptance criteria. We need to confirm that these stories represent the success criteria we visualized in the PRD.

Once agreed, the workflow writes all stories and epics to the document and runs validation checks:

- All functional requirements are tied to a specific epic
- All non-functional requirements are addressed within stories
- Stories are compliant with the architecture
- Stories have quality indicators and clear acceptance criteria
- Dependencies between stories are identified
- Epics deliver user value, not technical milestones

This last point is a mindset shift. We do not create stories and epics to deliver technical work — we create them to deliver user value. The user must be able to use what we are shipping to production; this is known as vertical slicing, which we will cover in more detail in the next sections.

Additional optional capabilities at this stage include an **Adversarial Review** workflow to find gaps in story coverage and an **Edge Case Hunter** to inspect acceptance criteria for missed edge cases. Those are specialist agent definitions that BMAD triggers to produce better outputs.

> **Note**
>
> An improvement over version 4: previously, epics and stories were created inside the `create-prd` workflow, which sometimes meant technical rules were not enforced because the stories were created before the architecture was defined. Now we have a consistent list of epics and stories that reflects both the product vision and the architectural guidelines. The bigger picture is broken down into smaller pieces of deliverable user value.

Validating implementation readiness

Before moving to implementation, there is one last quality gate: the BMAD check-implementation-readiness workflow. This is optional, but I always encourage running it to

identify any gaps across the PRD, stories, and architecture before starting to generate code. Time and tokens spent here are cheaper than finding these issues in working code.

We open a new agent and type `/bmad-check-implementation-readiness`. Sometimes, the workflow notes that it cannot find the architecture document in the `planning-artifacts` folder, since ours is under `docs (remember about /bmad-document-project workflow)`. We point it to the correct location and proceed:

```
Architecture is in docs/architecture.md
```

The workflow completes and produces a file listing all steps and the final validation. Some problems were identified. Specifically:

- Entities that do not exist in the current data model
- Missing date filtering properties in some data model components
- A technical limitation involving the AppProvider component, which will crash the application if not handled properly

These are exactly the kinds of problems this workflow is meant to catch before they appear in production. We evaluate each finding, confirm it is a real issue, and ask the workflow to propose fixes. After a few minutes it presents the proposed changes. We validate and approve, and the workflow marks the readiness check as complete.

We are now ready to start implementing working code.

Sprint planning

The last workflow of the planning phase is sprint planning. It creates the file that organizes execution of the stories and is a natural integration point with Jira or similar project trackers.

We open a new chat and type `/bmad-sprint-planning`. After a few minutes, it reads all information from the epics file and generates a `sprint-status.yaml` file under the `_bmad-output` folder. This file lists all epics, all stories, and the status of each. From here it is easy to track implementation progress as we work through the PRD.

This workflow can be extended to sync with external project trackers. For example, the workflow instructions can be modified so that when stories are created, they also create corresponding tasks in Jira via an MCP integration.

With sprint planning complete, we can finally begin implementing stories.

Creating test scenarios

Before starting implementation, I want to introduce one more optional workflow from the Test Enterprise Architecture module: the test design workflow. Its goal is to help us understand which tests to create, based on a priority pyramid, for the work defined in the epics and stories.

We open a new tab and type `/bmad-testarch-test-design`. This workflow can be used at the application level or the feature level.

Risk-based testing strategy

The Test Enterprise Architecture module works on a risk-based testing strategy; more details can be found here `https://bmad-code-org.github.io/bmad-method-test-architecture-enterprise/explanation/risk-based-testing/`. Traditional approaches apply equal test coverage to every feature regardless of impact, with no systematic prioritization. Testing becomes a checkbox exercise.

The TEA approach instead evaluates two dimensions: the probability that a particular scenario will fail and the impact if it does fail. These two scores are combined to calculate an overall risk score, and that score drives test prioritization.

The TEA methodology categorizes risks across six areas: technical debt, security vulnerabilities, performance degradation, data integrity, business logic errors, and operational issues. Within those categories it assigns test priorities: critical, high value, medium value, and low value. If a scenario scores higher than six and there is no test covering it, the TEA module ensures there is at least documentation explaining why it is not covered and how the risk will be mitigated.

This workflow is best run right after creating the PRD and generating epics and stories. From this point forward, when we run the ATDD workflow, it will read this test design file and generate test scenarios based on the priority levels identified here—which produces significantly better tests than relying on the specification alone.

Switching back to Cursor, we select both epics — visualization and filtering features — and let the workflow run. After a few minutes, a test-design file is created under the test-artifacts folder. The workflow identified some potential risks across our stories, and some of them are high priority.

Looking at the high-priority findings: one is about null segments being silently excluded — tasks where the client ID, project name, or tags are null may be filtered out during chart aggregation. This could hide information and lead to incorrect revenue conclusions. The other is about inline revenue recalculation — if a developer calculates billable hours times rate inline

instead of using established helper functions, it diverges from the authoritative formula. If that helper is later changed, the inline calculation will silently produce incorrect revenue figures.

The goal of this workflow is to force us to think through all the possible problems our epics and stories might face. For larger epics, run one at a time to maintain enough context.

> **Note**
>
> This workflow can be very expensive in terms of token usage, but the cost of letting these issues reach production is significantly higher.

Creating the story

With everything in place, it is time to draft the first story. We open a new chat and type `/bmad-create-story`. The workflow reads the sprint-status file, evaluates which epics and stories are in the backlog, and if no specific story is passed as a parameter, it picks the next one in sequence, reads the appropriate context, and generates the draft.

All stories start in backlog status in the `sprint-status.yaml` file. When `/bmad-create-story` runs for a particular story, it changes the status to `ready-for-dev`. It is our job to evaluate whether the acceptance criteria make sense — this is copied from the epics file we drafted earlier, augmented with the test design workflow.

The most important part of this draft: because the workflow reads the project context file, it generates a list of tasks and subtasks that respect all architectural and technical concerns from that file. It also reads the codebase to identify the specific points in the code that need to change to satisfy each acceptance criterion.

At the end of the story file, the references used to create it are listed — including the project context. This is why hallucination probability is reduced: the workflow is anchored to actual code and actual project rules.

There is also a section at the bottom of each story file for completion notes. After the developer agent implements the story, it may encounter things that only surface at runtime. These notes can be reused during the retrospective.

Vertical slicing and team extensibility

A real-world tip: the BMAD create-epics-and-stories workflow applies **vertical slicing**. Each story touches all the code layers necessary to deliver value to the customer — front-end, back-end, database, depending on the project. For larger teams working on the same codebase, the create-story workflow is a natural extensibility point where we can teach the workflow to generate stories sized appropriately for the team and structured to be parallelizable.

Because the process is sequential by default, only one person can work at a time when tasks depend on each other.

One additional best practice for larger teams: once the technical lead has reviewed an epic's stories and is confident in their direction, draft all stories at once. We can rerun this workflow with an explicit story number — for example, story 1.1 — and even though story 1.0 is still in `ready-for-dev` status, the workflow is smart enough to handle the explicit request. After all stories are drafted, distribute them to the team for implementation. Do not work on more than one story at a time unless they have no dependencies on each other.

Creating tests using ATDD

With the story in place, we run the ATDD workflow. We will open a new chat and type `/bmad-testarch-atdd`. We explicitly select the story we want to create tests for and point the workflow to it.

Because we ran the test design workflow earlier, we can now provide much richer context about which tests are most important. This workflow reads the files under the test-design folder and uses them when generating tests. Creating tests before implementation is what ensures the code delivered by the agent matches what the customer expects—the implementation fits the tests, not the other way around.

```
/**
 * RED-PHASE acceptance tests: Task Management - create and view tasks (ATDD).
 *
 * These scaffolds are intentionally skipped (TDD red phase).
 * Remove `test.skip` - `test` for each scenario when implementing the corresponding task.
 *
 * Standards enforced:
 *   1. Web-First Assertions - expect(locator).toBeVisible() / tohaveText() / tohaveValue()
 *   2. Explicit Locators - getByRole, getByTestId only
 *   3. No Static Maits - no page.waitForTimeout()
 *   4. Strict AAA - Arrange / Act / Assert separated
 *
 * Coverage:
 *   - Create a task via Add Task dialog
 *   - Pre-seeded task visible on board load
 *   - Billable task shows billing indicator
 *   - Opening a task shows its detail panel
 */
import { test, expect } from '../support/fixtures/merged-fixtures';
import { KanbanPage } from '../support/page-objects/kanban-page';
import { createTask } from '../support/factories/task-factory';
import { createDefaultColumns } from '../support/factories/column-factory';
import { buildAppState, seedState } from '../support/helpers/storage-helpers';

test.describe('Task Management (ATED - RED)', () => {
  test.skip('[P0] E2E-E1: user can add a new task via the dialog', async ({ page, log }) => {
    // THIS TEST WILL FAIL - Add Task dislog / task card not yet implemented
    // Arrange
    const kanban = new KanbanPage(page);
    const taskTitle = `Test task ${Date.now()}`;
    await log({ level: 'step', message: 'Navigate to board' });
    await kanban.goto();

    // Act
    await log({ level: 'step', message: `Add task: "${taskTitle}"` });
    await kanban.openAddTaskDialog();
    await kanban.fillTaskForm(TaskTitle, 'A description for the test task');
```

Figure 4.16 – Red-phase tests generated by ATDD

After a few minutes, the ATDD workflow completes. The red phase is done. Test scenarios are generated to cover this story—unit, integration, and end-to-end—aligned with the acceptance criteria and the priority levels from the test design phase.

We are now ready to implement.

Developing the story

We open a new chat and run the `/bmad-dev-story` workflow — not `/bmad-quick-dev`. These are different. We point it to story 1.0. If no story is specified, the workflow finds the first `ready-for-dev` story and begins there.

After a few minutes, the story is complete and its status is now under review. Looking through the workflow execution:

1. It created a plan listing all tasks to be performed:

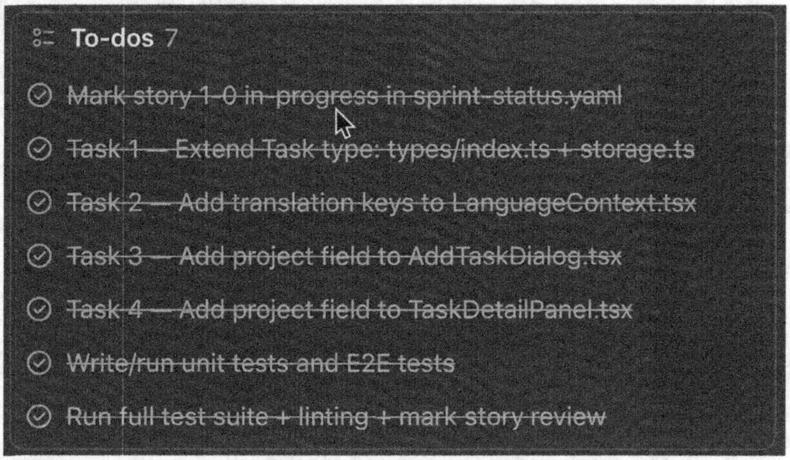

Figure 4.17 – Plan for tasks to be performed

2. It changed the story status from ready-for-dev to in progress:

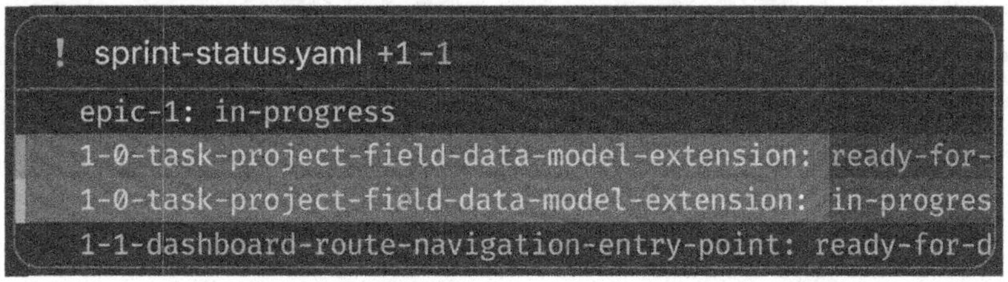

Figure 4.18 – Status changed to In-progress

3. It worked through the four tasks from the original story file:

```
- [x] Task 2 - Add translation keys (AC: #5)
  - [x] Add `project: string` and `enterProjectName: string` to the `Translations` interface in `src/
  context/LanguageContext.tsx`
  - [x] Add English values: `project: 'Project'`, `enterProjectName: 'Enter project name...'`
  - [x] Add Portuguese values: `project: 'Projeto'`, `enterProjectName: 'Digite o nome do projeto...
  '`

- [x] Task 3 - Add project field to AddTaskDialog (AC: #2, #4)
  - [x] Add `const [projectName, setProjectName] = useState<string>('')` near other field states in
  `src/components/AddTaskDialog.tsx`
  - [x] Add the "Project" Input field in the form JSX (place after Description, before Column -
  matching natural data-entry flow)
  - [x] Include `projectName: projectName.trim() || null` in the `dispatch({ type: 'ADD_TASK',
  payload: { ... } })` call
  - [x] Reset `setProjectName('')` inside the form reset block after dipatch

- [x] Task 4 - Add project field to TaskDetailPanel (AC: #3, #4)
  - [x] Add editable Input for `localTask.projectName` using the existing `handleUpdate` pattern in
  `src/components/TaskDetailPanel.tsx`
  - [x] Place field after Description, before Client - consistent position with AddTaskDialog
  - [x] On change: `handleUpdate({ projectName: e.target.value.trim() || nul })` so clearing saves
  `null`
```

Figure 4.19 – Completed the task from the original story

4. After implementation, it ran the test suites
5. It removed the skip directive from the ATDD-generated unit tests and activated the end-to-end tests
6. All unit tests passed
7. One end-to-end test failed, so the workflow auto-corrected, reran the suite, found another issue, proposed fixes, and verified all end-to-end tests are now passing

Completion notes are appended at the bottom of the story file, capturing what was done and what was found. These will be used in the retrospective. The story status is changed to under-review. The next recommended step — optional but encouraged — is to run the code review process, ideally using a different model to independently evaluate the work.

Reviewing the code

We open a new tab, run the `/bmad-code-review` workflow, and switch to a different model — for example, GPT-4.5 — to get an independent evaluation. We point the workflow to the story being reviewed, which is `1.0`.

The workflow confirms the story to review, reads the relevant files to understand what needs to be checked against the acceptance criteria, and then spawns three agents in parallel: one for edge case review, one to audit acceptance criteria, and one to view the difference between the state before and after implementation.

With all three reviews complete, it surfaces its findings. The workflow can find errors or patches needed for a story. Because we are in this workflow with sufficient context, these are things that should be fixed now before they accumulate as technical debt.

The workflow loads the context files, applies the fixes, reruns the tests, confirms everything is still passing, and changes the story status to done.

Automating tests

To close this story's loop, we run the `/bmad-testarch-automate` workflow one final time, pointing to the story, `1.0`. At this point, you can revert to your original model used to implement the features.

As a best practice for the TEA module, automate should always be called after a story is implemented and after the ATDD workflow has been run beforehand. If ATDD was not run first, automate should be called specifically for existing features to increase test coverage.

The workflow evaluates the story scope, reviews any pending tasks, implements the green phase — activating all components and layers of the application that the red-phase tests were waiting on — and then runs the full unit test and end-to-end test suites.

More tests were added in this round that were not covered in the first pass. The automation summary under test-artifacts is updated accordingly. All ATDD tests are passing, and the checklist is fully verified.

At this point the developer responsible for this story needs to run the application manually and confirm everything works as expected. We will run the following command:

```
npm run dev
```

Wrapping up the entire workflow

To summarize the complete story-level workflow: for each story, create the story file, run ATDD, develop the story, perform the code review, and run automate:

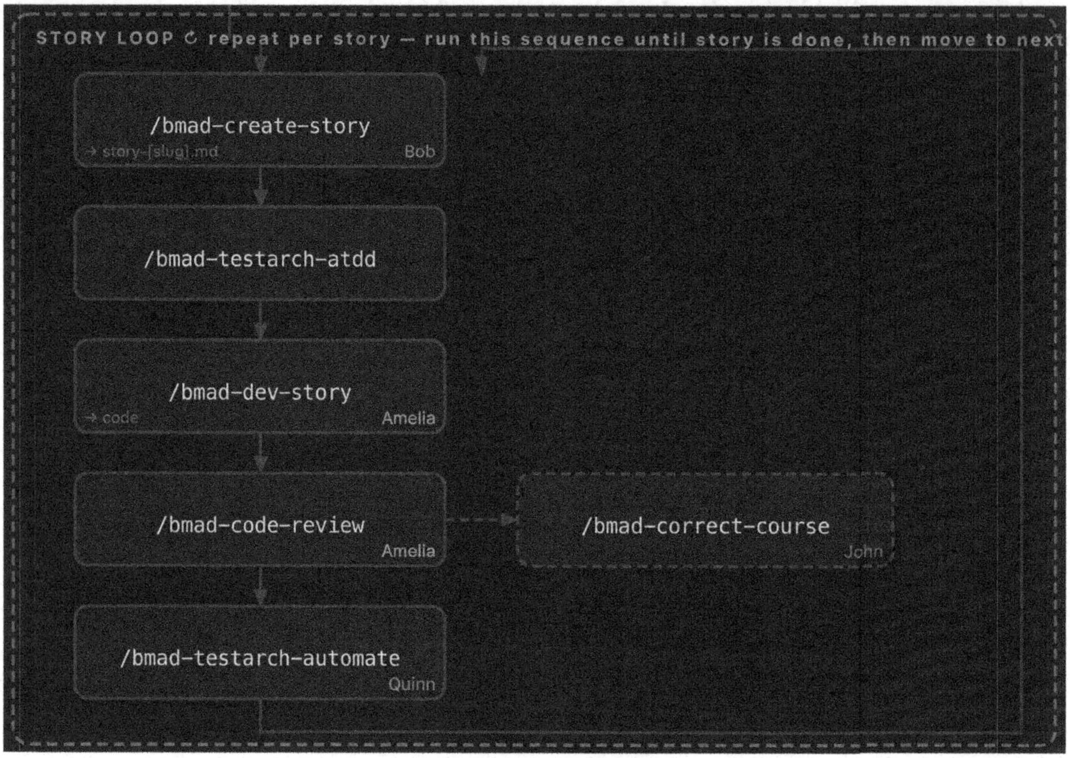

Figure 4.20 – Recommended workflow: /bmad + /tea

Repeat this for every story until the epic is complete.

This is time- and token-intensive. A more efficient approach is to use BMAD Loop—a custom framework developed by the community that develops all stages using an orchestrator agent. The orchestrator spawns each workflow in sequence for a given story, one after another, in the background. We trigger one workflow and after completion we review the results and apply any changes needed.

You can find more information here: `https://github.com/bmad-code-org/bmad-loop`. If it proves useful for building more efficient workflows, consider contributing back to the community.

Correcting the course during the sprint

What happens if, in the middle of a sprint, we evaluate our PRD with stakeholders or discover something in runtime, and need to change direction? BMAD provides the `correct-course` workflow for exactly this situation. It can be used to evaluate the impact of a change during PRD definition or at any point during implementation.

In our scenario: after reflection, the visualization by tag does not seem to add enough value. We want to remove that specific feature and deliver a more focused solution based on client and project views only.

We open a new agent and type the `/bmad-correct-course` workflow. The workflow finds the PRD and epics and stories, but might not find the architecture document in the default location. If this happens, we need to point it to the correct path under the `docs` folder.

The workflow asks whether this is a story blocker or a new stakeholder requirement. We confirm we want to remove the tag feature implementation with the following prompt:

```
I want to remove the tag feature implementation since it is not needed anymore.
```

BMAD asks us if we want to select the incremental mode or batch mode, and I always suggest incremental — this means the workflow reviews and refines each change one at a time. Incremental forces us to think carefully about each change without introducing unintended consequences.

The workflow asks us to clarify scope. It identifies the relevant features: the earnings-by-tag chart in the dashboard and the cross-dimension tag filter. We select both and proceed.

The output is a checklist evaluating the impact across all sections. Since no code has been written yet for these features, the effort is low and the risk is minimal. The workflow recommends adjusting the PRD and epics files directly. We approve and walk through eight confirmation steps as the changes are applied to both files.

After completion, a sprint-change-proposal file is created capturing all the changes made and providing a permanent record of the course correction.

Performing the retrospective

To close out this module, I want to show the final step after completing an epic: the retrospective workflow.

Looking at the `sprint-status.json` file, epic one is in progress and the first story is done:

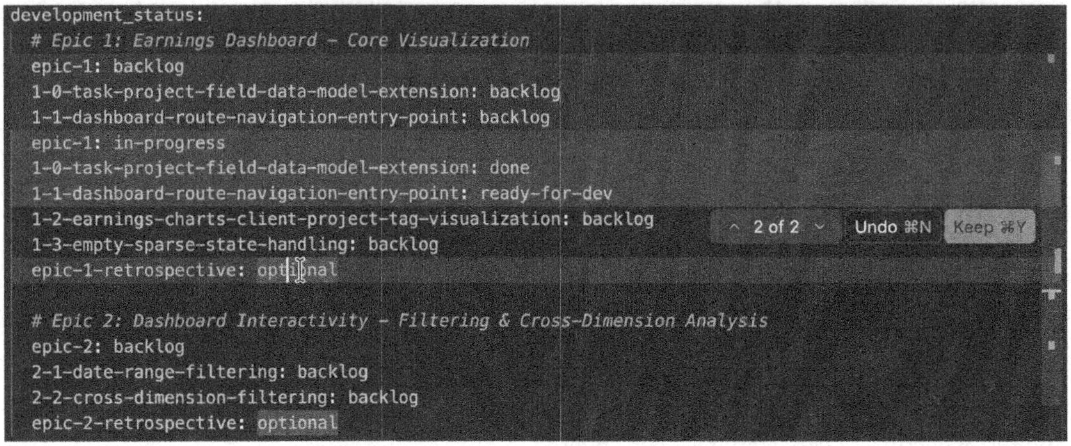

Figure 4.21 – Status of the project

If you open any story file with a status of done and scroll to the end, there is a section with completion notes written by the developer agent during the dev-story workflow:

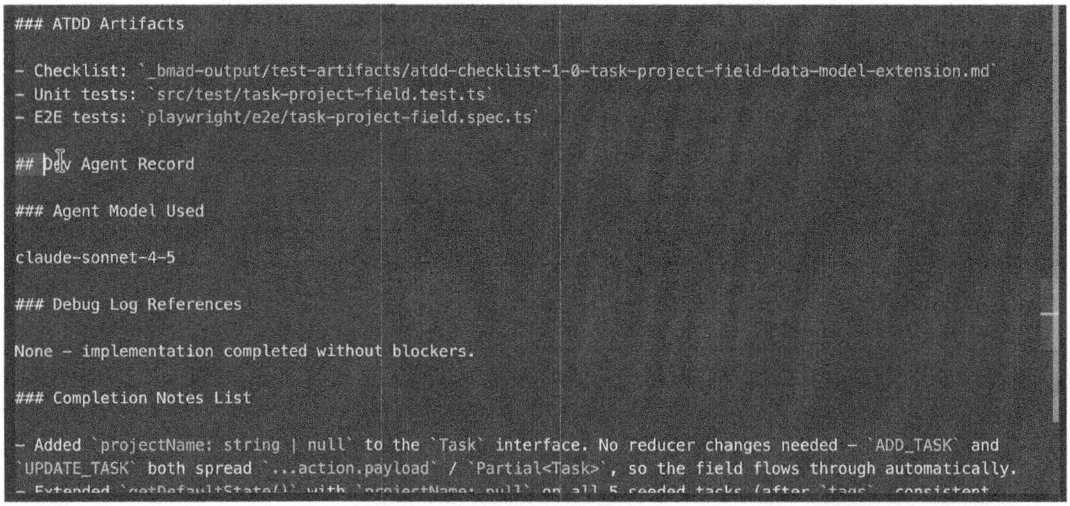

Figure 4.22 – Done story file screenshot

These notes capture findings and challenges encountered during implementation. When all stories in an epic are done, each of them will have notes in this format.

The retrospective workflow invokes party mode — bringing all relevant agents into the same conversation. Each reads the completion notes from every story in the epic and contributes its perspective on the findings. The workflow then synthesizes the key learnings that should be carried forward into the next implementation phases.

After the retrospective workflow completes, the output file can be used to update the project context. In a new agent session, we run `/bmad-generate-project-context` and point to the epic retrospective file, `epic-1-retro-YYYY-MM-DD`. This updates the project context with all the new learnings, so from that point forward, every BMAD workflow benefits from what was discovered during this implementation cycle.

This completes the entire workflow for this module. From installing BMAD on an existing project through creating documentation, project context, individual features, test coverage, full PRD-driven development, sprint planning, story creation, ATDD, implementation, code review, and retrospective—every step has been covered.

Summary

In this chapter, you learned how to apply the BMAD methodology to an existing project, taking it from initial documentation through feature implementation and continuous improvement. You explored how to document a brownfield application, generate project context, implement both simple and complex features using the appropriate BMAD workflows, and integrate the **Test Enterprise Architecture** (**TEA**) framework to create and automate unit and end-to-end tests. You also learned how to plan development through PRDs, epics, stories, and sprint planning, perform code reviews, manage changing requirements with course correction, and capture lessons learned through retrospectives. Together, these workflows demonstrate how BMAD enables AI-assisted development while maintaining quality, consistency, and traceability throughout the software development lifecycle.

5

Applying BMAD to a New Project

The true value of AI-assisted software engineering lies not in writing code faster, but in making better decisions before implementation begins. A well-defined idea, grounded in research and translated into clear product and technical specifications, provides AI agents with the context they need to generate high-quality, consistent results. In this chapter, you will apply the complete BMAD v6 upstream workflow to a brand-new project, following the journey from an initial concept to a fully documented implementation plan.

You will begin by using the Brainstorm workflow to explore and refine a product idea, then enrich it through market, domain, and technical research. From there, you will learn how to create a concise product brief, transform it into a comprehensive **Product Requirements Document** (**PRD**), and generate UX and architecture specifications that guide both human developers and AI agents. Finally, you will create a system-level test design and prepare the project for implementation by generating project context, epics, stories, and implementation readiness artifacts.

By following this structured workflow, you will learn how to replace ad hoc planning with a repeatable, specification-driven process that produces high-quality documentation before a single line of code is written. These artifacts not only improve collaboration and decision-making but also provide the context AI coding agents need to generate more accurate, maintainable, and production-ready implementations.

We will cover the following main topics:

- Recommended workflow
- Brainstorming session
- Research customers, competitors, and technology

- Creating the product brief
- Creating the PRD
- Creating the UX
- Creating the architecture
- Creating the test design and setting up the test framework
- Creating project context, epics and stories and wrapping up

By the end of this chapter, you will be able to take a new project from a rough idea to an implementation-ready state using BMAD. You will understand how each upstream workflow contributes to the overall development lifecycle, how the generated artifacts build upon one another, and how to establish a solid foundation that enables both developers and AI agents to implement software with greater confidence, consistency, and quality.

Recommended workflow

Applying BMAD to a new application becomes even more valuable when working on a medium to high complexity project, because this time we pass through the full BMAD workflow proposal, from the ideation phase all the way to implementation. This is where you spend most of your time sharpening the axe before actually starting implementation. For this book, we will rebuild the Freelancer Task Tracker that we used previously to learn BMAD, and we will work specifically on the upstream phase to create the documents that satisfy these features: time tracking per task to increase revenue, a Kanban board with an integrated timer, a web version without social features, and task persistence in local storage to avoid database complexity. You are welcome to apply all the workflows we cover in this module to your own project idea.

Set your goals and try BMAD, and you will see the power of this framework in practice. To wrap up the recommended workflow using the BMAD and TEA modules during the upstream phase, we will cover the brainstorm method, the research workflow, the create product brief workflow, the create PRD workflow, the create UX design workflow, and then move to the create architecture workflow:

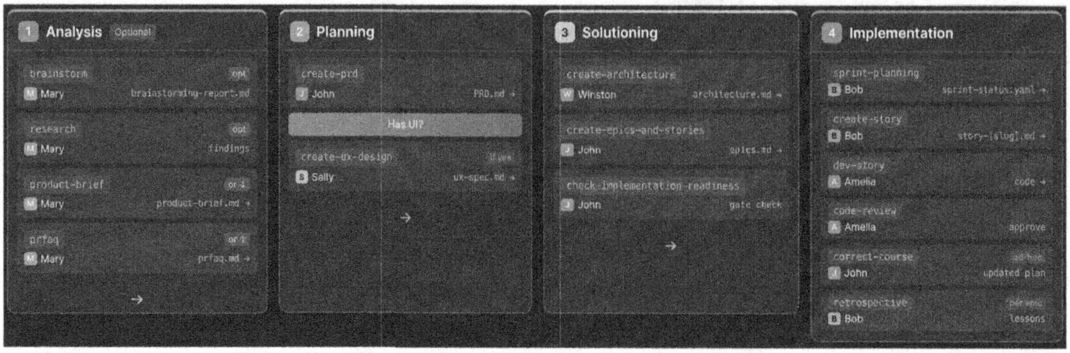

Figure 5.1 – Recommended workflow

Optionally, we can run the test design workflow from an application perspective rather than a feature perspective, as we learned in the previous module. From there, we create the epics and stories, check implementation readiness, and set up the framework and the /bmad-testarch-ci workflow, picking up from what we covered in the previous module. If you have not read the previous chapter, that is where sprint planning, create story, the ATDD workflow, dev the story, code review, automate, and course correction (if needed) are taught, finishing with the retrospective once everything is done.

In general, this is what we will cover in this chapter. It will have fewer lessons than the previous one, but we will focus especially on the upstream phase, where you sharpen your axe and see the power of BMAD to bring your ideas to life.

Brainstorming session

To start from scratch, let's open an empty folder. We are going to install BMAD and run the brainstorm workflow so we can see everything from the ground up, starting with a new terminal window inside Cursor.

Let's run `npx bmad-method install`, as covered in the previous chapters. Select BMAD Core, BMAD AI-Driven Development, and BMAD TEA modules. We are not going into a lot of detail since we already covered the installer previously; if you have doubts, refer back to *Chapter 1*.

With BMAD configured inside the application, we can run the brainstorm workflow by prompting `/bmad-brainstorming`. When you activate this workflow, it asks what we are brainstorming about and what specific outcome we are hoping for, opening the floor to a conversation with the workflow.

To start, use this prompt to kick off the workflow:

```
I want to create a web-based, local-first freelancer time tracking application
with Kanban, with an integrated timer for per-task hour tracking, and local
storage persistence, so I can have keep track of hours of service to my customers
as a freelancer.
```

After this point, the agent will start to discuss what we wanted to brainstorm, and you can use this workflow not just to discuss a particular feature, but any idea you want to turn into an application.

Our primary goal here is to discover creative features, UX flows, and implementation ideas that help accurately track billable hours per client task and increase revenue clarity. BMAD ships more than 50+ different brainstorm techniques, and you can select as many as you want to discuss better your idea. I always suggest selecting the AI-recommended option, since I think this is one of the most valuable parts of the workflow:

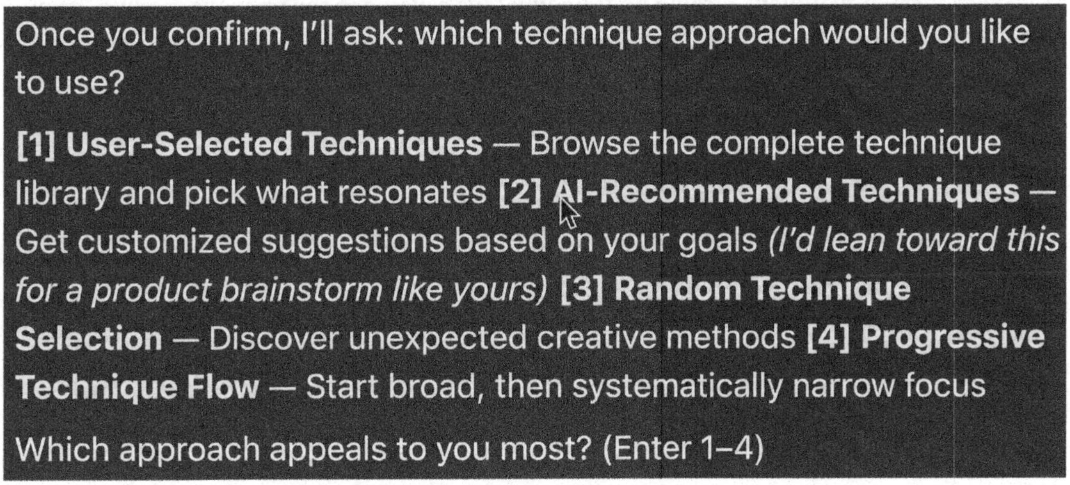

Figure 5.2 – Options provided by the agent

Based on your selection, the brainstorm technique library will show up. The categories include techniques to structure your thinking process, techniques for creative innovation, collaborative methods, deep analysis, theatrical exploration, wild thinking to push boundaries, introspective approaches, biomimetic and nature-based strategies, and some more esoteric and mythic frameworks for gathering unique perspectives. You are not bound to select just one technique; you can select multiple, as stated in the workflow. In our scenario, AI-recommended techniques are first principles thinking, the SCAMPER method, and what-if scenarios. The idea of this lesson is not to go into deeper detail about what this application could be, since we

already saw the application running and already learned how to apply BMAD to it. When we activated this workflow, it created a `brainstorming` folder under the `_bmad-output` folder, and stores each session there. Because this can take a significant amount of time, the workflow proposed that we spend at least an hour on it, so we will not cover the discussion in detail here. If you run out of context window, or want to pause and return later, you can always restart the workflow pointing to the existing session until you are satisfied with the result.

After a few hours discussing this workflow, here are the final results:

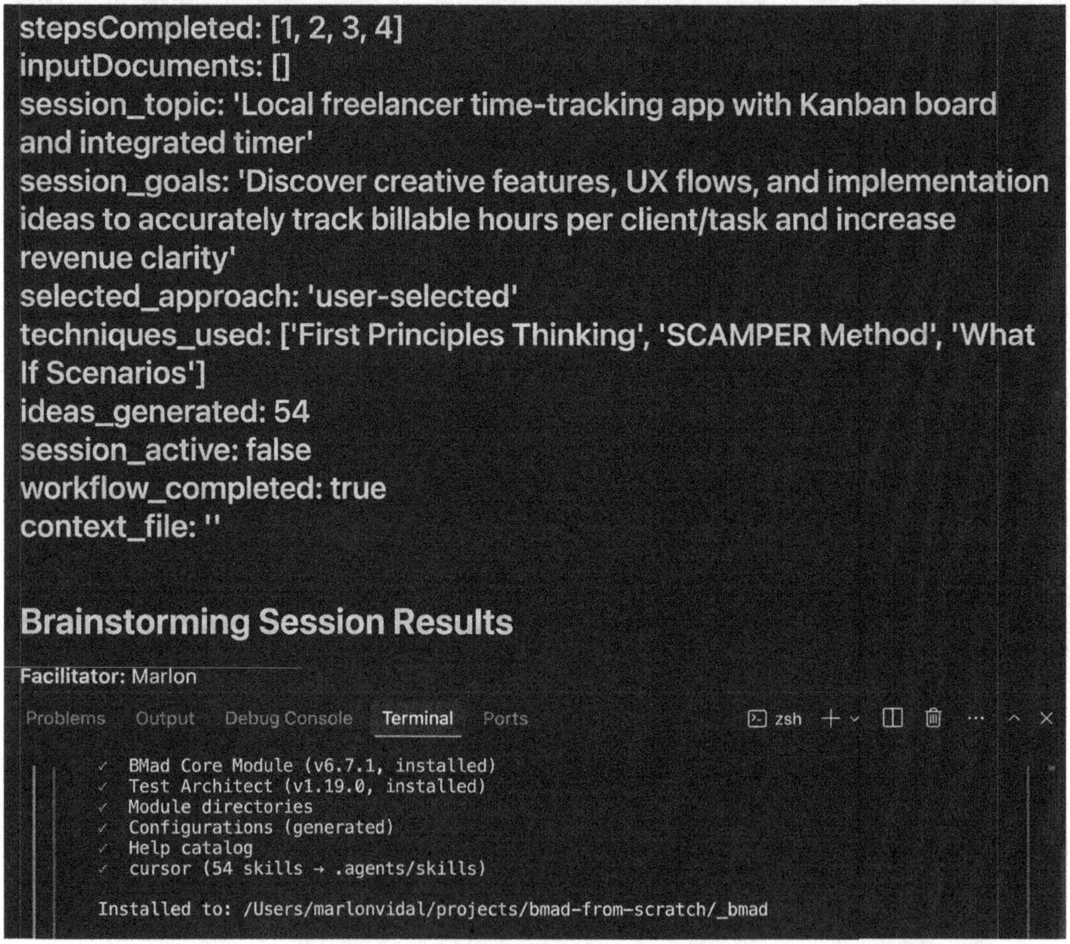

Figure 5.3 – Final results of the brainstorming session

The document states the topic we discussed, the goals we want to achieve, the constraints, and the techniques used. It proposed idea generation using the first principles thinking method.

Let us look at some examples. What do we actually know for certain about how freelancers lose money?

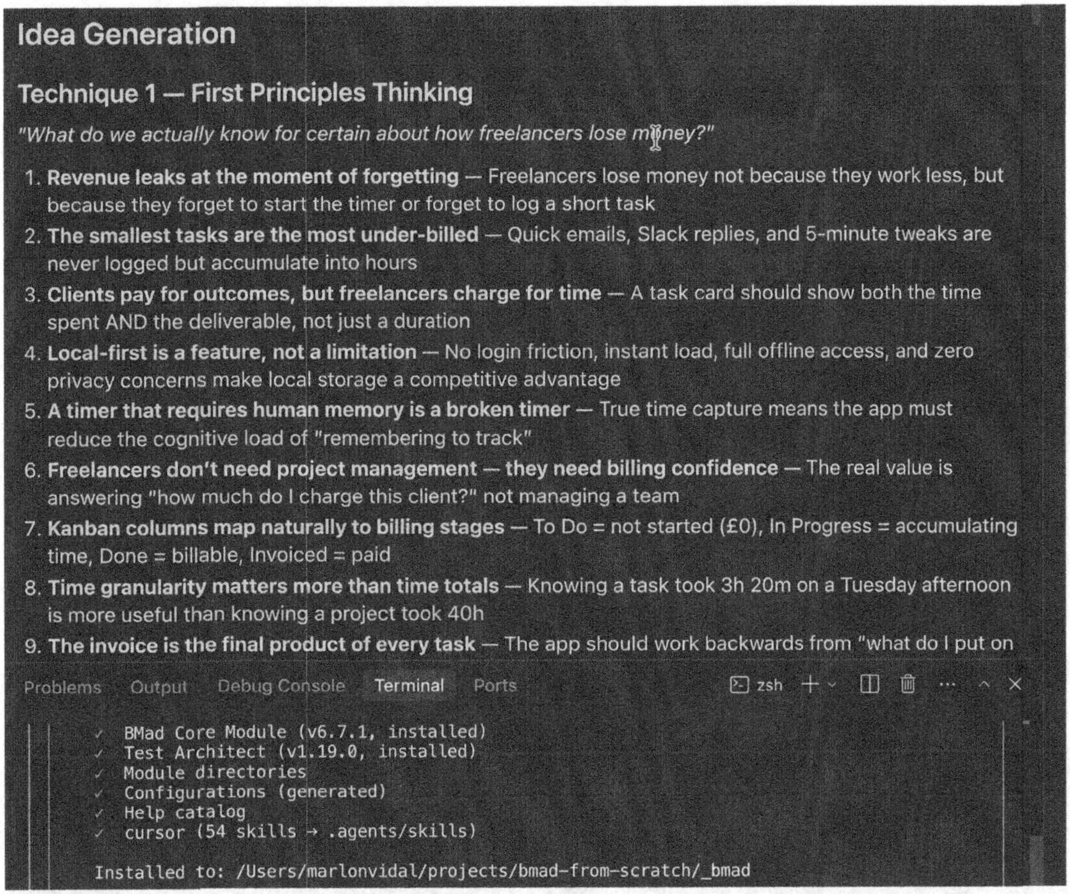

Figure 5.4 – Example scenario

Look at some ideas the workflow proposed to us applying first principles thinking: revenue leaks happen at the moment of forgetting, the smallest tasks are the most under-billed, the client pays for outcomes but freelancers charge for time, and we want local-first as a feature, not a limitation. A timer that requires human memory is a broken timer. Freelancers do not need project management, so we need something very simple. Kanban columns should map naturally to billing stages, so we can easily see work flowing through to completion. Time granularity matters more than time totals. The invoice is the final product of every task, and I completely agree with that. Some user data is noise; we want to focus on what we need to deliver in order to receive income from the customer.

Technique 2 — SCAMPER Method

Applying 7 lenses to the core features: timer, Kanban board, task card, and localStorage

S — Substitute

11. **Replace manual timer start/stop with a single-click "I'm working now" button** — One global action that assigns time to the currently focused card
12. **Replace task names with client-prefixed labels** — Format `[ClientName] Task Description` to make every card instantly scannable by revenue source
13. **Replace column names (To Do / In Progress / Done) with billing-stage language** — "Backlog / Billing Now / Ready to Invoice / Archived"
14. **Replace a flat task list with a collapsible client swimlane view** — Group all Kanban cards by client so revenue per client is always visible

C — Combine

15. **Combine the timer and the task card into one component** — The card itself has a start/stop button; no separate timer panel needed
16. **Combine daily time log + Kanban board in a split view** — Left: Kanban board. Right: today's time entries as a running log
17. **Combine the "Done" column with an auto-calculated invoice preview** — Moving a card to Done instantly shows the billable amount based on hourly rate × time logged
18. **Combine client color coding with the Kanban board** — Each client gets a color; every card, tag, and time entry inherits it — instant visual revenue mapping

Figure 5.5 – SCAMPER method

With SCAMPER method analysis applied, we can get into further detail in these topics:

- How can we substitute some of our workflow tasks with different perspectives?
- How do we combine concepts to make things easier to understand?
- What about adaptations or modifications?
- What perspectives from other people's usage apply here?
- What heavier concepts and friction can we eliminate?
- What happens if we reverse or rearrange the point of view to evaluate whether it still makes sense?

This approach makes us think about lots of different ways an user might use our application, challenging all the assumptions we might have about a freelancer time tracking application.

Technique 3 — What If Scenarios

Breaking every assumption about what a time tracker has to be

42. **What if the timer started automatically when you opened a task card?** — Auto-start on card focus, auto-pause on card blur. Zero clicks required to track time
43. **What if every task had a "minimum billable time"?** — Any task under 15 minutes rounds up to 15 minutes automatically. Configurable per client
44. **What if the app predicted how long a task would take?** — Based on similar past tasks, show "Tasks like this took you 1h 20m on average" on card creation
45. **What if there was a "panic button" to log forgetten time?** — A special entry mode: "I worked on [task] from [time] to [time] but forgot to track it" — adds a retroactive entry
46. **What if the board had a revenue thermometer?** — A visual goal indicator showing progress toward a monthly revenue target, updated in real time as time is logged
47. **What if time entries had confidence levels?** — "I'm sure about this" vs "This is an estimate" — logged differently so invoices reflect your certainty
48. **What if every client had a cap alert?** — Set a maximum monthly hours or budget per client; get a visual warning when approaching the limit
49. **What if the app had a "day view" mode?** — Flip from Kanban board to a timeline view of today — what you worked on, in chronological order, with gaps highlighted
50. **What if pausing the timer triggered a micro-journal entry?** — "Why did you stop? (break / client call / blocked / done)" — turns time data into a workday narrative
51. **What if archived tasks generated a one-click invoice draft?** — Select all "Ready to Invoice" cards for a client, click "Generate Invoice Text" — outputs clean, formatted text ready to paste into any invoice tool
52. **What if the board had a "dark hours" warning?** — Tracks how often you work outside declared work hours and shows a weekly summary — useful for freelancers managing work-life balance

Figure 5.6 – What-if method

With the what-if technique applied, it will make us think through some edge cases or non-trivial scenarios, expanding how we are going to approach the solution to our given problem. The answer will change based on your scenario, or even if you use the same prompt I used, you might get different answers. As you can see, there is a lot of ground to cover; our imagination is the limit here. After following this thinking process, the workflow consolidates your idea and helps you prioritize, so you end up with a much more well-thought-out process than simply saying "I just want to create a time tracking app." Invest a lot of time in this thinking process.

This is one of the most impressive workflows I have worked with so far. I encourage you to work through this feature so you can practice it, or apply this workflow to your own idea as I suggested in the previous chapters. The workflow proposed an action plan with priority one being the core timer and Kanban MVP, which I agreed with. Next is the revenue clarity layer, which connects to the dashboard from the previous module, giving a better understanding of where time is going and what the main revenues per client are. The roadmap also proposes an invoice output to generate invoices for customers, giving the full workflow inside the same application.

Apply this to your own ideas, see the results, and share them with other students so we can see what you are working on and how we can contribute.

Research customers, competitors and technology

Now that we have brainstormed what to build based on this book example, we are ready to perform some research to make our analysis phases richer before producing the PRD and architecture artifacts. Before that, I want to introduce the BMAD help workflow, which we have not touched yet, and show the different research methods BMAD offers.

If we open a new agent window and type `research`, BMAD offers three types of research workflows:

- Technical research, to research technology and solutions
- Marketing research, to look at competition and customers in general
- Domain research, to research industry behavior and competitors in the market.

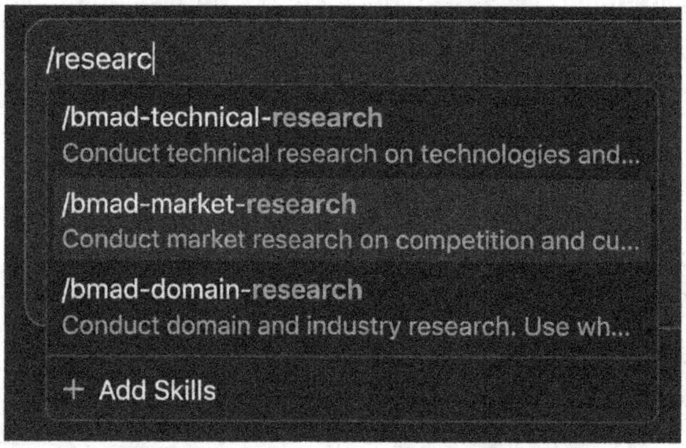

Figure 5.7 – Types of research workflows

Note

Under the hood, at the end of each workflow, `/bmad-help` is invoked to provide guidance on next steps. Whenever you are in the middle of a workflow or have cross-project questions, you can type `/bmad-help` and ask your question, and most of the time it will give you the correct information to keep track of where you are and what steps are needed to advance in the proposed workflow.

Comparing the three workflows: all three produce a research report saved inside the planning artifacts research folder, following a similar output file pattern:

Step-by-Step Comparison

Step	Market Research	Domain Research	Technical Research
1	Scope init (market focus)	Scope init (industry focus)	Scope init (tech focus)
2	Customer Behavior Analysis	Domain/Industry Analysis	Techrical Overview & Stack
3	Customer Pain Points	Competitive Landscape	Integration Patterns
4	Customer Decision Analysis	Regulatory Environment	Architectural Patterns
5	Competitive Analysis	Technology Trends	Implementation Research
6	Research Completion	Research Synthesis	Research Synthesis

Figure 5.8 – Comparing the workflows

Here is the output folders comparison:

Workflow	Output File Pattern
`bmad-market-research` `[MR]`	`research/market-{slug}-research-{date}.md`
`bmad-domain-research` `[DR]`	`research/domain-{slug}-research-{date}.md`
`bmad-technical-research` `[TR]`	`research/technical-{slug}-research-{date}.md`

Figure 5.9 – Comparing the output folders

The marketing research workflow asks about scope , then moves through customer behavior analysis, customer pain points, customer decision analysis, competitive analysis, and research completion. The domain research workflow guides you through domain and industry analysis, competitive landscape, regulatory environment, technology trends, and research synthesis; and technical research guides you through a technical overview and stack, integration patterns, architecture patterns, and implementation research.

Even if you are not a technical person, this workflow can help identify the best technologies to solve the problem you want to solve. If you are doing discovery on a new market or customer, go with marketing research. If you need to understand industry rules, players, and forces, try

domain research. If you are making a technology or architecture choice, go for technical research. These are optional, not required, but running them builds a very rich body of information that feeds the PRD and architecture workflows later. Feel free to skip them, but I highly encourage running these workflows to be more assertive in your research.

Let us open a new agent chat. In our brainstorming session, we run the `/bmad-market-research` workflow and hit *Enter*. Once the workflow loads, you can ask it to search based on the brainstorm document, which provides context for how you are approaching things from a market perspective.

> **Note**
>
> To load the document, hit @ and point to `_bmad-output/brainstorming/brainstorming-session-[current-date].md`.

The document gets created inside the `planning-artifacts/research` folder, following how BMAD always structures these workflows: stating the steps completed, what was used, what the current step is, and so on. As you proceed with the next steps, all the output gets appended to this document, so you can resume the session later or come back if you exceed your context window without losing the proper information.

I will not dive deep into this workflow with you here. Take a look at what was asked: do I want a geographic focus, should I look at specific competitors to prioritize, or do I want to perform research based on a particular business purpose? It is up to you to evaluate when this workflow should be run, but I truly recommend it, especially from a market and domain point of view, since it can completely change the direction of your solution or application, feeding into every next step.

Creating the product brief

Before talking about creating the product brief, let me show you the output of the marketing research workflow from the previous session. The workflow asked which topic to focus on, whether geographic, prioritizing competitors, or which business purpose I was trying to achieve. I answered: focus on Brazil only, base it on Asana as the main competitor, and I am performing this for product-market fit.

All the research workflows make use of the web search tool, performing searches on the topic and producing a document:

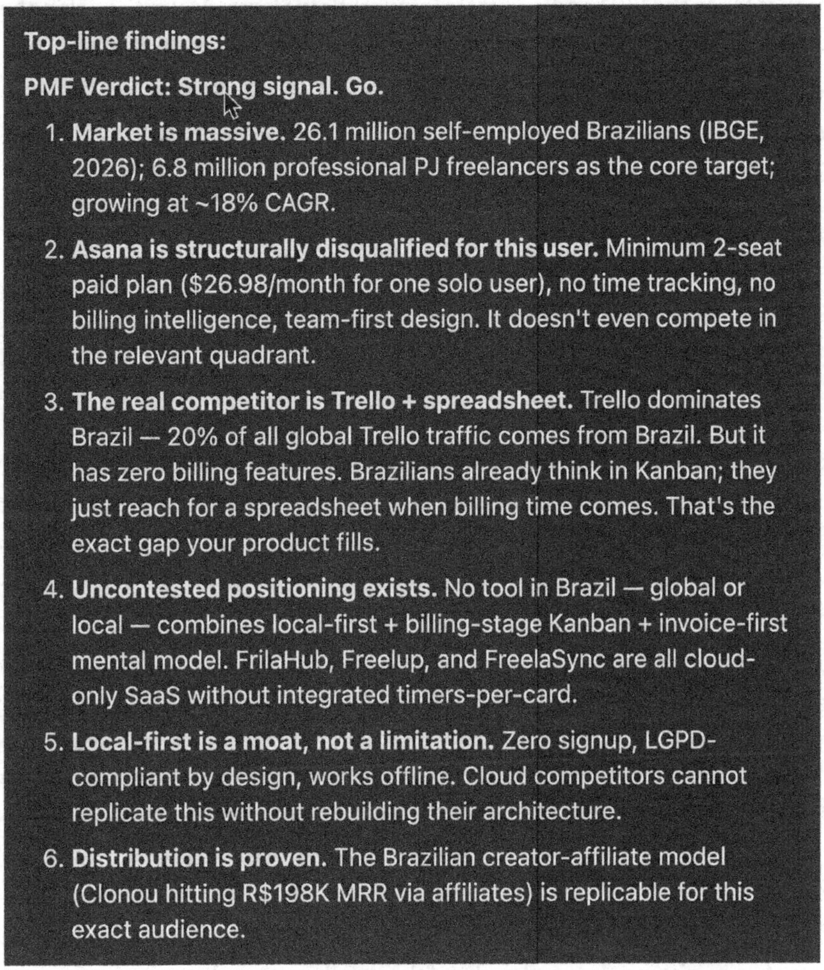
Top-line findings:

PMF Verdict: Strong signal. Go.

1. **Market is massive.** 26.1 million self-employed Brazilians (IBGE, 2026); 6.8 million professional PJ freelancers as the core target; growing at ~18% CAGR.
2. **Asana is structurally disqualified for this user.** Minimum 2-seat paid plan ($26.98/month for one solo user), no time tracking, no billing intelligence, team-first design. It doesn't even compete in the relevant quadrant.
3. **The real competitor is Trello + spreadsheet.** Trello dominates Brazil — 20% of all global Trello traffic comes from Brazil. But it has zero billing features. Brazilians already think in Kanban; they just reach for a spreadsheet when billing time comes. That's the exact gap your product fills.
4. **Uncontested positioning exists.** No tool in Brazil — global or local — combines local-first + billing-stage Kanban + invoice-first mental model. FrilaHub, Freelup, and FreelaSync are all cloud-only SaaS without integrated timers-per-card.
5. **Local-first is a moat, not a limitation.** Zero signup, LGPD-compliant by design, works offline. Cloud competitors cannot replicate this without rebuilding their architecture.
6. **Distribution is proven.** The Brazilian creator-affiliate model (Clonou hitting R$198K MRR via affiliates) is replicable for this exact audience.

Figure 5.10 – Research findings

From a product-market fit verdict, this research found strong signals to proceed with the idea: in Brazil there are 26 million self-employed professionals. Asana is structurally disqualified for this user because it charges a minimum two-seat plan, meaning a solo user pays at least $26, there is no time tracking, no billing intelligence, and the design is team-first. The real competitors are Trello and spreadsheets, which lots of people use. There is no tool in Brazil combining local-first, billing-stage Kanban, and an invoice-first mental model. Local-first is a mode, not a limitation—no signups required, LGPD-compliant by design, and works offline. From a distribution standpoint, the Brazilian creator affiliate model is replicable for this exact

audience. This does not necessarily represent a big business opportunity, but it shows the power of this workflow to help craft your ideas more effectively.

To wrap up this session, here is an overview of the brainstorm, research, and product brief workflows. The brainstorm workflow should be used in divergent mode, when you do not know what to build yet or want to explore before committing. It generates ideas, not decisions. That is exactly what we just discussed in this exercise: the document generated key insights, a session summary, and a proposed action plan, but nothing necessarily actionable yet. The research workflow should be used in grounding mode, when you roughly know the direction but need external facts, competitive landscape, domain terminology, or technical feasibility, which is what we just did with market research to enrich the analysis. Now we are in convergent mode: we are done thinking and want to distill everything into a tight, shareable concept document before writing the full requirements. The critical insight is that these three workflows serve three different cognitive modes, not three sequential steps. You can run brainstorm and jump straight to create PRD, run only the research workflows and feed into create PRD, run both brainstorm and research, or run just the product brief, it is up to you.

To see this in practice, we run the product brief workflow. Obviously your response may differ from mine. This is like a pre-PRD document, and because we already spent time on brainstorm and research, we can feed those right in, tagging the brainstorm session and the market research document. Based on these inputs, we converge on a tight view of what we should create.

The workflow already knows about the product, the current phase, and the market case, but asks about the stakes and purpose: is this to kick off a PRD, develop a sprint, share with someone, or just clarify our own thinking? It also asks for the product name, a central question we had not answered yet, and the capacity, whether I will solo build or have help. I answered: create a PRD, name it Freelancer Tracking Tool, and capacity is solo developer. The next questions covered UI language, which should be Portuguese since we are targeting Brazil, and the version one user, which is me, since I am building for myself.

After a few minutes, the brief document appeared inside the `planning-artifacts` folder. Inside, this is where all the convergent ideas wrap up so we can easily see what we are building: an executive summary, the problem, the solution, what makes it different, the scope, the success criteria, and the product vision. This is a very short version of what a PRD would be, and that is the expected output of this workflow, because within all the prior brainstorm and research sessions, this version is much more digestible and shows clearly what we are actually going to build. Feel free to share this with others to make sure all the fine details are captured, and now we are ready to move to the create PRD workflow.

Creating the PRD

With everything in hand, we are ready to pursue the PRD. Since BMAD is in constant evolution, what used to be separate workflows for create PRD, edit PRD, and validate PRD are now consolidated into a single workflow that automatically understands your intent and adapts accordingly:

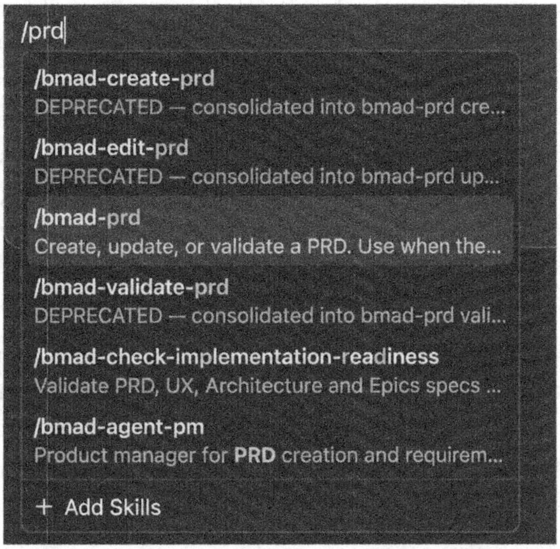

Figure 5.11 – PRD workflows

We run the `/bmad-prd` workflow and, as learned in the previous lesson, feed it directly the product brief (`brief.md`) we just created. If you do not have that, you could use the brainstorm session, the research, or any other document worth feeding into PRD creation.

After a few seconds, it loaded, identified the context, and started asking questions: some UX gut feelings, for example, I want this to feel like Notion, not like Trello. It asked about specific wording we care about in the UI, edge cases or constraints I had been thinking about since writing the brief, and anything about the tech stack that should inform the functional requirements. Like the product brief workflow, the PRD workflow also asks whether you want the fast path or the coaching path. The coaching path walks you through step by step, section by section, but because we already spent a lot of time in the analysis documents, I went with the fast path. I told it to just create the PRD based on the project brief, since I had already thought a lot about it. While I used the fast path here to speed up the demonstration, Greenfield projects should always use the comprehensive coaching path to ensure all functional, UX, and non-functional requirements are thoroughly evaluated by the PM agent.

After a few minutes, the PRD document was finished. The biggest difference between the PRD and the project brief is not just the vision, the target user, and the jobs to be done, but from a product perspective, the key user journeys. This matters because it clarifies what users will do while accessing the application. The PRD also lists the features the application should deliver, the functional requirements, giving clarity about what the application should deliver overall.

At the end of the process, the non-goals, the explicit ones, usually become the non-functional requirements that make the application work under the hood. It also describes what is in scope for the MVP versus what is out of scope, the cross-cutting non-functional requirements such as privacy, cost, and platform, the monetization approach, the success metrics, and any open questions still left to answer. Keep in mind that what the workflow shows me will not necessarily be what it shows you.

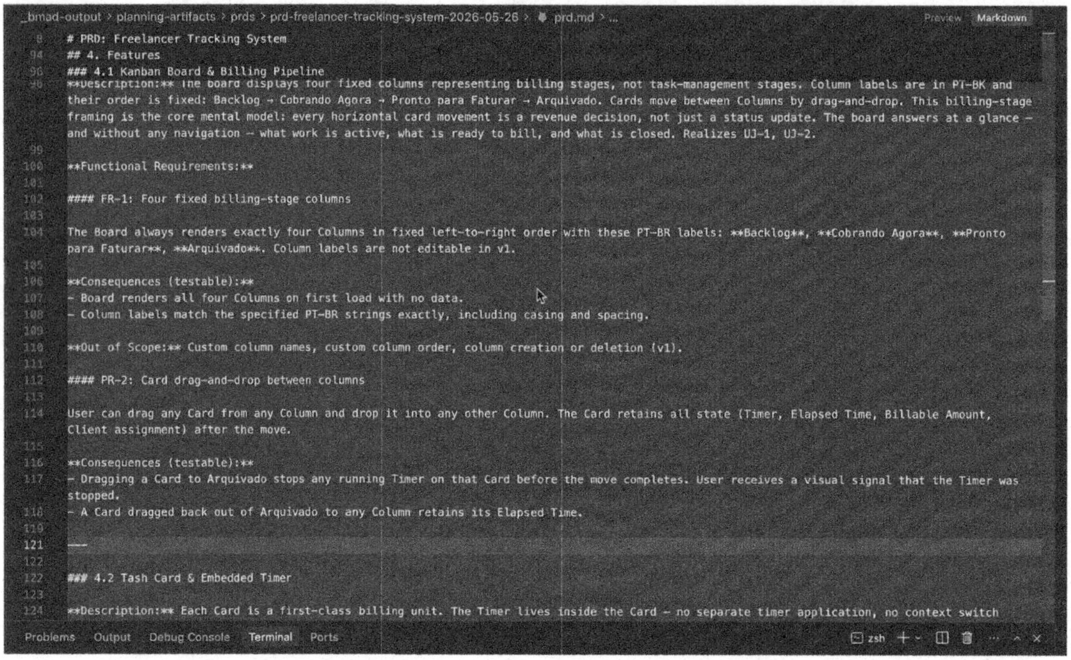

Figure 5.12 – Completed PRD document structure with functional requirements, scope, and success metrics

With this document in place, we are ready to proceed to create the UX design, an optional step, and from there to create the architecture document, giving us all the required documents to start building the solution.

I will not spend more time on the PRD workflow itself in this lesson, since we already covered it in much more depth in *Chapter 4*, including all the possible sections it can cover. I encourage you to revisit that section if you have not already. But for now, the PRD workflow helps create comprehensive product requirement documents for better quality and more focused products.

Creating the UX

In this section, we will learn how to leverage the `/bmad-ux` workflow. Once the initial steps load, it identifies files that can be used to generate this document (like the PRD), and you can provide additional documents if you have something usable. My tip: at this point, I loaded the published version of the Freelancer application, and you can also provide screenshots or brand guidelines for the workflow to use when crafting a better user experience. I took a screenshot, switched back to Cursor, and pasted the image into the chat as the interface I wanted to mimic:

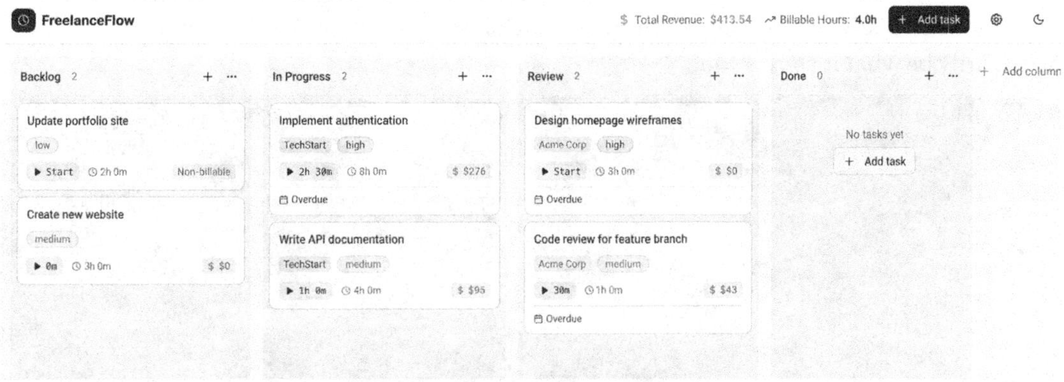

Figure 5.13 – Screenshot of the application

After a few seconds, the workflow responded. Something to keep in mind: if you have all your prototypes in Figma or a similar tool, or already have a design system in your application, where does the UX Design workflow fit in? This workflow produces comprehensive documentation used by the agents during development. It generates the guidelines for things like when a modal should be raised, or what color a badge should be depending on the action the user took. You might already have components implementing that behavior, but without these guidelines, the agents do not know when to use them. That is why this workflow is optional but highly encouraged if you want to keep consistency in the user experience you are providing to customers.

It is similar to the others: a single-canvas, browser-based Kanban board where every column is a billing stage. Let's take a look at the understanding of the workflow:

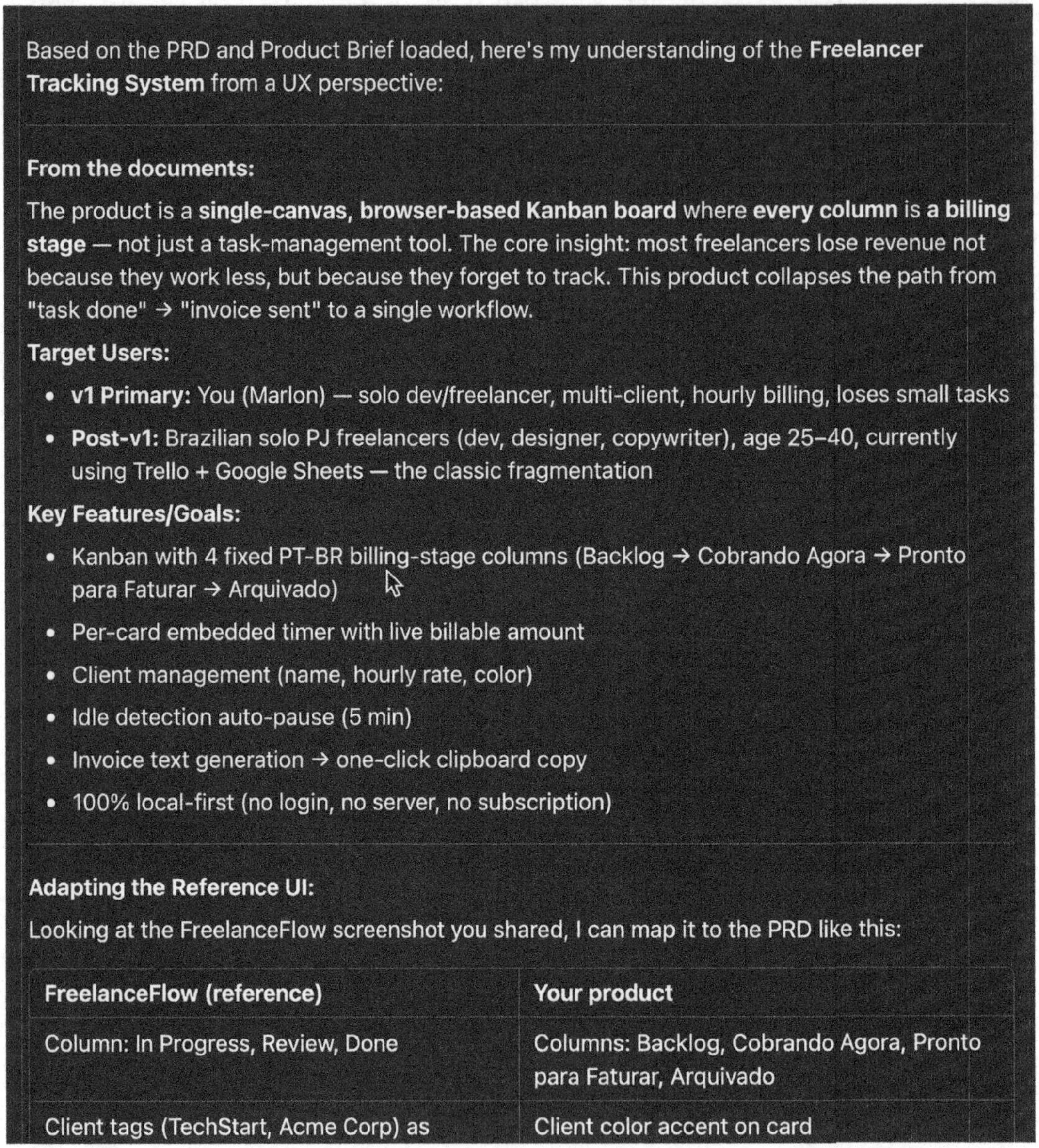

Based on the PRD and Product Brief loaded, here's my understanding of the **Freelancer Tracking System** from a UX perspective:

From the documents:

The product is a **single-canvas, browser-based Kanban board** where **every column** is **a billing stage** — not just a task-management tool. The core insight: most freelancers lose revenue not because they work less, but because they forget to track. This product collapses the path from "task done" → "invoice sent" to a single workflow.

Target Users:

- **v1 Primary:** You (Marlon) — solo dev/freelancer, multi-client, hourly billing, loses small tasks
- **Post-v1:** Brazilian solo PJ freelancers (dev, designer, copywriter), age 25–40, currently using Trello + Google Sheets — the classic fragmentation

Key Features/Goals:

- Kanban with 4 fixed PT-BR billing-stage columns (Backlog → Cobrando Agora → Pronto para Faturar → Arquivado)
- Per-card embedded timer with live billable amount
- Client management (name, hourly rate, color)
- Idle detection auto-pause (5 min)
- Invoice text generation → one-click clipboard copy
- 100% local-first (no login, no server, no subscription)

Adapting the Reference UI:

Looking at the FreelanceFlow screenshot you shared, I can map it to the PRD like this:

FreelanceFlow (reference)	Your product
Column: In Progress, Review, Done	Columns: Backlog, Cobrando Agora, Pronto para Faturar, Arquivado
Client tags (TechStart, Acme Corp) as	Client color accent on card

Figure 5.14 – Understanding of the workflow

The target user is loaded from the PRD, along with the key features, also loaded from the PRD and brief documents, and the workflow already started making definitions. It evaluated the screenshot I provided and proposed translations to Portuguese since I had stated that explicitly in the PRD. It also proposed key UX design challenges and opportunities for the application. What I am seeing here is not necessarily what you will see on your screen, but you should get something similar following this process.

As a reminder, you can always use advanced elicitation, which activates different points of view to discuss the same topic, or bring in party mode for the discussion.

The next step is the core experience definition, covering the main actions the user should perform in the application and guiding how those experiences should be defined to improve the user experience. I reviewed it and it made sense to me, tackling what should happen automatically versus where friction forces extra steps that could be eliminated, which gives leverage. It also covers the critical success moments and the principles for the entire experience in the application. This matters because, since it is written as a principle, every interaction with other agents takes it into consideration. How you expect the user experience to be is not just in your head; it is written into a clear document that the AI agents read and follow, reinforcing the importance of this workflow for keeping consistency in the user experience.

I want to highlight one step from this workflow: the design direction.

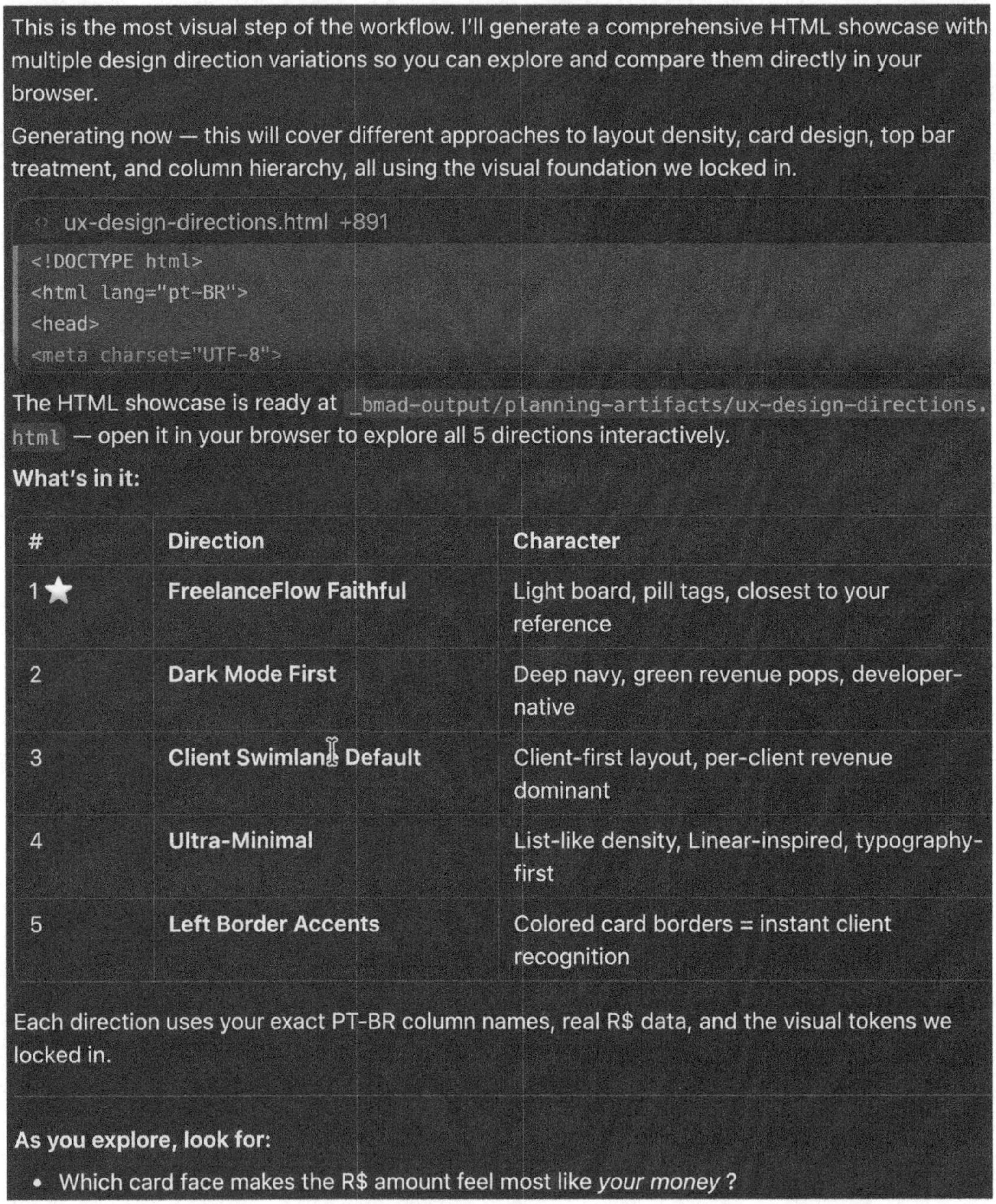

This is the most visual step of the workflow. I'll generate a comprehensive HTML showcase with multiple design direction variations so you can explore and compare them directly in your browser.

Generating now — this will cover different approaches to layout density, card design, top bar treatment, and column hierarchy, all using the visual foundation we locked in.

ux-design-directions.html +891

```
<!DOCTYPE html>
<html lang="pt-BR">
<head>
<meta charset="UTF-8">
```

The HTML showcase is ready at `_bmad-output/planning-artifacts/ux-design-directions.html` — open it in your browser to explore all 5 directions interactively.

What's in it:

#	Direction	Character
1 ★	**FreelanceFlow Faithful**	Light board, pill tags, closest to your reference
2	**Dark Mode First**	Deep navy, green revenue pops, developer-native
3	**Client Swimlane Default**	Client-first layout, per-client revenue dominant
4	**Ultra-Minimal**	List-like density, Linear-inspired, typography-first
5	**Left Border Accents**	Colored card borders = instant client recognition

Each direction uses your exact PT-BR column names, real R$ data, and the visual tokens we locked in.

As you explore, look for:

- Which card face makes the R$ amount feel most like *your money* ?

Figure 5.15 – The Design directions

Since we are creating a visual experience using only text, this step answers the question of what the output will actually look like, while also letting you provide guidance on how the application should look from your perspective. It creates a `ux-design-direction.html` document under the `planning-artifacts` folder, which you can preview. Based on all the inputs gathered, it shows which direction the UX should follow from this point forward:

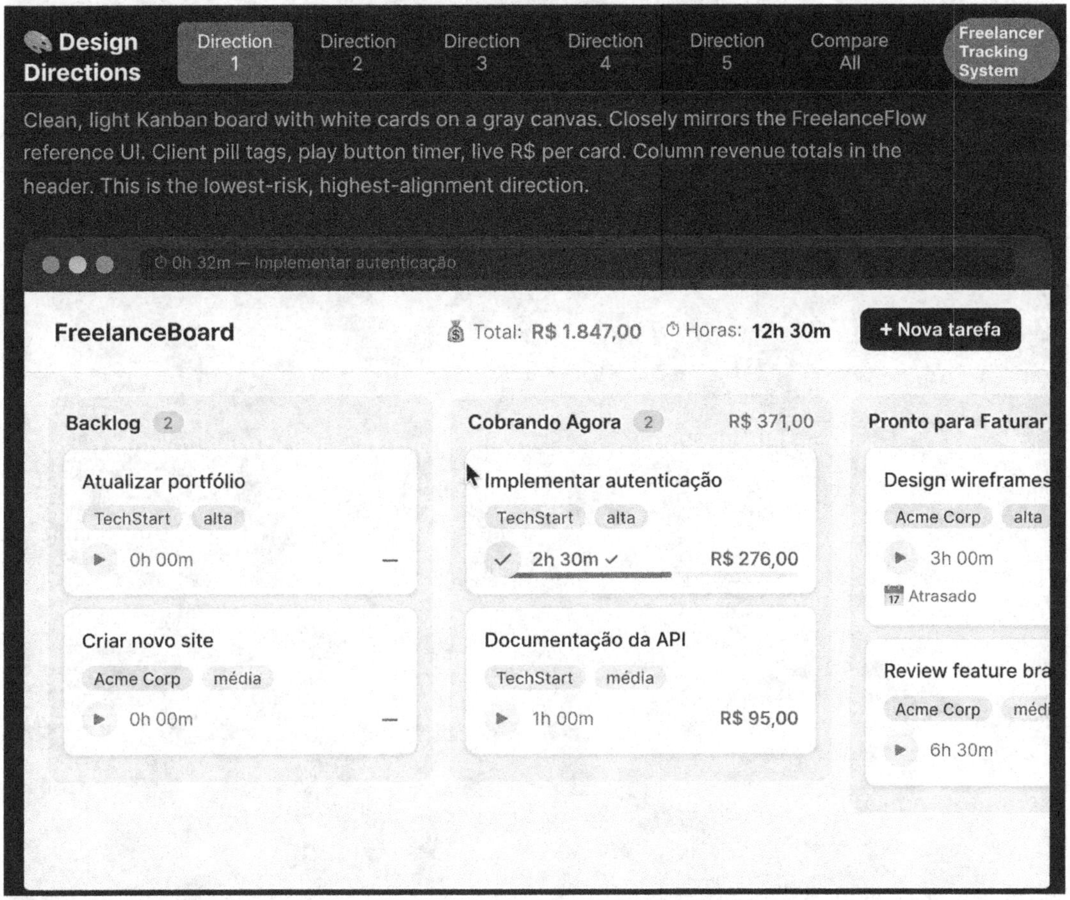

Figure 5.16 – Application sample

One of the proposed directions was quite close to the screenshot I shared, with a dark theme. A third direction took a completely different approach, with a Kanban view and a per-customer view, an interesting option I had not considered:

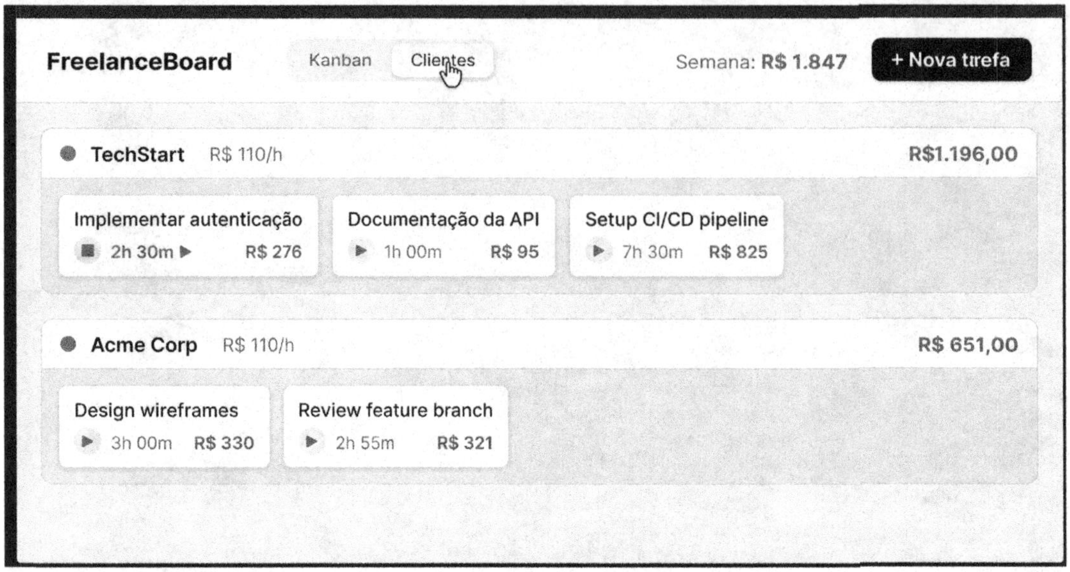

Figure 5.17 – Kanban view

Another proposed a much cleaner approach, with cards and information more easily viewable. If you want to compare all the proposed options, you can also see the pros and cons for each and decide which one you are more comfortable following:

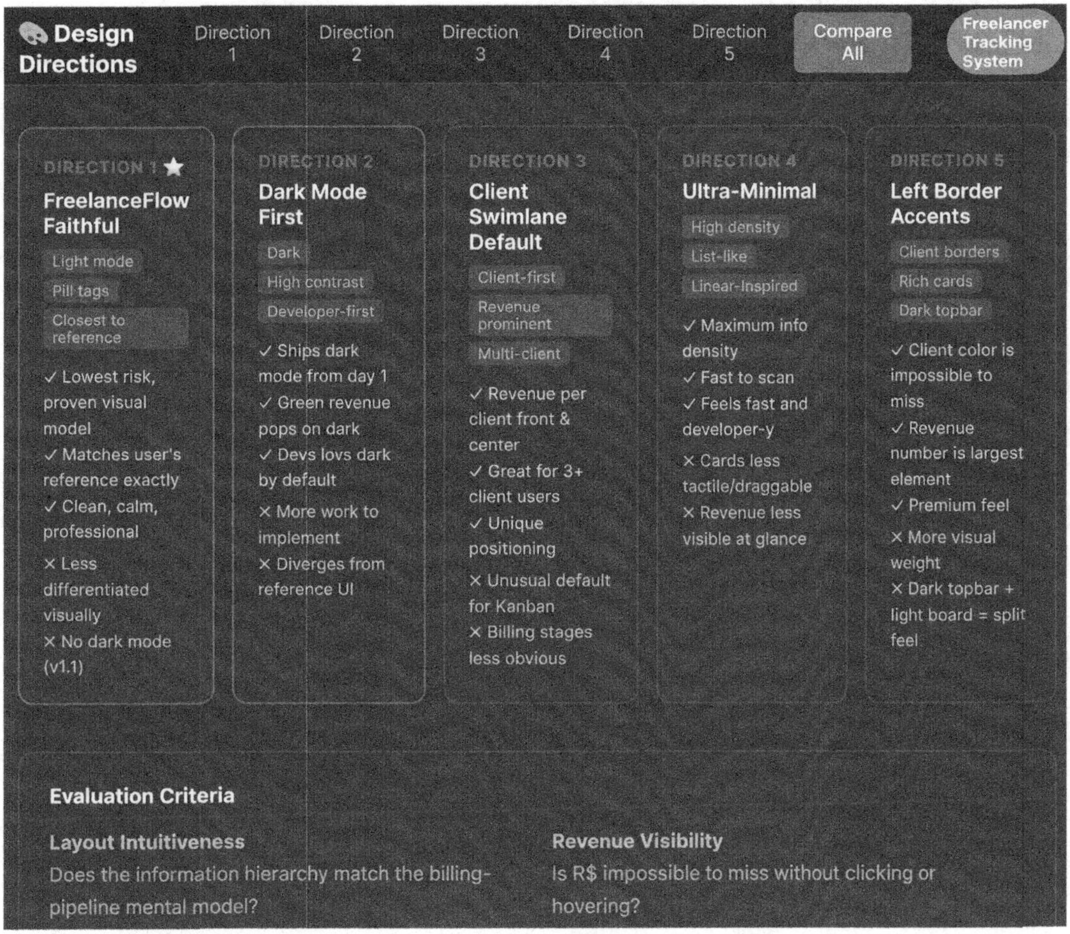

Figure 5.18 – Comparison of the UI

The next step worth exploring is the user journey flow:

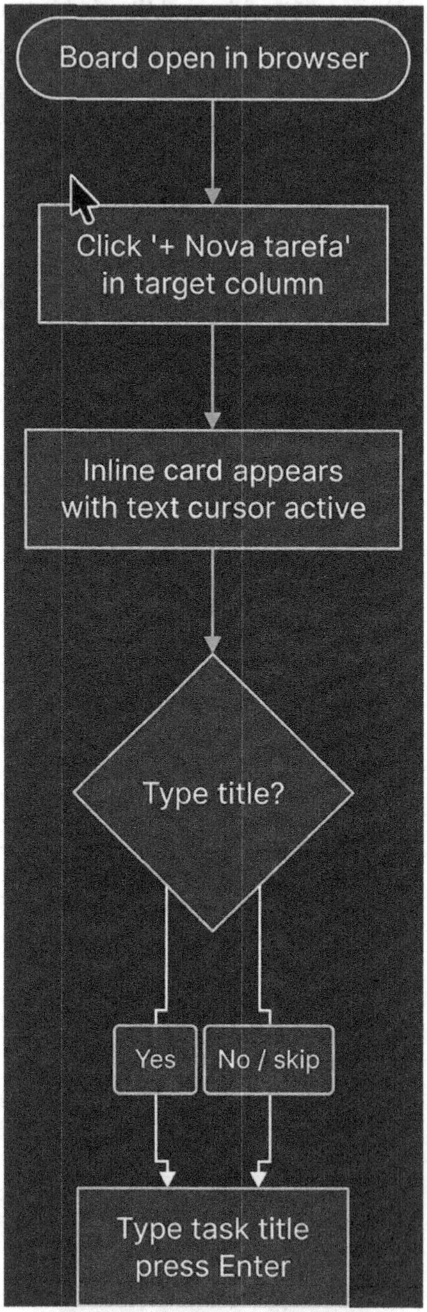

Figure 5.19 – User journey flow

If you do not already have this in your PRD, this workflow helps you evaluate the user journey, showing whether the application flow really works as expected. For example look at the following image:

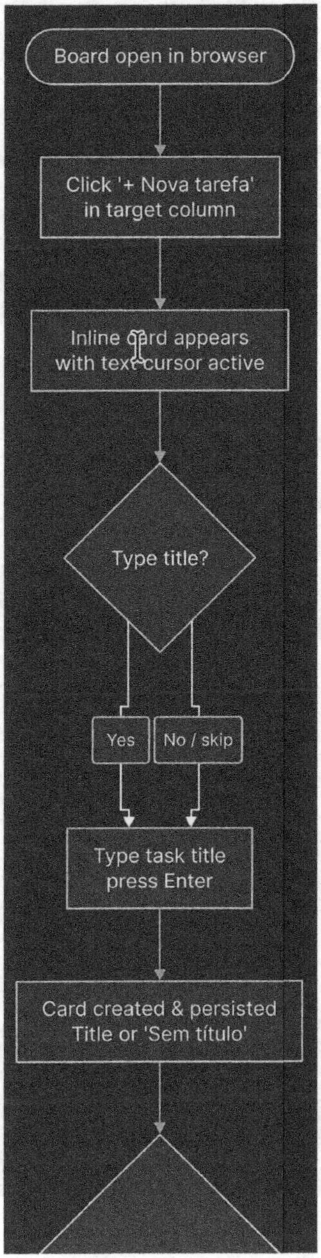

Figure 5.20 – Workflow to evaluate user journey

Without any of the functionality actually implemented, I can already see how this workflow will render after this user journey proposal, and we can repeat this for the rest of the application.

This step is very rich in defining how the experience should be, and these behaviors get implemented based on what is being created. This workflow has a dozen different steps. Since it is a pretty intensive workflow, keep track of your token usage, and you will probably need to resume this workflow from time to time and revisit the sections already created in the document.

This workflow will output two files: `EXPERIENCE.md` and `DESIGN.md`. `EXPERIENCE.md` draws out the core user experience you want to address and the desired emotional response while using the application, a thoughtful touch in my opinion. It also covers UX partner analysis and inspiration, how the application compares to existing benchmarks or references, and the foundations of the design system. If you are creating a design system from scratch, this workflow helps set up the proper rules for the agents to follow; if you already have one, it reinforces its usage during development.

On the other hand, `DESIGN.md` covers the visual design foundation, including all the tokens, colors, fonts used, spacing, layout foundation, and accessibility considerations. It documents the chosen design direction, the user journey as a Mermaid diagram you can share with your team and correct as needed, and the application's components, buttons, badges, dropdown menus, supporting atomic design based on your front-end framework. It also covers UX consistency patterns, ensuring all agent implementations follow similar patterns: feedback patterns, form patterns, navigation patterns, so you can expect consistency as new features are implemented. Finally, it covers responsive design and accessibility guidelines, including breakpoints based on screen size and the accessibility strategy, targeting WCAG 2.1 AA, the industry standard, along with a testing strategy. This is a very comprehensive document, and it is important for keeping consistency in the user experience the agents implement.

Even though it is an optional workflow, I truly recommend using it. The quality of what you implement will improve significantly by following these patterns.

Creating the architecture

We are almost there. Let's use the `/bmad-create-architecture` workflow. As with the other workflows, following the demand process phase by phase, the architecture workflow automatically loads the previously produced documentation: the PRD, the UX design, the research, and the product brief. Since we do not have project context yet, and have not run `/bmad-create-documentation` workflow because this is a brand-new application, that step is not needed, so we are ready to create the architecture document.

Especially if you are not a technical person, this might feel overwhelming, but this is where we really dive into, based on the functional requirements, which technology choices solve each problem. For example, we have the Kanban board with billing stages, task cards with embedded timers, client management, and revenue visibility. Based on the functional and non-functional requirements, this workflow guides the choice of technology to solve those problems. Since this is a front-end-only single-page application, we will not need a backend, authentication or robust infrastructure, but that does not mean the application is simple: there is meaningful reactive state complexity, live timers, cascading rate recalculation, drag-and-drop, and real technical complexity to manage. And even though we don't have a backend or traditional authentication, the Architect must still address client-side security, like ensuring data serialized to local storage is strictly sanitized to prevent **Cross-Site Scripting (XSS)** vulnerabilities.

> **Tip**
>
> Frontend security sanitization is crucial because it serves as the browser's primary defense against XSS attacks. When an application renders untrusted user input, like comments, search queries, or rich text, without cleaning it first, attackers can inject malicious JavaScript capable of stealing session tokens, hijacking user accounts, or defacing the site. By stripping or escaping unsafe HTML tags and scripts before they reach the DOM, sanitization ensures that user-supplied content is treated strictly as passive data rather than executable code, preserving application integrity, and protecting sensitive user privacy.

To solve this, the application gets broken down into smaller components: a store, a timer engine, a drag-and-drop adapter, a persistence layer, a clipboard service, a notification service, an invoice generator, a weekly summary computer, and i18n, the internationalization standard that adapts an application to multiple languages, currencies, and cultures. We can spend a lot of time here, but the main point is choosing which technology solves each problem proposed in the PRD. I identified cross-cutting concerns here, things that get reused across the application, which is important from an architectural perspective. If you are a technical person, review this carefully to make sure it holds up.

The next section covers the starter template: how we create this project from scratch. It proposes using the Shadcn framework as our design system framework, alongside Vite as our build tool and Next.js as our fullstack framework. I will proceed to the end of this workflow without going deeper into the architecture itself here, since that is not the focus of this lesson, but you can see the amount of detail this workflow provides, ensuring your implementation

stays consistent and delivers quality standards. Remember, you can always use advanced elicitation and party mode if you want to go deeper into these technical conversations.

Technology Stack

Category	Technology	Version	Justification
Language	TypeScript	5.8	Type safety across all layers
Build Tool	Vite (SWC)	5.4	Fast HMR, ES module native
UI Framework	React	18.3	Component model, hooks
Component Library	shadcn/ui	various	Copy-in Radix UI primitives with Tailwind
Styling	Tailwind CSS	3.4	Utility-first, co-located styles
Routing	React Router DOM	6.30	Declarative client-side routing
Server State	TanStack Query	5.83	Present in dependencies; not actively used for remote data
Drag & Drop	dnd-kit	6/10	Accessible, keyboard-capable DnD
Animations	Framer Motion	12.28	Smooth panel/card transitions

Figure 5.21 – Architecture document

Looking at the final output, the main topics covered include project analysis, acquired from every workflow, the starter template evaluation, how to create things from scratch, and core architecture decisions covering decision priority analysis, data architecture, authentication, security and API communication patterns. It also covers implementation patterns and consensus rules. Just as the UX workflow ensures UX consistency, this workflow ensures technical consistency. It covers project structure, boundaries, and architecture validation. Looking deeper at the document: it discusses technical constraints and dependencies to consider in the solution, and the cross-cutting concerns, the components reused across the application. The starter template evaluation covers how we create the scaffolding for the application. Architectural decisions cover the language, the runtime, the styling solution, and the build tooling. It covers how to approach the testing framework, since we will use the TEA test design module in the section, so no worries there yet. It covers how to organize the code and the development experience, for example running a dev server with instant feedback, so changes show up in real time in your local environment.

It also covers architectural decisions about state management, the data schema, and deployment. Since this application revolves around time, it covers the timer engine and deferred decisions such as a multi-device sync strategy, progressive web app worker configuration, and whether to support JSON imports.

For the data architecture, how the entities should be modeled and mapped to the domain. We have the client, a timer session, a card, the app state, and app settings, with some properties that should be computed and never stored, since they change based on the current application state, such as elapsed seconds and billable amount, with everything else stored in local storage. We will not have authentication or security to worry about, and the document covers which browser APIs we will interact with.

It also covers the state management library, deployment infrastructure hosted on Vercel with GitHub Actions for the CI pipeline, and how implementation will be sequenced through the construction phase. Very importantly, it covers implementation patterns and consistency rules: how to name components, TypeScript files, design tokens, and CSS classes, how the project is structured from a folder and file perspective, data formats for hours and IDs and how to display them in the UI, how the state management library stores those patterns, error handling, loading states, and enforcement guidelines, which matter for keeping the agent from hallucinating or deviating while implementing code in the repository. It also covers boundaries around which files represent the functional and non-functional requirements.

An important point I want to call attention to, especially if you are working with BMAD v4, is that this document, even though extensive, is far more flexible than the previous version of BMAD. We do not handle topics like observability, monitoring, or testing here, because now the TEA module handles those, but the v4 architecture workflow did handle those scenarios directly. If you do not have technical knowledge, this workflow is much more flexible, letting you start implementing features without evaluating all those additional long-term concerns up front. We created a comprehensive document, and most of the time we discover the rest during the implementation phase. The purpose of this workflow is to think before implementing: what are the technical constraints, what is the data model, and what implementation patterns should the agent follow. Now that we know how we should implement, let us make sure we are handling quality by calling the test design workflow from the TEA module.

Creating the test design and setting up test framework

In this section, we run the test design workflow as suggested by the architecture workflow, typing the `/bmad-testarch-test-design` command from the TEA workflows. This follows the TEA naming convention.

A few minutes later, this workflow, which most of the time does not require input from us, produced a fairly long list of output. I will not re-explain the concepts behind the Test Engineering Architecture module here, since we already covered them in *Chapter 3*. I encourage you to revisit those if this is new to you. The main point of this workflow is that, since we are in a greenfield project and triggering it before anything is implemented, this is a system-level test design. The Test Architect agent reviews the application from a general perspective and creates a plan grounded in risk assessment, testability analysis, and quality architecture decisions.

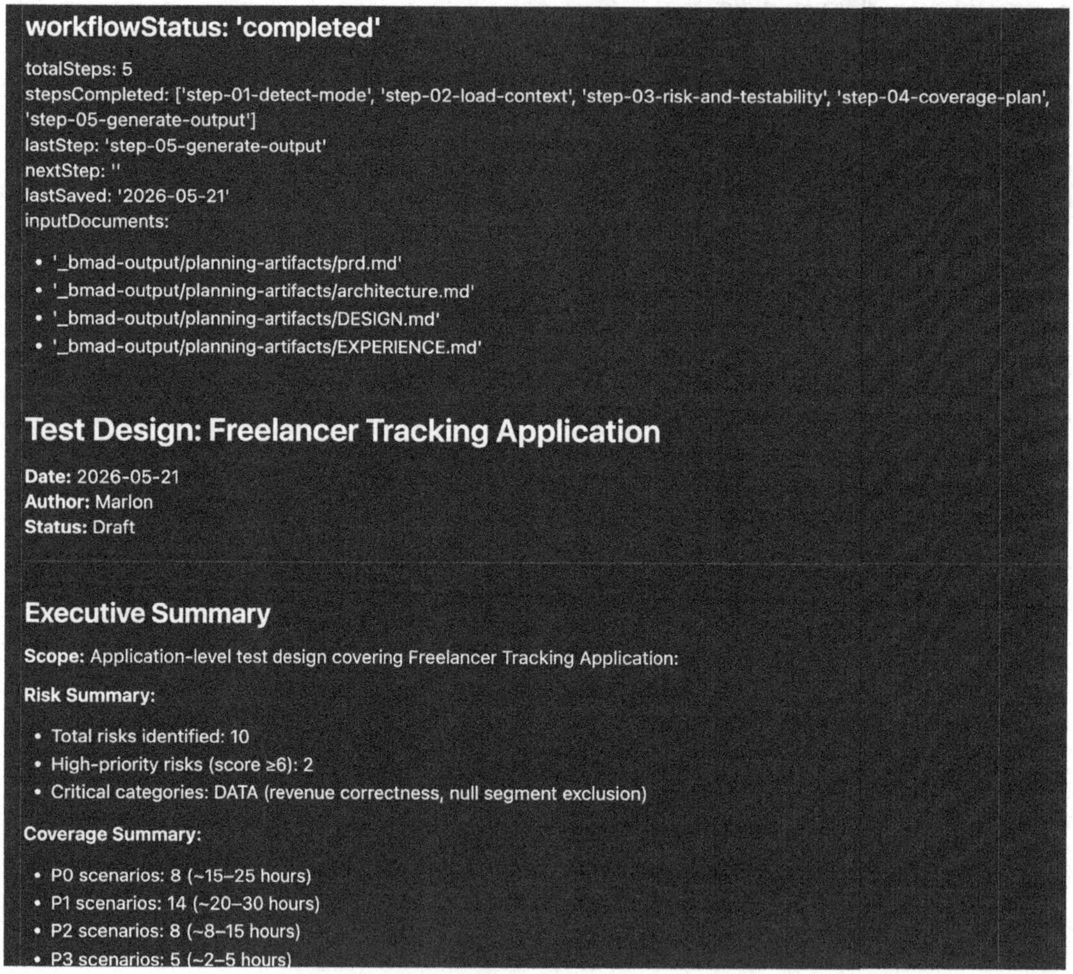

workflowStatus: 'completed'

totalSteps: 5
stepsCompleted: ['step-01-detect-mode', 'step-02-load-context', 'step-03-risk-and-testability', 'step-04-coverage-plan', 'step-05-generate-output']
lastStep: 'step-05-generate-output'
nextStep: ''
lastSaved: '2026-05-21'
inputDocuments:

- '_bmad-output/planning-artifacts/prd.md'
- '_bmad-output/planning-artifacts/architecture.md'
- '_bmad-output/planning-artifacts/DESIGN.md'
- '_bmad-output/planning-artifacts/EXPERIENCE.md'

Test Design: Freelancer Tracking Application

Date: 2026-05-21
Author: Marlon
Status: Draft

Executive Summary

Scope: Application-level test design covering Freelancer Tracking Application:

Risk Summary:

- Total risks identified: 10
- High-priority risks (score ≥6): 2
- Critical categories: DATA (revenue correctness, null segment exclusion)

Coverage Summary:

- P0 scenarios: 8 (~15–25 hours)
- P1 scenarios: 14 (~20–30 hours)
- P2 scenarios: 8 (~8–15 hours)
- P3 scenarios: 5 (~2–5 hours)

Figure 5.22 – Test design document

Looking at the produced output, inside the `test-artifacts/test-design` we find the `test-design-architecture` document, very rich in detail about what should be tested and where the bottlenecks or most impactful points of the application are. It includes an executive

summary, the blockers, the high-priority items, and the info-only topics to be aware of, different scenarios across high and low priority, testability requirements for non-functional requirements, and a risk mitigation plan based on high-priority risks, especially those scored six or above. It is up to you to dig into these must-decide blockers and understand what each represents for your application. For example: there is no seeding API, since this application is being built from nothing, which is correct, but from an integration test perspective, we will need to create those functions; otherwise, integration tests might fail. That is an important perspective from this workflow.

> **Note**
>
> Another important point: since the entire application revolves around time passing, we need an easy way to create a fake timer, so we can test and confirm everything works as expected without relying on real time.

Another edge case: our PRD states that local storage should warn when it reaches four megabytes, but it does not specify the behavior when the quota is actually exceeded.

This is an example of the kind of edge case this workflow brings to light. You should review, evaluate, and confirm that the proposed scenarios and priorities are real problems, and that you can cover the quality needs of your application. With this file in place and the test design architecture created, we can open a new agent window and run the framework workflow. I will not cover this workflow here also, since we already have a lesson in the previous module showing its output, but it basically creates the initial infrastructure needed to run tests for the application, both unit tests and end-to-end tests, the ones proposed by the TEA module.

Let us move to the final section to wrap up this chapter.

Creating project context, epics and stories and wrapping up

To wrap up this book, I hope you have already noticed some patterns. Once everything is in place, the next step is generating the project context. I will not go into detail here, since we already have a lecture covering it in the previous chapter.

After generating the project context, we create the epics and stories, then check implementation readiness, and then run the sprint planning workflow. We will use the following commands:

```
/bmad-create-epics-and-stories
/bmad-check-implementation-readiness
/bmad-sprint-planning
```

As a reminder, what we did in this chapter, and what we move into from this point forward, is: run the brainstorm, the research, and the create product brief workflows, then create the PRD and the UX design:

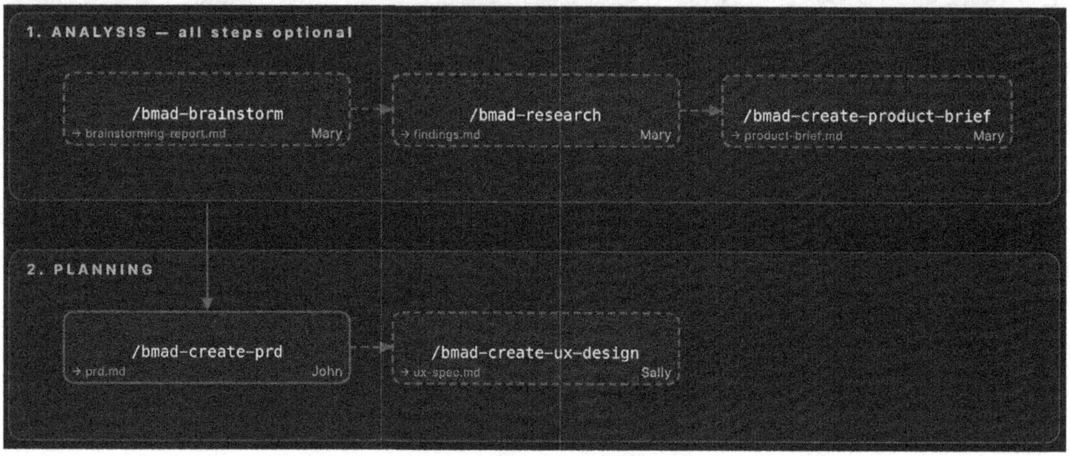

Figure 5.23 – Analysis and planning phase workflows

Then, we created the architecture and the test design, and from there created the epics and stories and checked implementation readiness. After that, we ran the TEA framework workflow to set up the testing strategy framework, and optionally you can run the TEA CI workflow to create our continuous integration pipeline. And to finish the upstream phase, we run sprint planning to start developing the stories.

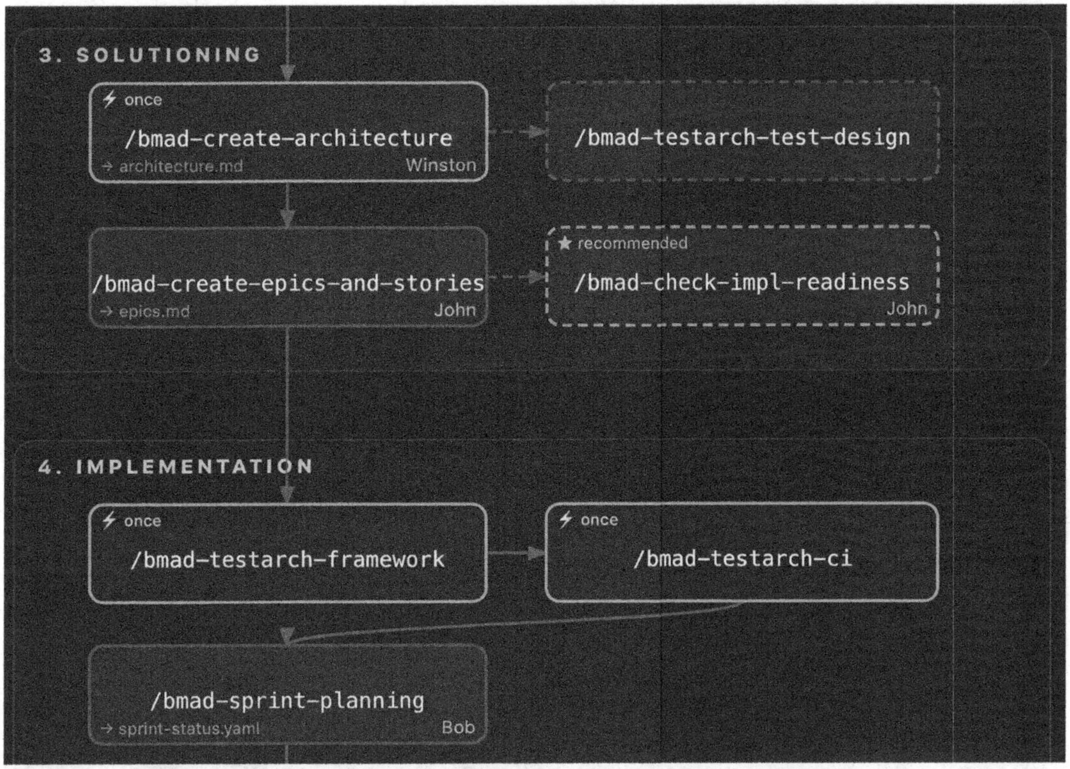

Figure 5.24 – Solutioning and implementation phase workflows

In the downstream phase, we run the story loop sequentially, as shown in the previous chapter: create a story, run ATDD, develop the story, perform the code review and finally run TEA automate. Before starting a new story, you can always run correct course to change how a story should behave, When you finish this process for a given epic, you run the retrospective and feed the project context again, updating the rules based on the learnings from the developer agent.

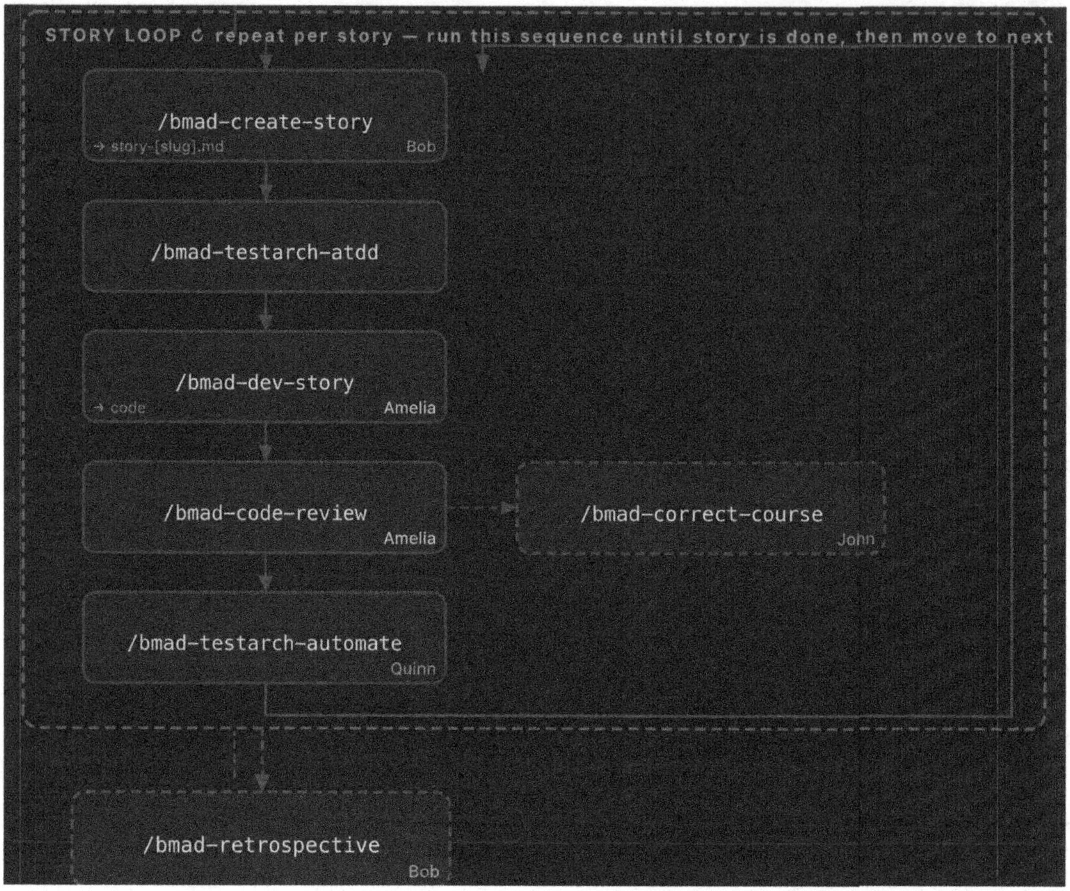

Figure 5.25 – Development loop workflows

Please revisit the previous chapter, where I go into detail about how to run each of these workflows, so you can start producing your stories, your epics, and the actual code, following all the standards we defined throughout this chapter.

Summary

In this chapter, we applied the complete BMAD v6 upstream workflow to a new project, moving from brainstorming and research through product brief creation, PRD development, UX design, architecture planning, and test design. We also prepared the project for implementation by generating project context, epics, stories, and implementation readiness artifacts. By following this structured, specification-driven approach, you learned how to create the documentation and context needed for both developers and AI agents to build software more consistently, efficiently, and with higher quality.

6

BMAD in Practice: Answers to Real-World Questions

Every other chapter in this book walks through a BMAD workflow step by step. This one works differently. Rather than a guided walkthrough, it is built from questions that real teams asked while putting BMAD into practice for the first time, and the answers those teams were given in the room.

The following questions were collected across four live training sessions where a team of approximately eighty practitioners, including product managers, engineers, UX designers, and quality engineers, worked through BMAD for the first time on real projects. The sessions covered PRD creation, UX specification, architecture, and testing, in that order.

What follows is an edited synthesis. Questions were grouped by theme rather than by session, because the same underlying concern often surfaced in multiple sessions in different forms. Where one question clarifies another, they have been placed together.

The questions are grouped into eight themes, each corresponding to a stage or concern in the BMAD workflow:

- On Skipping Steps
- On Structuring Work
- On Context Management
- On Teams and Process
- On Architecture
- On UX and Design Systems
- On Quality and Testing
- On Governance and Maintenance

A closing section pulls together the patterns that surfaced across all eight themes, regardless of which session the question came from.

On skipping steps

Can I skip stages if context already exists?

Yes. The upstream phases — brainstorm, research, UX design — are all optional. The PRD and architecture plus everything that follows it is not. Think of the left side of the BMAD workflow as context-building: you run those steps when you need to generate context that doesn't already exist. If your team already has a validated design system, you don't need to recreate it. If your architecture is already established, you don't need to generate it again.

The practical rule: always ask what documentation the downstream agents will need to do their work. If that context already exists, reference it. If it doesn't, run the workflow that generates it.

When is it acceptable to skip the UX step entirely?

Skip it only when there is no interface to design — APIs, data integrations, backend services that expose no UI. For anything with a user-facing interface, even if you have a validated prototype, the UX workflow is still valuable. It doesn't redesign your interface; it transforms it into a structured specification that the implementation agents can consume.

Does a validated Figma prototype mean I can skip UX?

No — but it changes the nature of the work. When you already have a prototype, the UX workflow functions as a compliance check rather than a creative process. It reads your existing design and produces a markdown specification: colors, typography, spacing rules, component behavior, and accessibility constraints. That specification becomes the context all implementation agents reference. Without it, agents interpret the design from whatever partial information is available, and you will see inconsistencies.

One team summarized it well after testing: they achieved roughly eighty percent adherence to their design system when they ran the UX workflow and injected the output as a "source of truth" with an explicit instruction not to reinterpret any existing component. Without that, adherence was noticeably lower. Two hours of upstream work replaced continuous manual correction downstream.

When does running the UX step cost more than it delivers?

The breakeven calculation changes depending on reuse. If you run the UX workflow once for a shared design system and replicate the output across every project that uses that system, the per-project cost approaches zero. If every team runs it independently for the same design system, you're paying repeatedly for the same result. The recommendation: treat the UX

specification document the same way you'd treat central architecture guidelines—generate it once, version it centrally, distribute it to all projects.

What about quick dev – does it replace the UX step for small changes?

Quick Dev is designed for small, targeted changes where running the full upstream process would be disproportionate overhead. It works, with one important caveat: by default, Quick Dev may decide that a task is simple enough to implement without generating a specification first, and it will write directly to code. If you want it to produce a spec before touching implementation, say so explicitly: "I want you to generate a specification".

Use Quick Dev for genuinely isolated changes. For anything that touches shared components, layout behavior, or user flows, favor the full process; the specification it generates is the last checkpoint before implementation, and it will catch things that aren't visible until agents start working.

On structuring work

How should I break up PRDs? By user journey, by feature, or by epic?

By feature. A user journey is typically too large to be a single PRD. It encompasses multiple features, each of which may require different people, different timelines, or different repositories. An epic is too small. It is a subdivision within a feature, not a planning unit.

The practical test: if you had to assign a PRD to a specific team for a specific sprint, would the scope make sense? If the answer is "this is two teams' worth of work," split the PRD. If the answer is "this is one story," the PRD is too narrow.

A concrete example: an e-commerce checkout journey would produce roughly four PRDs — product listing, product selection, payment, and delivery. Each of those features can stand alone as a deliverable, can be assigned to a team, and can be tested independently.

Should I generate all stories for all epics at once, or epic by epic?

Generate stories for a full epic before starting development on that epic. This allows you to distribute work across the team as soon as the stories exist, rather than waiting for each story to be created before handing it off. Within the development loop, work sequentially through stories in an epic: implement, test, review, then move to the next. Don't proceed to the next epic until the current one is complete and a retrospective has been run.

Generating all epics and all stories simultaneously before starting any development is not recommended. Learnings from the first epic — captured in retrospectives and project context updates — should inform the next.

Can I run multiple stories in parallel?

Yes, but you need to customize the workflow behavior. The default story shape in BMAD is a vertical slice: each story touches all layers (frontend, backend, data). That creates dependencies that make parallelization difficult. If you override the story generation behavior to decompose by layer instead, separating frontend tasks from backend tasks, for example, you can parallelize across team members. One team shared a custom configuration that forced the story generator to identify which tasks could be made independent, and they successfully ran front and backend stories in parallel. Another approach is to assign epics that don't depend on each other to specific owners; this way you can have one responsible per epic and can parallelize work.

How complex should a single PRD be? We have a product with dozens of sub-features

Each sub-feature that carries its own complexity — its own rules, its own edge cases, its own test surface — merits its own PRD. Think of the parent document as an index: it describes the product's scope at a macro level and links to the PRDs for each capability. Think about a random product with key management, account limits, and dispute resolution — each of those is its own PRD.

This structure serves two purposes. For humans, it makes navigation manageable. For LLMs, it enables progressive disclosure: the agent loads the index, identifies the relevant section, and loads only that file rather than ingesting the full document. When you have a single PRD with hundreds of lines, every agent call carries the full cost of that context even when only ten percent of it is relevant.

The BMAD agent asked me about endpoints and request parameters during PRD creation. is that appropriate?

It depends on what you want to include. From a pure product perspective, those decisions belong in the architecture phase. You can defer them: tell the agent the technical details will be defined later, and it will continue.

However, if the integration contract is already known — you have a Swagger spec, an existing API — including it enriches the PRD. Epics and stories generated from a technically-complete PRD will be more precise, and the implementation agent will have less to invent. The key point: this is collaborative territory between product and engineering. The PRD is primarily a product

document, but it benefits from a technical sign-off. Don't leave the architecture phase to discover that a requirement described in the PRD cannot be implemented as specified.

What's the difference between a product brief and a PRD?

A Product Brief captures a hypothesis — it's pre-validation, exploratory, and carries significant uncertainty. A PRD is a commitment: it describes what is going to be built, and the expectation is that it will be developed. If you're still discovering whether something should be built at all, you're in Product Brief territory. Once the decision is made and you're planning execution, you're writing a PRD.

On context management

Our PRD is picking up technical context we didn't include – it seems biased toward certain technology choices even after we cleaned it

Two likely causes. First, check your repository for an `agents.md` or `CLAUDE.md` file in the project root. If one exists and contains architecture directives ("this project uses .NET, SQL Server"), that context is injected into every session before BMAD loads. Second, if a prior session generated architecture documents and placed them in the `docs/` folder, the PRD workflow will load them because they're present in the expected locations. Running the PRD workflow in a contaminated session can produce these effects.

The fix: always start a clean session before running a new workflow. Never chain — "I just ran the PRD, now let me do architecture in the same session." Terminate the session, open a new one, run the next workflow from zero.

We work across three separate repositories. How do we share context without duplicating everything?

Treat each repository as an island. When you need cross-repository context for a workflow — generating a PRD that involves both a frontend and a backend — refer to the relevant context document from the related repository, use it provisionally during that planning session, then discard it. You're not maintaining a synchronized copy; you're borrowing context for the duration of a workflow.

The cleaner long-term solution is a monorepo, where all context exists in a single location and there is no copying. If a monorepo is impractical, the copy-and-discard approach is the recommended fallback. Accept that your copies will diverge — they're not meant to stay in sync — and refresh them at the start of each workflow session.

Should the _bmad artifacts be versioned in git?

Yes. Unlike `node_modules`, which can be regenerated from a manifest, BMAD artifacts contain the workflow definitions that make BMAD work in your repository. If you add it to `.gitignore`, anyone who clones the repository and runs a workflow will get nothing. The folder must be committed.

If your organization maintains a corporate fork of BMAD with custom configurations, the standard installation command should point to your internal repository rather than the upstream source. This ensures everyone who installs BMAD gets your organization's version, with your customizations, without needing to manually configure each project.

On teams and processes

What team composition works best with BMAD?

Three roles: a product leader, a technical lead, and one to two developers. There's no need for three separate people — in smaller teams, one person often covers product and technical leadership. The important constraint is that each role represents a perspective: product (what should be built and why), technical (how it can be built and what constraints exist), and execution (building it).

Larger teams can work with BMAD by parallelizing at the story level, but the coordination overhead grows. Most successful adoptions have been in small, focused teams working on well-bounded initiatives.

How do we handle work cycles? Do we still do sprints?

Most teams that have adopted BMAD have moved toward Kanban-style flow rather than fixed sprints. Pull the next story when the current one is complete. The reasons are practical: stories in BMAD are granular enough that completion times vary widely — some take hours, some take days — and forcing them into fixed sprint boundaries creates artificial waiting.

The rhythm that has emerged in practice: one-hour end-of-day demonstrations within the team, where each person shows what they completed. Weekly release notes compiled from those demonstrations. Milestones set for external communication.

The one ceremony that remains essential is the retrospective. Run it at the end of each epic. The outputs — learnings, discovered edge cases, corrected assumptions — go back into the project context file so they inform every subsequent story.

How do multiple product managers work with BMAD? Do they share PRD creation?

Each PM owns the PRDs they're responsible for. When one PRD is handed off to development and in flight, the PM moves on to the next PRD in their queue. BMAD doesn't create a bottleneck on PRD creation — a PM can be working upstream on the next initiative while the current one is being implemented downstream.

Collaboration matters most during PRD review: product, technical lead, and quality representative should all sign off before the PRD is broken into epics and handed to development.

On architecture

We're trying to evolve our data architecture from an existing pattern to a reference architecture. Can BMAD help?

Yes, and the process is the same as product development. Document the current state of the system using `/bmad-document-project`. Then write a PRD that describes the desired end state — performance, security, stability improvements — with the justification in business terms (transaction volume, error rates, compliance requirements). Break that PRD into epics and stories. The architecture evolution is an initiative like any other; it just happens to have technical objectives rather than user-facing ones.

The benefit of framing it this way is that you get the same traceability and planning discipline, and you can present the work to leadership using the same artifacts you would use for a product initiative.

Should I provide architecture context before generating the architecture document, or let BMAD suggest one?

Provide context. If your organization has established technology choices — language, framework, database, deployment patterns — inject them before running the architecture workflow. If you don't, BMAD will generate an architecture based on common market defaults, which may conflict with your standards.

A corporate-level `agents.md` or a shared architecture reference document (maintained in a central repository and referenced in each project) is the most scalable approach. Every team that starts a new project gets the same baseline constraints without anyone having to configure them manually.

We want to reuse corporate components across all applications. How do we prevent teams from building things that already exist?

Embed that knowledge in your corporate BMAD fork. The organization that maintains the internal BMAD installation can add instructions to the workflow agents that prompt for component discovery. "If this feature involves account operations, check whether components X, Y, Z exist before generating new implementations." This turns the discovery workflow into a knowledge propagation mechanism: the right information surfaces at the right moment in the process, without requiring every developer to know the full catalog upfront.

Who should own each workflow?

Based on field experience, a practical assignment looks like this:

- **Project Context**: AI Engineer. This file governs how all agents behave and must reflect the technical architecture. A product manager should not be responsible for its content.
- **Brainstorm / Research**: Anyone. These are expansive thinking tools with no direct downstream impact. Run them independently, in any combination.
- **PRD**: Product Manager, validated by AI Engineer. Product owns the requirements; engineering validates feasibility before the document is treated as final.
- **Architecture**: AI Engineer.
- **Test Design**: Quality Engineer, with product validation. The quality engineer generates the risk matrix; the product owner confirms that the identified scenarios match business priorities.
- **Create Epics and Stories**: Product Manager. This is where the product, technical, and quality perspectives are merged into executable work.
- **Development loop**: AI Engineer primarily.

On UX and design systems

Our design team works directly in HTML rather than Figma. Does the UX workflow still apply?

Yes. The input format is flexible. You can pass your HTML components, your CSS variables, your component documentation — whatever describes the visual and interaction rules of your system — as context for the UX workflow. The workflow transforms that information into the same kind of specification regardless of where it originates.

How do we ensure BMAD doesn't generate components that contradict our design system?

Two mechanisms work together. First, include an explicit instruction in your project context file — in uppercase if necessary — that the design system specification is the source of truth and must not be reinterpreted. Second, if your organization maintains a BMAD fork, you can add a UX compliance check as a pre-delivery step in the development workflow. Before an agent marks a story as complete, the check runs and confirms that no new components were created outside the design system's existing primitives.

One team tested both approaches. With just the instruction, they achieved roughly eighty percent adherence. When they added the pre-delivery check, violations became explicit rather than silent, and developers could correct them before delivery rather than discovering them in review.

The UX workflow didn't help us explore unhappy paths. It mostly validated what we already had.

The UX workflow is designed for specification and conformance, not for scenario exploration. For unhappy paths, alternative flows, and edge cases, use the Brainstorm workflow. Load your existing flow documents, specify that you want to explore scenarios beyond the primary path, and ask for non-conventional alternatives. The Brainstorm workflow has over sixty techniques available, including specific patterns for "what if" scenarios. You can also engage the analyst agent directly, ask it to act as an adversarial reviewer, and challenge your existing flows.

We receive prototypes from stakeholders built in informal tools. Can we use those as a BMAD starting point?

With caution. A prototype built ad hoc — especially one that was iterated rapidly without architectural discipline — will likely have structural patterns that conflict with your reference architecture. If you load that code directly into a BMAD project and start generating stories, you pay twice: once for the agent to reconcile the conflicting contexts, and once for the implementation work itself. The more productive approach is to treat the prototype as a proof of concept that validates the interaction model, then build the implementation fresh from a PRD and architecture derived from your standards. Use the prototype as a benchmark to confirm that the final result behaves as expected.

How do we validate early concepts without going through the full BMAD process?

Use BMAD only to generate the PRD. Then take that PRD into a plain Claude session and ask for an interactive HTML prototype based on the requirements. Claude's Playground feature can

generate animated, navigable HTML from a markdown document — enough to demonstrate a concept to stakeholders and gather feedback. Validate with real users, refine the PRD if necessary, then run the full BMAD implementation workflow. Don't use BMAD to generate throwaway prototypes; its process cost is only justified when you're building for production.

On quality and testing

What is the recommended sequence for the testing workflow?

Before any development begins on an epic, run `/bmad-testarch-test-design`. This analyzes the epic as a whole and produces a risk matrix: which scenarios have a high probability of failure, which have high business impact, and which fall at the intersection of both. This is the primary input for everything that follows.

Once development starts on an individual story, run `/bmad-testarch-atdd` per story — not per epic, and not for all stories at once. ATDD generates acceptance tests in the red phase: tests that describe the expected behavior but fail because the code doesn't exist yet. The implementation agent then writes code that makes those tests pass.

After all stories in an epic are complete, run the `/bmad-testarch-automate` workflow to confirm that everything that was generated passes and to add coverage for any scenarios that were missed.

Why not generate all ATDD tests at the beginning of an epic?

Because what you learn in story one should affect how you write the tests for story two. ATDD is part of the development cycle for each story. Running it all upfront means you're writing tests without the benefit of the implementation learnings that accumulate as you work through the epic. It also creates a false sense of completeness — you have a full test suite on day one, but the suite was written before anyone touched the code.

What is the relationship between test design and ATDD?

Test Design produces the plan: here are the scenarios that matter, ranked by risk. ATDD consumes that plan: for each story in the current epic, it generates test code that covers the scenarios identified in the plan. If Test Design identified "payment processing failure when balance is insufficient" as high probability and high impact, ATDD will generate a test case for that scenario when you reach the story that implements payment processing. The two workflows are designed to be used together in sequence.

We tried running ATDD on a legacy system and most of our tests failed immediately

The likely cause is sequence: Test Design should have run before ATDD, and Test Design should have been validated before ATDD was called. The test failures suggest the generated test scenarios don't match the actual behavior of the existing code—which is expected if you're generating tests without first analyzing what the code does.

For legacy systems, start with `/bmad-document-project`. Use the exhaustive mode if the codebase is large and unfamiliar — it reads every file and produces comprehensive documentation at the cost of time and tokens. Once the system is documented, run Test Design against that documentation to understand the risk surface. Validate the test plan with a product owner. Then run ATDD against individual stories using the validated plan as input.

Can test design documents be modified after the fact?

Yes. Test Design is a living document, not a contract. As the application evolves and new constraints are discovered during implementation, update it. Just be aware that if ATDD has already generated test code from an earlier version of the document, there may be divergence between the existing tests and the updated plan. A periodic review of the test artifacts against the Test Design document catches this drift before it compounds.

Should test coverage percentages be configured in BMAD or in the pipeline?

In the pipeline, BMAD generates the scenarios; the CI/CD pipeline enforces the thresholds. Configure your coverage gates in your build configuration, not in BMAD's workflow definitions. When a build fails because coverage is below threshold, the path forward is to implement additional scenarios from the Test Design document — specifically the ones that BMAD identified as lower priority and that you chose to defer.

We want to use our organization's custom test framework, but BMAD keeps generating tests for the default frameworks

You need to teach BMAD what your framework looks like. This requires two additions to your project's architecture document: a description of the framework itself (what it is, how it's imported, what annotation patterns it uses), and examples of the expected test structure. Once those are documented, ATDD will generate test code that follows your organization's patterns rather than the defaults. The architecture document is the authoritative reference BMAD uses for technology choices — if your framework isn't described there, BMAD doesn't know it exists.

Our test repository is separate from our application repository. Can BMAD generate tests there?

It can, but the coordination overhead is significant. BMAD needs access to the acceptance criteria (in the application repository) to generate meaningful test scenarios. If the repositories are separate, you either copy acceptance criteria between them—which introduces staleness risk—or you accept that the test generation agent can't see what it's supposed to be testing.

The recommended approach is to bring the test repository into the application repository as a folder within a monorepo structure. Configure independent pipelines per folder so that changes in the application code and changes in the test code trigger separate build processes. This preserves your operational separation while giving BMAD the unified context it needs to do its work.

Does BMAD support the concept of tests that must pass before code is accepted?

This is the direction the industry is moving toward. The core idea: an agent's delivery is not considered complete until end-to-end tests pass. The agent does not mark a story complete, does not move to the next story, and does not stop iterating until the acceptance criteria are demonstrably met by a passing test suite. This is a configuration decision in your workflow definitions — you're setting a success criterion that the agent must meet, not just a checklist it can self-report on.

The practical implication: code generated to satisfy a test tends to be more correct than code generated independently. Writing tests before code is not just a quality practice; it improves the quality of the code itself, because the agent optimizes toward passing the test rather than toward its own interpretation of the requirements.

On governance and maintenance

How do we prevent teams from using different versions of BMAD and getting inconsistent results?

Create a corporate fork and distribute it from an internal repository. All teams install from the internal URL rather than from the upstream source. The fork includes your organization's default configurations, architecture guidelines, and custom workflows. When you update the fork, teams pull the update the same way they would pull any other dependency.

One important difference from typical package management: BMAD artifacts should be committed to each project repository. It is not analogous to `node_modules`. If you add it

to `.gitignore`, the next developer who clones the repository will not be able to run any BMAD workflows. Version the folder; update it deliberately when your corporate fork changes.

How do we handle breaking changes when BMAD releases new versions?

The team responsible for the corporate fork absorbs the update, validates it against internal projects, and distributes it when stable. Teams using the fork are insulated from upstream breaking changes. The risk of updating too aggressively is workflow disruption mid-sprint; the risk of updating too conservatively is missing meaningful improvements. The fork maintainers make that tradeoff on behalf of the organization.

The BMAD help command – is it actually useful for day-to-day questions?

Yes, and it's underused. The help system contains the complete workflow reference: which workflows exist, what inputs they expect, what outputs they produce, and what the recommended sequence is. Many operational questions — "which workflow do I use here," "what files does this generate," "what should I run next" — can be answered directly without going to documentation or asking a colleague.

Crosscutting themes

Several patterns recur across all four topic areas:

- **Context is everything.** The quality of BMAD's output is bounded by the quality of its input context. Skipping the UX specification means implementation agents will interpret your design. Skipping architecture documentation means they'll invent technology choices. Skipping Test Design means test generation will be unfocused. Each upstream artifact reduces the interpretive latitude of the downstream agents.
- **Sessions should be clean.** Contamination between workflow sessions — context from a PRD session leaking into an architecture session — produces inconsistent, biased output. Start a new session for each workflow. The cost of starting fresh is seconds; the cost of contaminated output is debugging time you can't easily trace back to the source.
- **Retrospectives close the learning loop.** Every epic produces discoveries: edge cases that weren't anticipated, constraints that weren't visible in the PRD, implementation patterns that should become rules. The retrospective is the mechanism for capturing

those learnings and inserting them into the project context. Without it, the same issues recur in every subsequent epic. With it, the process improves continuously.

- **BMAD is a team process, not a solo tool.** Its value is in coordinating multiple roles — product, engineering, quality — around shared artifacts. The PRD requires product and engineering sign-off. The Test Design requires product validation. The architecture requires technical ownership. The tools exist to make that coordination efficient, not to replace the judgment of the people doing the work.

7

Unlock the Code Bundle and the PDF Version

Your copy of this book includes the following exclusive benefits:

Complete Code Bundle

Download the full source code for this book's examples and projects.

DRM-Free PDF Version

Download DRM-free PDF and ePub copies of this book.

7-Day Packt Library Access

Get 7-day unlimited access to 8,000+ books and videos. No credit card required.

Available for first-time Packt+ trial users only.

Next-Gen Reader Access

Read this book on Packt Reader with progress sync, dark mode and note-taking.

Follow this guide to unlock them. The process takes only a few minutes and only needs to be completed once.

Unlock this book's free benefits in three easy steps

Step 1

Have your purchase invoice ready for *step 3*. If you have a physical copy, scan it using your phone and save it as a PDF, JPG, or PNG.

For more help on finding your invoice, visit `https://www.packtpub.com/unlock-benefits/help`.

> Note
>
> **Note**: If you bought this book directly from the Packt website, no invoice is required. After *step 2*, you can access your exclusive content right away.

Step 2

Scan the QR code or go to `packtpub.com/unlock`.

On the page that opens (similar to *Figure 7.1* on desktop), search for this book by name and select the correct edition.

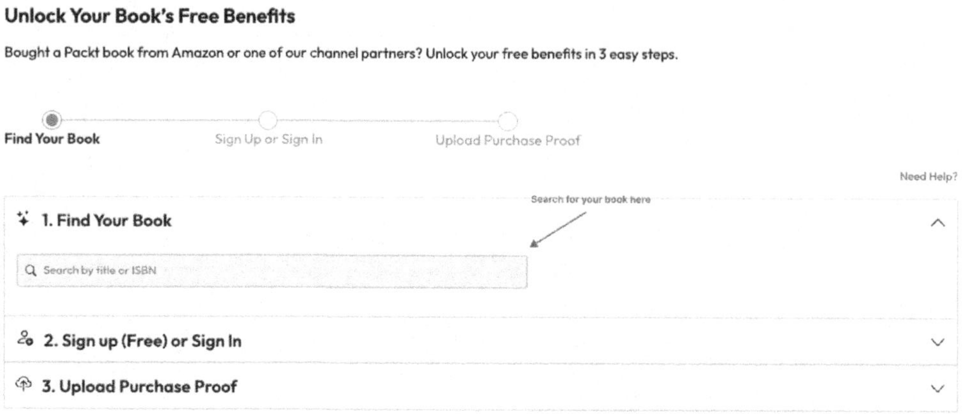

Figure 7.1: Packt unlock landing page on desktop

Step 3

After selecting the book, sign in to your Packt account or create one for free. Then, upload your invoice (PDF, PNG, or JPG, up to 10 MB). Follow the on-screen instructions to finish the process.

Need help?

If you get stuck and need help, visit `https://www.packtpub.com/unlock-benefits/help` for a detailed FAQ on how to find your invoice and more. This QR code will take you to the help page.

> Note
>
> **Note**: If you are still facing issues, reach out to `customercare@packt.com`.

Other Books You May Enjoy

If you enjoyed this book, you may be interested in these other books by Packt:

Agentic Coding with Claude Code

Eden Marco

ISBN: 9781806022595

- Design agentic coding workflows in the terminal and IDE using Claude Code
- Build custom automations with reusable slash commands and hooks
- Use Claude Code with a Next.js project to implement AI-driven workflows
- Create persistent AI memory using Claude Code memory files
- Apply MCP for structured context sharing across tools and agents
- Design multi-agent systems using subagents and orchestration patterns
- Enforce coding standards using project documentation and context control
- Scale AI pair programming while keeping code maintainable

Web Dev with an AI Sidekick

Mark J. Price

ISBN: 9781806111251

- Optimize your chatbot to act as your web development learning mentor
- Structure, style, add images, and animate content with HTML, SVG, and CSS
- Add web page interactivity with JavaScript and TypeScript
- Store and query data using practical SQL exercises
- Build backend features in Python and Django step by step
- Collaborate with an AI coding expert: Codex, Claude Code, or Copilot
- Create surveys, gather responses, and show results in charts
- Test, debug, and deploy your app with AI support

Packt is searching for authors like you

If you're interested in becoming an author for Packt, please visit `authors.packtpub.com` and apply today. We have worked with thousands of developers and tech professionals, just like you, to help them share their insight with the global tech community. You can make a general application, apply for a specific hot topic that we are recruiting an author for, or submit your own idea.

Share your thoughts

Now you've finished *Spec-Driven Development with BMAD*, we'd love to hear your thoughts! Scan the QR code below to go straight to the Amazon review page for this book and share your feedback or leave a review on the site that you purchased it from.

`https://packt.link/r/1808086074`

Your review is important to us and the tech community and will help us make sure we're delivering excellent quality content.

Index

Symbols

/bmad-create-story workflow
- creating 109

/bmad?dev?story workflow
- developing 112, 113

A

AAA validation **51**

Acceptance Test-Driven Development (ATDD) workflow
- tests, creating 110

Acceptance Test-Driven Development (ATDD) workflows **6**

Amelia, developer
- working with 56 – 58

Architecture Decision Records (ADRs) **45**

analysis phase, BMAD workflow **26 - 28**
- market research, performing 31, 32
- PRFAQ workflow 34
- product brief, creating 33
- product idea, brainstorming 28 – 31

architecture
- creating 143 – 146

B

BMAD **4**
- _bmad-output folder 15
- configuring 12 – 15
- full feature, building with 10 – 12
- implementations, answers to real-world questions 153
- modules 5
- progressive disclosure 16
- v4 and v6, comparing 15, 16
- workflows 4

BMAD Agile **18**
- analysis phase 18
- implementation phase 20
- planning phase 19
- solutioning phase 19

BMAD Builder **5**

BMAD check-implementation-readiness workflow
- validating 107

BMAD document project workflow **85 - 88**
- creating 88, 89

BMAD help command **165**

BMAD new version
- breaking changes, handling with 165

BMAD v6
- Help 17
- installation 23, 80
- installation prerequisites 23
- installed folder structure 81
- modular architecture 17
- Party Mode 18
- problems 80
- project context 18
- QuickSpec workflow 17
- setting up 80
- upgrading, from v4 23
- workflows, without agents 17

BMAD workflow, themes
- on context management 157
- on governance and maintenance 164
- on quality and testing 162 – 164
- on structuring work 155, 156
- on UX and design systems 160, 161
- skipping steps 154, 155
- teams and processes 158 – 160
- themes 153

brainstorming session **121 - 127**

C

Correct Course workflow **20**

Creative Intelligence Suite (CIS) **6**

Cross-Site Scripting (XSS) **144**

clarify-and-route step **92 - 94**

code
- reviewing 114

context engineering **7**
- context drift 7
- context gap challenge 7

customers
- adding, via quickspec 91

D

development cycle, implementation phase
- code, reviewing 62, 63
- story, creating 59 – 61
- story, implementing 61, 62

E

E2E tests
- creating, with TEA automate 94, 95

G

Game Design Documents (GDDs) **6**

Game Dev Studio (GDS) **6**

I

implementation phase **56**
- Amelia, working with 56 – 58
- development cycle 59
- Mid-Sprint changes, handling 65, 66
- quick-dev workflow 64, 65
- sprint plan, initializing 58, 59
- testing cycle 66

K

Kanban application
- dependencies, installing 79

L

large language models (LLMs) **1**

M

Mid-Sprint changes
- handling 65, 66

N

non-functional requirement (NFR) **6**

O

object-oriented programming (OOP) **4**

output folders
- comparing 128

P

PRD workflow
- advanced elicitation 102, 103
- creating 105, 106
- dashboard, creating 101, 102
- party mode 104, 105

PRFAQ workflow **34**

Product Requirements Document (PRD) **25, 119**
- creating 132, 133

phase workflows
- creating 148 – 151

planning phase, BMAD workflow **35**
- PRD, creating 37, 38
- PRD, updating 39
- PRD, validating 39
- product manager, working with 35, 36
- UX design, creating 40 – 43
- UX designer, working with 39, 40

product brief
- creating 129 – 131

project context
- creating 148

project-context.md **22**

Q

quick-dev workflow **64, 65, 77**
executing 101
quickspec
customers, adding 91

R

recommended workflow **120, 121**
research workflows
types 127, 128
retrospective workflow
performing 116 – 118

S

Spec-Driven Development (SDD) **3**
solution phase, BMAD workflow **43**
architect, working with 43, 44
architecture, creating 45, 46
epics, creating 51, 52
implementation readiness, checking 53, 54
project context, generating 46, 47
stories, creating 51, 52
test architect, working with 48, 49
test strategy, designing 49 – 51
sprint
course, correcting 116
sprint plan **107**
initializing 58, 59
story-level workflow **115**

T

TEA ATDD
using, to generate tests 97
TEA automate
using 98, 99
using, to create E2E tests 94, 95
TEA framework
running 82 – 84
Test Enterprise Architecture (TEA) **77**
tags
adding, via quick spec 96
test design
creating 146 – 148
test design workflow
epic-level 49
system-level 49
test enterprise architect (TEA) **6**
workflows 21, 22
test framework
setting up 147, 148
test scenarios
creating 108
risk-based testing strategy 108
testing cycle, implementation phase
CI pipeline, configuring 68, 69
coverage gate 73, 74
coverage, expanding 71 – 73
epic retrospective 74 – 76
test framework, setting up 67, 68
test scaffolds, generating 69 – 71
tests
automating 114
scenarios 100
validating 100

U

UX
creating 134 – 136, 139 – 143
upstream context **8**
pillars 8, 9
real-world context example 9

V

vertical slicing **110**

Spec-Driven Development with BMAD

Portfolio Director: Ashwin Nair
Portfolio Manager: Sneha Shinde
Project Manager: Vishnu Priya R
Content Engineer: Nithya Sadanandan
Technical Editor: Rohit Singh
Copy Editor: Nithya Sadanandan
Indexer: Pratik Shirodkar
Proofreader: Nithya Sadanandan
Production Designer: Ajay Patule
Growth Lead: Anamika Singh

First published: September 2026

Production reference: 1140826

Published by Packt Publishing Ltd.
Grosvenor House
11 St Paul's Square
Birmingham
B3 1RB, UK.

ISBN 978-1-80808-607-6
`www.packtpub.com`

Spec-Driven Development with BMAD

Master Agentic Workflows using Cursor, BMAD, and Context Engineering

Marlon Vidal Ferreira

<packt>